DATE DUE

ENGLISH ROMANTICISM

ENGLISH ROMANTICISM

The Grounds of Belief

John Clubbe and Ernest J. Lovell, Jr.

Northern Illinois University Press
DeKalb, Illinois

Library of Congress Cataloging in Publication Data

Clubbe, John.
  English romanticism.

  Includes bibliographical references and index.
  1. English poetry – 19th century – History and
criticism. 2. Romanticism – England. I. Lovell,
Ernest James, 1918–   . II. Title.
PR590.C56   1983   821'.7'09145   82–22586
ISBN 0–87580–092–0

To

J. A. Bryant, Jr

Contents

Preface

'Romanticism is still the most vexing problem in literary history,' wrote Morse Peckham in 1965, 'even more irritating than the problem of the Renaissance.'[1] This book makes no pretence to solving that problem or even to answering the question, 'What is Romanticism?' But it does examine the beliefs of the six major Romantic poets, not only in the chapters devoted to each poet – where we make connections with the other poets and suggest interrelationships among them – but also in the two chapters of synthesis (Chapters 5 and 9) that group the poets by generation. The operative thesis behind this study is that Romanticism is what it is because writers wrote poems and prose works – writers who lived at a particular time in history and within particular human and social contexts – and not because subsequent literary historians have organized these writers and their works into a movement and so labelled it.

Also underlying our argument is the notion that the intellectual affinities among the Romantics are greater, more interesting, certainly less explored, than the differences. The differences are of course obvious and striking, and thus have been accorded more attention. For example, Earl R. Wasserman has stated that the Romantics 'vigorously disagreed on central issues and that their works differ in vastly more essential and interesting ways than they are similar'.[2] Before him, Walter Jackson Bate affirmed that 'few generalizations consistently apply to the outstanding exponents of romanticism'.[3] We believe otherwise. Without minimizing the undeniable differences among these writers, we venture to make a 'few generalizations' that argue for the fundamental coherence of the Romantic movement in England. The similarities among the Romantics suggest to us the validity of considering 'Romanticism' (whatever its deficiencies as an inclusive term) as a whole rather than discriminating among romanticisms. We attempt to offer a context within which readers may freshly consider, not oversubtle nuances of interpretation, but elemental questions about the ethical, aesthetic and spiritual qualities of life that the Romantics raise in their beliefs. We have written this book (designed as an extended 'essay') not only for professional students of Romanticism but also for those students (of any age) who wish to understand why we still read Romantic literature, what its basic assumptions and characteristics are, what values it embodies. Such readers, we hope, will find challenging our interpretation of 'the grounds of belief' that underlie the achievement of the major Romantic poets.

When Ernest J. Lovell, Jr, died from cancer on 22 June 1975, he left behind a rough draft of eight chapters (the present Chapters 2 to 9) of this book, along with much other material in incomplete and note form. I had known that Ernest was working on a general study of English Romanticism, for during a week I spent in Austin at the Humanities Research Center in July 1972 we talked about it on several occasions. In October 1976 Ernest's widow, Chris, asked me if I would take over the manuscript, revise and edit it, and add whatever introductory matter I thought it needed. As I read over what Ernest had written, I soon realized that he had undertaken a large-scale revaluation of Romanticism as a complex body of ideas, ideas that he interpreted within a broader humanistic framework than did most other studies I knew of. It struck me immediately that, incomplete as was his manuscript, such a viewpoint was too valuable to lose. Furthermore, I perceived that our positions on crucial issues of Romanticism were close enough to permit collaboration without fundamental disharmony of viewpoint.

Ernest Lovell had attempted a synthesizing study of English Romanticism only after several decades of specialized scholarship and of thinking about poets and poems. The manuscript was, in effect, a departure from his previous work, much of which had centred on Byron and was oriented toward biography and complex problems of editing. After thinking over various possibilities for expanding the manuscript, I decided that it had unity as it stood. Thus, aside from writing this Preface and most of the first chapter, I have retained Ernest's basic structure.

The eight chapters he left behind have been extensively rewritten, however, in places restructured, and I have added whenever necessary passages to flesh out the argument. Almost every sentence of the manuscript has been altered in some way and a good many sentences are new. I am also responsible for the book's title and its chapter titles. My notes direct the reader's attention as much to other relevant works by the poets themselves as to the voluminous secondary literature. This study is thus in a full sense a collaboration, though for whatever errors of fact and inadequacy of interpretation it retains I accept sole responsibility.

In working on this volume, I acknowledge with gratitude a number of debts: to Chris Lovell, for her encouragement and support; to Anne Lovell Matsen, for her careful decoding of the handwritten rough draft of her father's manuscript; to Patricia L. Skarda, for an informative letter detailing Ernest's hopes for his manuscript as she remembered them in conversation; and to Dorothy Roberts, at whose hospitable premises in Crewe, Virginia, I worked on the Coleridge and Keats chapters. I also thank friends and colleagues – J. Robert Barth, William R. Campbell, Mary Robbins Duncan, Richard Harter Fogle, Donald M. Hassler III, Frank Jordan, Jerome Meckier – from whom I have learned much through exchange of ideas. Never once did they balk when I inflicted chapters upon them. The University of Kentucky Research Foundation provided funds for the preparation of the manuscript, and Barbara Coleman typed it with professional competence. My colleague in Classics, Jane E. Phillips, made many detailed suggestions for improving both its content and its style, as did official readers on both sides of the Atlantic, and I am very grateful to her and to them for their comments. Julia Steward, Timothy Fox and Barbara Harford at Macmillan and Mary Livingston at Northern Illinois University Press have been unfailingly helpful. Earlier versions of Chapters 7 and 8 appeared in *Prose Studies* and *The Kentucky Review*, as did several paragraphs of the Introduction in *Mosaic*, and I gratefully acknowledge permission from the editors of these journals to reprint our words here. Lastly, during the years that I worked on this book I benefited greatly from the unstinting support of my departmental chairman, J. A. Bryant, Jr. My debt to him for his continuing interest in my research and for his many kindnesses is incalculable.

Pat Skarda, once a doctoral student of Ernest's, characterized his attitude to literature thus: 'His major contention with the critics was narrow-mindedness. He loathed the riding of hobby-horses, and he espoused no single approach to poetic texts or to the poets themselves. He wanted his students to taste everything sound, eschew anything small, and note everything the poet said with attention to the manner in which it was said.' If readers find these virtues even intermittently evident in this book, its authors will have succeeded in their purpose.

University of Kentucky   J. C.

Works Frequently Cited

After the first reference, page (and volume) numbers to standard editions are not stated in the Notes and References but given parenthetically in the text; for the poetry, line numbers are given. Standard editions that we have used infrequently we cite in full in the notes. For others we have adopted the following abbreviations and short titles. Full bibliographical details are given for books from which quotations are taken; for other books only date of publication is given.

BLAKE

BPP   *The Poetry and Prose of William Blake*, edited by David V. Erdman, revised edn (Garden City, New York: Doubleday, 1970)

BL   *The Letters of William Blake*, edited by Geoffrey Keynes (Cambridge, Mass.: Harvard University Press, 1970)

WORDSWORTH

Prelude   *The Prelude or Growth of a Poet's Mind*, edited by Ernest de Selincourt, revised by Helen Darbishire (Oxford: Clarendon, 1959). Quotations (unless indicated otherwise) are from the 1850 text

WPW   *The Poetical Works of William Wordsworth*, edited by Ernest de Selincourt and Helen Darbishire, 5 vols (Oxford: Clarendon, 1940–9)

WL   *The Letters of William and Dorothy Wordsworth*, edited by Ernest de Selincourt, 6 vols, 1935–9; revised by Chester L. Shaver *et al.*, 2nd edn (Oxford: Clarendon, 1967–   )

COLERIDGE

CPW *Complete Poetical Works of Samuel Taylor Coleridge*, edited by Ernest Hartley Coleridge, 2 vols (Oxford: Clarendon, 1912; reprinted 1957)

CCW *The Complete Works of Samuel Taylor Coleridge*, edited by [W. G. T.] Shedd, 7 vols (New York: Harper, 1853)

CCL *Collected Letters of Samuel Taylor Coleridge*, edited by Earl Leslie Griggs, 6 vols (Oxford: Clarendon, 1956–71)

Biographia   Biographia Literaria, with his Aesthetical Essays, edited by J. Shawcross, 2 vols (London: Oxford University Press, 1907; reprinted 1958)

Shakespearean Criticism   Shakespearean Criticism, edited by Thomas Middleton Raysor, 2 vols, 2nd edn (London: Dent, 1960)

The Friend   The Friend, edited by Barbara E. Rooke, 2 vols (London: Routledge and Kegan Paul; Princeton: Princeton University Press, 1969)

CMP *Coleridge's Miscellaneous Prose,* edited by Thomas Middleton Raysor (London: Constable, 1960)

BYRON*

BP *The Works of Lord Byron: Poetry*, edited by Ernest Hartley Coleridge, 7 vols (London: John Murray, 1898–1904; reprinted 1922)

BPW *Lord Byron: The Complete Poetical Works*, edited by Jerome J. McGann, 3 vols to date (Oxford: Clarendon, 1980–1)

LJ *The Works of Lord Byron: Letters and Journals*, edited by Rowland E. Prothero, 6 vols (London: John Murray, 1898–1901; reprinted 1922)

BLJ *Byron's Letters and Journals*, edited by Leslie A. Marchand, 12 vols (London: John Murray, 1973–82)

---

*As Marchand's edition of Byron's letters and journals has superseded Prothero's, so McGann's of the poetry will, when completed, supersede Coleridge's. But because Marchand's does not contain much of Byron's prose (including his important critical essays) and because McGann's is still incomplete, we have used the older editions when the newer do not contain the texts cited.

SHELLEY

SPP *Shelley's Poetry and Prose*, edited by Donald H. Reiman and Sharon B. Powers (New York: W. W. Norton, 1977, Norton Critical Editions)

SP *Shelley's Prose or The Trumpet of a Prophecy*, edited by David Lee Clark, revised edn (Albuquerque: University of New Mexico Press, 1966)

SL *The Letters of Percy Bysshe Shelley*, edited by Frederick L. Jones, 2 vols (Oxford: Clarendon, 1964)

KEATS

KP *The Poems of John Keats*, edited by Jack Stillinger. (Cambridge, Mass.: Harvard University Press, 1978)

KL *The Letters of John Keats, 1814–1821*, edited by Hyder Edward Rollins, 2 vols (Cambridge, Mass.: Harvard University Press, 1958)

1 Introduction

Disguise it not – we have one human heart –
All mortal thoughts confess a common home.
Shelley[1]

Art / Is complete when it is human.
Charles Tomlinson[2]

The importance of understanding the nature and theory of
English Romanticism is by now sufficiently well known that
we need suggest here only our method of approach. We address
ourselves to the beliefs of the six major poets, the manner in
which they arrived at these beliefs, and their importance within
each poet's critical theory. It is not everyone who can say *I
believe* or who can affirm the same belief all the years of his or
her life. Belief, or faith in that which cannot be empirically
demonstrated or verified, rests finally on grounds that are
broadly religious, and a religious experience may be quite different from the memory of it or the record of it. Probably no
one believes with the same intensity on Tuesday that he or she
did on Monday or will on Wednesday. The Romantic poets
were, furthermore, to a remarkable degree and in more ways
than one, poets of process whose vision of the truth continued
to grow and develop. Thus it is with some trepidation that
literary historians should contemplate erecting, for any of the
Romantics, a structure of belief built out of their scattered utterances.[3]

We find a fundamental coherence in the beliefs of these poets,
beliefs that in their maturity do reveal a remarkable consistency.
With the Romantics, the blossom and the bole of their thought are
recognizably of the same branch-charmed tree. But in analyzing
this thought literary historians must themselves exercise some
imagination. They must concern themselves with statements of

belief about matters of importance, statements not resolutely contradicted elsewhere in the poet's mature writings, that is, statements in harmony with the great body of the poet's thought; and probably they should limit themselves to statements expressed in a tone of intensity or with deep conviction or vividness of phrase. It is helpful, too, to observe chronology and to avoid imposing a rigid ideological scheme upon the beliefs of these poets, all of whom still remain alive to us.

The Romantic poets had a tremendous interest in the nature of perception. Blake, Wordsworth and Coleridge agreed that man was capable of seeing more than the bodily eye permitted him to see. The act of human perception was, for all three, a creative act in the sense that man perceiving creates the world in which he lives. Although Byron, Shelley and Keats were nearly as interested in the nature of perception as the first generation of poets, they were less persuaded that a redeemed nature would result from improved perception. All the Romantic poets, understanding that the reader who gives nothing learns nothing, rejected the idea of the mind as a passive machine. Newton's passive theory of perception, as Coleridge for one recognized, did not explain the creative process or the existence of poems. These poets came eventually to believe in an active theory of perception, and, in writing poems about intellectual or spiritual growth, intended that their readers' minds should also grow.

The Romantic poets identified the creative with the ethical imagination. This identification is, in our view, one of the central assumptions or doctrines of English Romanticism. For Blake, the highest form of imaginative vision – the fourfold vision of the artist – was also the highest ethical vision; for Coleridge, the poetic imagination was an ethical imagination that recognized the sameness and kinship in all men; for Shelley, the poetic imagination cannot exist unless it arises out of an ethical imagination – that is, a visionary, spiritual and redeemed imagination.

In this study we consider the relationship of each poet's beliefs to his poetry and find, among other evidence of their beliefs, that the poets stood closer to orthodox Christianity than they realized or than we have since. However unorthodox Blake, Wordsworth and Coleridge may at times appear, they were deeply Christian and shared an enthusiasm for the Bible and *Paradise Lost* as great poetic storehouses. Each of them viewed man as a fallen creature partaking in original sin but believed also that man possessed divine potentiality and was capable of visionary redemption. Although the second generation of Romantic poets were more sceptical in the realm of belief, they too, like their predecessors, accepted as fact the fallen, basically imperfect state of man.

The Romantic poets, more than generations of poets before and since, wrestled with the problem of selfhood. They viewed the fall as due essentially to the sin of pride, Blake's selfhood, the absence of love for others. The true poetic genius must annihilate self, Blake insisted again and again, and this Blakean annihilation of self is close to the Shelleyan sympathetic or ethical imagination. The annihilation of self was *the* Romantic experience. It was an expansionistic experience that involved the loss of the sense of personal identity by absorption or union or reconciliation with that which is greater than or outside of the self.[4]

Though not in a strict sense philosophers, the Romantic poets offer some of the most original thinking in existence about man, his position in the universe, his imaginative powers and his potential for creativity. The range and intensity of their ideas, their focus on the individual, their subjectivity, signify a major literary revolution. That fact has now gained widespread recognition despite sceptics like T. S. Eliot, ostensibly hostile to Romanticism but affected by it at every turn. Recently, Jerome J. McGann has written:

> I do not really doubt that all the Romantics share a definable community of attitudes and procedures. But, by the same token, I do not see that their work uniformly adheres to this communal project: and, even more importantly for criticism and scholarship, I do not see that scholars and critics have yet gained a clear grasp of what these communal elements are, except in the most general way.

McGann observes that 'we have leaped toward the Unity of Romantic Being without being fully aware of the problems that must be solved before such an idea, or set of ideas, can be properly – i.e., usefully – categorized'.[5] He presents the situation squarely: despite a sense of the essential unity of the Romantic movement, we have not yet made an adequate case for it. We need synthesizing studies, to be sure, but synthesizing studies that bring the poets together on clearly demarcated grounds.

Several of the Romantic poets knew they lived amidst something larger than themselves, both a *Zeitgeist* and a literary community of which they were a part. Shelley, for example, hymned most fervently in *A Defence of Poetry* the 'spirit of the age', and Hazlitt picked up the phrase, a common one at the time, for the title of his famous book of 1825. Earlier, in the Preface to *The Revolt of Islam*, Shelley had argued for 'a resemblance, which does not depend upon their own will, between all the writers of any particular age. They cannot escape from subjection to a common influence which arises out of an infinite combination of circumstances belonging to the times in which they live.'[6] Shelley felt that, as in Milton's time, literature was intimately connected to society, a connection fostered by the common inheritance writers shared in the French Revolution. Never did he doubt the greatness of the literature of his own age. 'It is impossible to read the compositions of the most celebrated writers of the present day,' he concluded in the *Defence*, 'without being startled with the electric life which burns within their words' (SP, 297). Everyone alive at the time partakes in the current of this creativity, he claimed in the Preface to *Prometheus Unbound*, for no one 'can conscientiously assure himself that his language and tone of thought may not have been modified by the study of the productions of these extraordinary intellects' (SP, 327). The writers Shelley had in mind included Wordsworth, Coleridge, Byron, Hazlitt, Hunt, possibly Godwin, possibly Keats (he never knew of Blake). Not that he thought his own generation more endowed than others – 'the mass of capabilities remains at every period materially the same'. But 'the circumstances which awaken it to action perpetually change' (ibid.), and in the decades following the French Revolution extraordinary 'circumstances' became the norm. Military involvement abroad, political repression at home, currents of ideas let loose, produced an epoch charged with tension. The result was the flood of magnificent literature that poured forth after 1789.

Shelley was not the only contemporary who realized that unusual achievement was in the air. Observers as far apart in their views as Hazlitt and Jeffrey, De Quincey and Thomas

Noon Talfourd, testify to the vital interaction between the French Revolution and the tumultuous literature that came into existence in its wake. Coleridge, for example, sensed the impact that the 1790s had upon Wordsworth long before Wordsworth read to him *The Prelude*. So stunning is the achievement of contemporary poets, beginning with *Songs of Innocence* in 1789 and continuing through the mid-1820s with the later cantos of *Don Juan*, that it left even astute observers bewildered and awed. Macaulay, not usually identified as a partisan of Romanticism and never thinking to apply the term 'Romantic' to particular poets, recognized the unity of the movement when as early as 1830 he spoke of it (in characteristic hyperbole) as 'the most enlightened generation of the most enlightened people that ever existed'.[7] De Quincey, looking back in 1838 on what he had lived through, thought it 'a revolution more astonishing and total than ever before happened in literature or in life'.[8] Another decade, and Charlotte Brontë in *Jane Eyre* has St. John Rivers (not, one would have thought, a friend to the Romantics) recall the earlier part of the century as 'the golden age of modern literature' (ch. 32).

The lives and art of the Romantic poets evince the richness of their humanity, and they are read today in large part because they thought deeply about significant areas of human endeavour and art. Literature was important to them, but more important than literature was life. One reason we keep returning to their works is that they knew so much about humanity, both the particular humanity that was themselves and that of others whom they observed, were curious about and learned from. 'Our very words "human" and "humanity", and all the words that have developed from them,' Walter Jackson Bate has reminded us, 'come from the [Latin] word meaning "earth" (*humus*)'.[9] Out of this concern with *humus*, with the ways human beings are – and can be – emerges a poetry suffused with imaginative empathy into human emotions and into the human mind.

'For poetry to be great,' Donald Davie has written, 'it must reek of the human, as Wordsworth's poetry does. This is not a novel contention; but perhaps it is one of those things that cannot be said too often.'[10] The Romantic poets did something the originality of which we can never too much insist upon: they brought poetry back to the human. By and large it has stayed there, for the Romantic focus on individual (as opposed to generic) man remains paramount in modern literature. Astute contemporaries recognized at the time something of what was happening. Hazlitt exaggerated but captured essential truth when he said of the (yet unnamed) Romantics, 'there is nothing interesting, nothing heroical, but themselves. To them the fall of gods or of great men is the same.'[11] Exploration of the dimensions of man's being, particularly of his psychology, emerges as the dominant interest of Romantic poetry. 'It is in relation to [the] great *moral* capacities of man that the literature of power . . . lives and has its field of action', De Quincey insisted. 'It is concerned with what is highest in man.'[12] Echoing Milton in *Paradise Lost,* Blake, Wordsworth and Coleridge praised 'the human form divine'; poets, for Keats in *The Fall of Hyperion,* 'seek no wonder but the human face' (I, l. 163). For all the Romantics, man was vital and organic, an integral part of a universe equally vital and organic. Even the unformed child is part of process. 'Emphatically such a Being lives', Wordsworth declared in the 1805 *Prelude,* 'An inmate of this *active* universe' (II, ll. 265–6). In such a universe man's primary responsibility is to other humans and to the human community of which he is a member. 'Everything that lives, / Lives not alone, nor for itself', wrote Blake in *The Book of Thel,*[13] and the other Romantic poets, though they never read these lines, celebrated marriage, union potential or achieved, and universal brotherhood.

With the Romantic poets we confront what is still basically a religious vision, one that was the inheritor of the Christian humanism of the Renaissance. This vision posits a close inter-relationship among the ethical, aesthetic and spiritual qualities of life. The giant figure looming behind the Romantics is Milton, but before him stand Sidney, Spenser and Donne. For Sidney, the poet, unlike those engaged in other pursuits, makes 'things either better than Nature bringeth forth, or quite a newe formes such as never were in Nature'.[14] His *Apologie for Poetrie* argues that inseparably intertwined with the aesthetic is the ethical: poetry both delights *and* teaches. The poet's goal should be 'knowledge of a mans selfe, in the Ethicke and politick consideration, with the end of well dooing and not of well knowing onely' (ibid., 19). The word 'Poet', Sidney explains, derives from the Greek for 'maker' (ibid., 14), and for him the 'maker' assumes a role like God's except that it is on a lower plane. Sidney, by equating poetry with the profoundest religious experience, anticipates the Romantics' conception of the poet as creator. Spenser, in Book I of *The Faerie Queene,* superimposes Parnassus upon Mount Sinai and the Mount of Olives. On Parnassus, the old man Contemplation allows the Red Cross knight a vision of the Heavenly City, a vision that also suggests that poetry and deep religious experience are one.[15] Donne in *Meditation* XVII speaks of the interconnectedness of all life in terms that foreshadow the Romantic position: 'The *Church* is *Catholike, universall,* so are all her *Actions; All* that she does, belongs to *all.* When she *baptizes a child,* that action concernes mee; for that child is thereby connected to . . . that *body,* whereof I am a *member.* . . . All *mankinde* is of one *Author,* and is one *volume.*'[16] Two centuries later the Romantic poets affirmed, in language saturated with religious imagery and symbolism, a similar vision of union between man and other men and between man and Nature.

'Poets are not ideal beings; but have their prose-sides', Hazlitt once wrote.[17] His observation, however we take it, retains value. Nowhere better than in a poet's prose side do we find clues to aid us in interpreting his beliefs and his poetry. We do not deny that the Romantic poets often *thought* in their poetry, that their poems explore ideas, separately or in conflict, or that in poems the poets work out epistemological, ethical and aesthetic problems. Still, by using their prose as well as their poetry we may gain a clearer perspective on their achievement. 'The study of Shelley's ideas in the prose [is] the best approach to the understanding of his poetry', David Lee Clark declared in 1954; more recently, Kenneth Neill Cameron has affirmed that 'Shelley's prose works provide important keys to his poetry. But they are significant in their own right also.'[18] What Clark and Cameron say about Shelley has validity for the other major Romantics. Only in the eighteenth century did prose become, as John Hollander has observed, 'an authentic vehicle of imaginative expression'.[19] Romantic prose we read for its intrinsic merit and as a complement to Romantic poetry. We need not agree with Auden when he claims that Keats's letters outshine his poetry, but we should recognize that Romantic prose – of the other poets no less than that of Keats – represents an extraordinary achievement, virtually as rich and varied as Victorian prose. Although in this study we discuss the beliefs of the Romantics as evidenced in their poetry, we make even fuller use of their prose works, whether they be full-dress treatises like the *Biographia Literaria*, hortatory essays like Wordsworth's 1800 Preface and Shelley's *Defence,* gnomic utterances like Blake's 'There is No Natural Religion', or the letters of Keats and Byron, written with apparent spontaneity and (in Keats's case at least) without thought of publication.

Certain writers on Romanticism today believe that to offer evidence in support of a generalization is a sign of bad taste. We do not. Rather, we believe that readers will follow an argument supported by ample quotation more willingly, and with more conviction, than one not so supported. E. D. Hirsh has criticized M. H. Abrams for dosing readers of his major study, *Natural Supernaturalism: Tradition and Revolution in Romantic Literature,* with 'a superfluity of instantiation and quotation'.[20] Abrams replied – rightly, we think – that 'any large historical generalization . . . called for a good deal of instantiation to back it up'.[21] This book uses each writer's words as much as possible for the reason that each expressed himself more accurately (and eloquently) than any paraphrases we can offer. We return again and again to certain key texts, not because others would not sometimes do as well, but because by returning to those already familiar we can explore their implications with different poets and from different perspectives. Readers may consider each chapter, in part, as a meditation upon a number of carefully chosen passages. The shifting perspectives from which we regard these passages will, we hope, elucidate the critical premises behind each poet's beliefs and suggest his intellectual affinities with the other poets.

Were this another kind of book, it might have attempted to chart in detail each writer's awareness of and response to the others with the aid of biography and through study of ascertainable literary influence. Every one of these poets had a character of great vitality, knew of the others as physical beings, met or unmet, and often reacted significantly to specific writings, ideas and opinions, as well as to personalities. (The major exception is the other poets' almost total unawareness of Blake, who, in turn, remained unaware of several of them.) '[Modern poets] are always talking of themselves and one another', wrote Hazlitt in *The Spirit of the Age* (1825), which, though opinionated, remains the best starting-place from which to gain a sense of the writers' personalities, their interactions among themselves and their response to the age. Despite recent studies,[22] this personal and literary context remains a radically neglected area in Romantic scholarship.

One cannot insist too strongly upon an awareness of biographical context for adequate comprehension of each poet's art: they gave of themselves intensely and received in return love, affection and support. Coleridge spoke in 1809 of his 'twelve years' intercommunion' with Wordsworth,[23] and he, Blake and Byron inspired loyalty of an uncommon kind, as did Keats, whose circle of friends actively sustained him. Even Shelley, the most theoretically inclined of the younger Romantics, brought out intense devotion in others – such that Byron, utterly unlike him in personality and style of life, exclaimed on at least four occasions that no one in his experience had equalled him in goodness of character.[24] De Quincey spoke for others as well when he described his regard for Wordsworth and Coleridge as 'in no respect short of a religious feeling: it had, indeed, all the sanctity of religion, and all the tenderness of a human veneration'. These men were, for him, 'not so much mere literary preferences as something that went deeper than life or household affections'.[25]

More significant even than biographical relationships is the nature of each poet's actual *literary* interaction with the others and with the intellectual climate of the age. For example, Shelley, in rethinking Wordsworth and Coleridge, made himself into a poet in *Alastor*, 'Hymn to Intellectual Beauty', and 'Mont Blanc'; Byron, in *English Bards*, reacted against Scotch Reviewers, but, more important, formed himself in defiance of the first generation of Romantic poets. Throughout the period, literary influence interweaves with biographical interaction in most subtle ways. We have only begun to explore the patterns of this tapestry.

It has been suggested that our conventional division of the Romantic poets by generations – Wordsworth and Coleridge, Shelley and Keats – is largely accidental, and that we would do better to emphasize, for example, the correspondences between Shelley and Coleridge on one hand, and Keats and Wordsworth on the other.[26] Certainly we should emphasize these correspondences, but the conventional division has even more validity if, instead of using it to separate each poet from the others, we approach them in ways that suggest the links among the poets of each generation and the relationships between the generations. In courses on English Romanticism in America the poets are usually taught in isolation (the older generation from the younger, each from the others), sequentially, three a semester. Jack Stillinger, evaluating the pedagogy of the field in 1971, put the situation thus: 'I think our current curricula, even in departments that have only historically oriented programs, very likely give the impression that Blake, Wordsworth, and Coleridge wrote in one semester, and Byron, Shelley, and Keats wrote in another – and that not only were these the sole writers of the period, but that the poets of the first semester and those of the second semester had very little to do with one another.'[27] The situation has not changed appreciably since Stillinger wrote. So vast does the bibliography attached to each figure loom nowadays that few scholars specializing in one figure or subject risk excursions into others. Only when we can escape the prevailing compartmentalization of knowledge about the Romantic poets will we find ourselves in a position to grasp the larger implications that their interactions and reciprocal influences, biographical and literary, have for English literature.

A book on Romanticism by two Byron scholars, one presumably with a Byronic perspective – what might this imply? Such a perspective (assuming that it exists) does *not* imply, first of all, that we share Byron's attitude toward 'those poor idiots of the Lakes' who he fervently believed were polluting contemporary literature.[28] It *does* imply, we hope, a respect for the provisional and relative rather than for the definitive and certain, for lucidity and common sense, and for fact ('words are things' in Byron's view and in ours).[29] The eclecticism of our approach indicates an indifference to systems of whatever ilk or fashionableness. We wish to embody a perspective that takes its stand not in a chosen methodology but in a regard for human life in all its bewildering complexity. Such a perspective may become a strength if readers find fewer traditional biases in this avowedly revisionist study than in comparable books.

'I hate all mystery', wrote Byron in *Don Juan,* 'and that air of claptrap, which your recent poets prize' (II, st. 124). The mystery and claptrap that so annoyed him among his contemporaries have yielded to the mandarin prose and convoluted argument of some recent practitioners of Romantic criticism – with, alas, no Byron to guy them.[30] A Byronic perspective also implies that we view Byron as a Romantic poet, taking his place securely with the other Romantics because he shares with them a number of characteristic assumptions and positions. Some critics of Romanticism, even the most astute, do not seem to know what to do with the poet of *Don Juan*. M. H. Abrams, for instance, though admiring him immensely, left him out completely of *Natural Supernaturalism* because he did not wish to complicate further his already complex argument.[31] We urge that Byron be brought into the larger Romantic context, argue that he was (in his special way) as much a Romantic as the other poets, and suggest affinities, discordances and relationships between him and the writers who were more than his contemporaries.

In confining the arena of our investigations to the six major poets and to familiar examples of their writings, chiefly prose, we knowingly omit much. We do not consider huge areas within each writer's work, we largely neglect the important Enlightenment background, we make almost no mention of Romanticism in other lands,[32] and, even within the English tradition, we scant major critics such as Hazlitt. In defence of these choices, we say only that we wished to write a short book, one that by focusing on essentials suggests more than it establishes, one that provokes rather than defines.

We have structured the book as a series of interlocking triads. In the chapters that follow this one (2–4) we discuss Blake, Wordsworth and Coleridge one by one. We set Blake beside Wordsworth and Coleridge, Wordsworth beside Blake and Coleridge, Coleridge beside Blake and Wordsworth. After pointing out their most evident and indisputable points of contact and swift interchanges of thought, we then take up thematically in the intercalary Chapter 5 the similarities within the pattern that has developed. This chapter attempts a preliminary synthesis of the beliefs of the first generation of Romantic poets. Coleridge in *The Friend*, developing an analogy between writing a literary work and going up a staircase, speaks of the 'LANDING-PLACES' that he interposes between the 'main divisions' of his work (I, 149). The landing-places function as reminders of an altered perspective brought about through progress up the stairs. Coming upon such landing-places in this book, the reader can presumably better grasp what he or she has already read and, after the landing-place that is Chapter 5, is prepared to go on with this new perspective in mind. In the subsequent discussions of Byron, Shelley and Keats (Chapters 6–8), we observe a similar procedure, suggesting analogies among their writings as well as to those of the first Romantic generation. Chapter 9, 'the last and highest' of the landing-places, surveys the grounds of belief shared by all six poets. By seeing English Romanticism whole and coherent, the parts not merely parts but parts of a whole, this chapter recapitulates the common elements within the intellectual positions of the major poets. The overall result of our investigation will be, we hope, a fresh and persuasive interpretation of English Romanticism.

Although the Romantic poets vigorously disagreed on central issues and would have been astonished to find themselves lumped together in university courses on 'Romanticism' (a term none of them would have dreamed of applying to themselves), they nonetheless did respond vitally and often passionately to each other's work, often defining their own position in the intensity of this reaction. Their writings, viewed within this larger context, embody similar concepts and suggest major interrelationships. We contemplate this dome of many-coloured glass again and again, examining its numerous facets from different points of view. Our focus invariably moves outward from the poets to the larger subject of Romanticism, not, as all too often in recent studies, inward from 'Romanticism' to the poets, a procedure that scants works in favour of theory. Whatever English Romanticism may signify, its meaning can only derive validity when it emerges from sustained contemplation of the six major poets who are its glory.

The initial chapter on Blake we have made less comparative than the discussions that follow it because it is intended in part to provide a foundation for them, a foundation all the more remarkable for the reason that Blake exerted almost no influence upon the other Romantics. The similarity of his thought and theirs suggests in startling fashion the fundamental unity or coherence of the English Romantic movement. None of this is meant to imply that we will give the other poets and their poems a Blakean reading or interpret them through the eyes of Blake. As he himself clearly understood, all men do not see alike, and he perhaps more than any of the other Romantics sang and celebrated the infinite variety of men and poets.

2 Blake and the Nature of Perception

In many ways, Blake's first engraved works, 'There is No Natural Religion', which exists in two versions, and 'All Religions are One' ushered in the Romantic movement ten years before the publication of *Lyrical Ballads*. This series of three was probably engraved in 1788. We know that thirteen copies exist, but, significantly, 'in no known copies . . . is the grouping of axioms complete or consistent'.[1] The natural religion of Blake's titles is deism, conceived as a mechanistic world-view, like 'a mill with complicated wheels' (BPP, 2) or, to use a figure that he does not use, like a great and perfectly running watch, the existence of which demonstrates the existence of a great Watch-Maker.[2]

But few poets have wished to worship a Watch-Maker, and Byron alone among the Romantics gave his faith, intermittently at least, to distinctly deistic principles. These principles are dualistic, imagining a Creator distinct and separate from the created universe, from which He has withdrawn as from a work completed, not evolving, and which may be understood only in terms of Newtonian and other science denying supernatural revelation. God is to be worshipped not in man-made churches but in His great outdoors. As Byron wrote in his juvenile poem 'The Prayer of Nature' of late 1806:

> Shall man confine his Maker's sway
>   To Gothic domes of mouldering stone?
> Thy Temple is the face of day;
>   Earth, ocean, heaven thy boundless throne. . . .
> Father! no prophet's laws I seek, –
>   *Thy* laws in Nature's works appear; . . .
> Thou, who can'st guide the wandering star
>   Through trackless realms of aether's space;
> Who calm'st the elemental war,
>   Whose Hand from pole to pole I trace. . . .
> To Thee, my God, to Thee I call![3]

Such freethinking, like Blake's own, rejects organized clergy or priesthood along with the physical church and its dogma. Coleridge alone of these poets in their period of greatest poetic achievement regarded himself as a member of an organized church, but even he, perhaps as late as 1820, could write a sonnet 'To Nature', in which he was his own priest: 'So will I build my altar in the fields, / And the blue sky my fretted dome shall be, / . . . Even me, the priest of this poor sacrifice.'[4] All this should remind us of what we know: that even within the thought of the most philosophically minded of the major Romantic poets we may easily find inconsistencies. Coleridge's ideas are so eclectic that plagiarism became for him a mode of composition, it has been said, a new prose genre.[5]

When Blake in 1788 engraved his first short works, he was a mature man of thirty-one years who had thought seriously about serious matters and had reached conclusions that foreshadowed much of his later work, as well as attitudes or ways of thinking that we will find in the other Romantic poets. We may observe, for example, in 'There is No Natural Religion', both series of maxims, his tremendous interest in the nature of perception, a word that appears here in its several forms at least nine times. This interest is shared by all the other Romantics, who agree that man is capable of seeing more than the bodily eye alone, mechanistically understood (like a *camera obscura*), will permit him to see. At least implicit in the thought of these poets is the distinction between see-er and seer, who is also sayer or singer. This being true, they agree, in their optimistic moments or moods, upon the infinite or nearly infinite potentialities of man, whatever his present state may be or however agonizing the process of his elevation to a higher vision. In the 'Conclusion' to the first series of 'There is No Natural Religion', Blake equates the Poetic or creative faculty with the Prophetic power (usually conceived in a religious context), the seer's power to see into the true life of things or to see things in a time dimension not present to the sight of others, to see into eternity, that is, to see as God sees, in Whose mind all things have always existed. Although the voice of Blake's prophetic bard is distinct and unique, all these poets can at times assume or create the role of poet as priest or priestly lawgiver. The Poetic-Prophetic faculty of perception, which sees beyond the limits of this world, Blake places in conflict with 'the

Philosophic & Experimental' faculty, the power to construct abstractions – mental abstracts that stand for and may become confused with living things, thus becoming the ghosts of living things in a universe of death.

In the second series, Blake's non-ironic, point-by-point rebuttal of the first, he reveals the philosophic and experimental faculty to be that of the 'Reason or the ratio of all we have already known', the great binding or limiting power of man's mind and personality and clearly anticipating the figure of the fallen Urizen. The greatest achievement of this power is the worst of all possible achievements for man: to reduce man's vision of the entire universe, in all its rich and immense variety, to a single abstraction. (The word *reason*, we may recall, is related to the Latin *ratio*, meaning *calculation* or *computation,* which gave us *rationalize, rationalization,* etc.) But, Blake asserts, 'Mans perceptions are not bounded. . . . The bounded is loathed by its possessor.' Thus it becomes imperative to assert the possibility of escape from this Promethean bondage, and the means are visionary, the way of the seer, the reward the escape from the misery and sin of selfhood into an expanded vision of 'the Infinite in all things'. Thus may the daily life of man be transformed or redeemed, much as Wordsworth described it in his 'Prospectus' to *The Recluse.* Although Blake's dramatic context or frame of reference is religious, the foundation of his structure is in his psychology, for 'less than All cannot satisfy Man'. 'The desire of Man being Infinite the possession is Infinite & himself Infinite'. The word *desire* is important in both maxims VI and VII, for 'if any could desire what he is incapable of possessing, despair must be his eternal lot'. That this is the condition of the damned Blake made clear in one of his marginalia to Lavater's *Aphorisms on Man* (1789): 'mark that I do not believe there is such a thing litterally. but hell is the being shut up in the possession of corporeal desires' (BPP, 579). Such an unregenerate man is then possessed by his desires, as by demons. However, the 'desire of Man' in maxim VII, the possession of which makes man himself 'Infinite', is that of redeemed man, and Blake's argument takes its form from the terms of the Christian concepts of the fall of man and the promise of redemption. The enemy is thus seen to be the true Satan, identified in plate 5 of *The Marriage of Heaven and Hell* as 'the restrainer [of desire] or reason', the 'Governor or Reason', that is, unredeemed Urizen. Blake equates Urizen (whom he does not specifically mention in this context) with 'Miltons Messiah' (BPP, 34).

Inherent in such argument, then, and logically implied by it, is a clear and convinced belief in the doctrine of the fall, for without such conviction there is no possibility of redemption.[6] To deny this doctrinal view of human nature is to deny or destroy the deepest foundations of the Christian system and to take away the very reason for Christ's coming upon earth. All this becomes evident in Blake's address 'To the Deists' in *Jerusalem* (BPP, 198–9), where deism '*is* Natural Religion' (italics added) and 'teaches that Man is Righteous in his Vegetated Spectre: an Opinion of fatal & accursed consequence to Man'. Deism 'is the Worship of the God of this World by the means of . . . Natural Religion . . . and of Natural Morality or Self-Righteousness, the Selfish Virtues of the Natural Heart. This was the Religion of the Pharisees who murderd Jesus.' Blake's Christianity, unlike deism, must believe that 'Man is born a Spectre or Satan & is altogether an Evil, & requires a New Selfhood continually & must continually be changed into his direct Contrary.' Hence the need of 'Forgiveness of Sins continually'. Here Blake writes, interestingly, not of 'the Religion of Jesus, Forgiveness of Sin', but of friendship, which 'cannot exist' without such forgiveness. 'Vengeance for Sin' thus becomes the denial of forgiveness of sin and the religion of Satan. Shelley was equally firm in his abhorrence of 'Revenge', and Byron at one time in his life thought that 'the basis of [the Anglican] religion is *injustice*', the God of that church 'a tyrant'.[7] A poet's view of the essential nature of human nature influences in the most important ways, then, his views on other major matters, including his ethics and his art. Subsequent chapters will consider the views of the other Romantics on man. All of them saw him as a fallen creature who needed to be redeemed. Not one of them, as Blake wrote of Rousseau, 'thought Man Good by Nature' (BPP, 199).

The only other work that Blake engraved in 1788, also a kind of elaborate miniature on momentous matters, 'All Religions are One', asserts by implication the common inheritance of all humanity. In Blake, where this aspirational dream takes the form of a religious-poetic community, all men, both living and dead, are potentially united by the presence of a poetic genius in every man. The mood is subjective, as in 'There is No Natural Religion' and elsewhere in Blake. We have in effect another vision of potential union, marriage, universal brotherhood, some form of which we shall find in all the Romantic poets. Blake's 'Argument' announces his subject: 'the true faculty of knowing' is that which 'experiences'. Poetry thus becomes not only a way of knowing but the 'true' way. The method is metaphorical, equating dissimilars, and circular, metaphorically circular, returning in the last sentence to the first sentence of Principle 1st. (Coleridge, we remember, thought all the best poems – and paintings – circular in structure.) In between these poetical bounds, Blake demonstrates, using the outward form of reasoned or geometric argument, that the one source of all religions is 'the true Man', who has within him the Poetic Genius, which, in turn, 'is every where call'd the Spirit of Prophecy', itself the source of the Old and New Testaments, the true word of God. In other and more human words, 'All deities reside in the human breast', as Blake wrote in *The Marriage* (BPP, 37), and speak out of the human breast, redeemed, even though 'an universal Poetic Genius exists' also (2). Blake associates the God of Ezekiel and the Poetic Genius in similar fashion in the second Memorable Fancy of *The Marriage,* where, however, he also states, 'God only Acts & Is, in existing beings or Men' (39). But in Blake's 'Additions to [his] Catalogue of Pictures', describing in 1810 his 'Vision of the Last Judgment', we read, 'Imaginative Art & Science & all Intellectual Gifts all [are] the Gifts of the Holy Ghost' (544). The Holy Ghost speaks through the divinely inspired poet.

To return more directly to 'All Religions are One'. In Principle 5th all religions are 'derived from . . . the Poetic Genius'; so also in Principle 1st 'the body or outward form of Man is derived from the Poetic Genius'. That is, both the vegetated body and the organized religion of churches are the external or imperfect expressions of the inner vision. After this, it may seem anti-climactic to observe that for Blake not only 'all religions' but 'all similars have one source'. Here Blake has defined the central function of the poet: to make metaphors, or as Coleridge repeatedly said, 'to reconcile opposites', finding unity in multeity.[8]

Thus far had Blake proceeded in 1788. The next year would see presumably *Songs of Innocence* and perhaps *The Book of Thel.*

It remains now to examine certain other interesting expressions of Blake's critical theory in his letters in order to consider the fundamental coherence of his thought early and late. The first extant letter of essential importance is that of 23 August 1799 to the Rev. Dr John Trusler, author of *Hogarth Moralized* and *The Way to be Rich and Respectable.* Trusler had disliked Blake's design illustrating Malevolence, showing a helpless wife and child 'watch'd by Two Fiends incarnate' intent on murder.⁹ One might predict the nature of Blake's response to such an author: 'What is Grand is necessarily obscure to Weak men. That which can be made Explicit to the Idiot is not worth my care. The wisest of the Ancients consider'd what is not too Explicit as the fittest for Instruction, because it rouzes the faculties to act. I name Moses, Solomon, . . . Homer, Plato' (BL, 29).

Among the Romantic poets there is a less than general agreement on the importance of the implicit, 'what is not too Explicit', for the reason that, as Blake phrased it, 'it rouzes the [reader's] faculties to act'. 'The grandest efforts of poetry', Coleridge explained in a lecture on that subject in 1811, 'are where the imagination is called forth . . . to produce . . . a strong working of the mind. . . . keeping the mind in a state of activity'.¹⁰ If 'Genius is the introduction of a new element into the intellectual universe', as Wordsworth stated, then the reader must 'exert himself; for he cannot proceed in quiescence'.¹¹ These poet-prophets, all seriously interested in that which is 'fittest for Instruction', truths that are operative on the minds of men, understood that the merely passive reader learns nothing, that the poem that only keeps 'the fancy amused without the trouble of thought' changes nothing (WPW, 429). They wrote poems about growth, spiritual or intellectual, and they expected the reader's mind to grow too.

In his letter to the Rev. Dr Trusler, Blake understands that Homer and the Bible are 'more Entertaining & Instructive than any other book[s]' for the reason that 'they are addressed to the Imagination, which is Spiritual Sensation, & but mediately to the Understanding or Reason' (BL, 30). Blake's terminology is by no means consistent, but his use of the term 'Understanding' here is at least roughly equivalent to the faculty represented by the fallen Urizen and is probably synonymous with the phrase 'Corporeal Understanding' as he used it in his letter to Thomas Butts of 6 July 1803, perhaps referring to his *Milton:* 'Allegory address'd to the Intellectual powers, while it is altogether hidden from the Corporeal Understanding, is My Definition of the Most Sublime Poetry' (BL, 69). The same letter links 'Understanding' with memory and dissociates it from Blake's own 'affections'. Here again the term 'Understanding' seems to refer to a calculating faculty that deals with the sum of things already known. In 'A Vision of the Last Judgment' Blake tells us that 'Mental Things are alone Real what is Calld Corporeal Nobody Knows of its dwelling Place ⟨it⟩ is in Fallacy & its Existence [is] an Imposture'; that is, it exists 'in the Mind of a fool' (BPP, 555) but not in the mind of Blake, a man of imagination. This view is by no means unlike Shelley's position that nothing exists except as it is perceived.[12]

Turning back to the earlier letter to Trusler, we read, 'But to the Eyes of the man of Imagination, Nature is Imagination itself. . . . To Me This World is all One continued Vision of Fancy or Imagination' (BL, 30). Imagination is then defined as 'Spiritual Sensation', that is, presumably, a sensation or sensing, primarily a seeing or visual imaging of the world so that the sun, for example, may be transformed from 'a round Disk of fire somewhat like a Guinea' into 'an Innumerable company of the Heavenly host crying Holy Holy Holy is the Lord God Almighty'. The substance of this vision is spiritual, as Blake looks through and not with his 'Corporeal or Vegetative Eye' (BPP, 555).[13] Although Blake had not anticipated Coleridge's distinction between fancy and imagination, using them synonymously in his letter to Trusler, we may be reminded of T. S. Eliot's early statement: 'many men will admit that their keenest ideas have come to them with the quality of a sense-perception; and that their keenest sensuous experience has been "as if the body thought" '.[14] Blake phrased it another way in *The Marriage:* 'my senses discover'd the infinite in every thing' (BPP, 38).

We have now arrived in the midst of the problem of perception, about which so many critics of Blake have written.[15] Probably we should rejoice in the products of his spiritual sensation rather than try to understand much more than Blake has told us about the process or workings of it. For the sad fact of the matter is that the science of perception has advanced little since Blake's time. Sir Peter Medawar, a distinguished biologist, Nobel prize winner, and for a long time director of the National

Institute for Medical Research in Great Britain, wrote not too long ago concerning an interpretation of Romanticism that denied Blake's distinction between the imaginative faculty and reason: 'anyone who thinks otherwise [than Blake] is a fool or a knave'.[16] Richard Gregory, head of the Brain and Perception Laboratory of the University of Bristol, puts the problem in a wider perspective:

> Theories of perception – of what happens to bridge the extra-ordinary gap between sensory stimulation and our experience of external objects – have a long history, of astonishing variety. . . . How we see remains essentially mysterious after a century of intensive experiment, on animals and on men, by such a variety of scientists that aims and communication can be lost between them.[17]

In 'Neural Connexions and the Life-Cycle of the Senses', John G. Taylor, a professor of applied mathematics at King's College, University of London, observes further: 'The mechanisms by which these changes of sensation [during the span of man's life] and sensations in general are experienced are still not understood. The basic problem is to understand how a sensation is perceived or felt.'[18]

Perhaps so – for the scientist. But for the critic of literature this 'basic problem' is pre-literary, an aspect or branch of psychology, and, when focused on a single poet, a form of biography. Taylor continues, 'We start life, then, as a passive unconscious machine, responding to the streams of energy of different forms impinging on our various sense organs.' Blake would have violently disagreed. He had in fact responded to this argument in the second series of 'There is No Natural Religion': 'Mans perceptions are not bounded by organs of perception. he percieves more than sense (tho' ever so acute) can discover.'

All the Romantic poets rejected the idea of the mind as a passive machine. Their battles against this concept are still being fought. Richard Gregory explains: 'Perceptual theories form a spectrum – from *passive* to *active* theories. Passive theories suppose that perception is essentially camera-like, conveying selected aspects of objects quite directly, as though the eyes and brain are undistorting windows.' Blake knew better: 'I question

not my Corporeal or Vegetative Eye any more than I would
Question a Window concerning a Sight. I look thro it & not
with it' (BPP, 555). Coleridge, who had been reading Newton's
Optics, also argued against passive theories of perception: 'Newton was a mere materialist – *Mind* in his system is always passive – a lazy Looker-on on an external World. If the mind be not
passive, if it be indeed made in God's Image, & that too in the
sublimest sense – the Image of the *Creator* – there is ground for
suspicion, that any system built on the passiveness of the mind
must be false, as a system.'[19] Such a mind clearly has no place in
it for Coleridge's primary imagination, which, in the famous
definition at the end of chapter 13 of the *Biographia*, is the 'prime
Agent of all human Perception, . . . a repetition in the finite
mind of the eternal act of creation in the infinite I AM' (I, 202).
The secondary or poetic imagination is an 'echo' of the primary.
Newton's passive theory of perception, then, cannot explain the
act of poetic composition, the existence of poems.

Richard Gregory's summary of active theories of perception
thus becomes of particular interest. These theories

> suppose that perceptions are constructed, by complex brain
> processes, from fleeting fragmentary scraps of data signalled
> by the senses and drawn from the brain's memory banks –
> themselves constructions from snippets from the past. On
> this view, normal everyday perceptions are not selections of
> reality but are rather imaginative constructions – fictions –
> based (as indeed is science fiction also) more on the stored
> past than on the present. On this view all perceptions are
> essentially fictions. . . . Here we should not equate 'fiction'
> with 'false'. Even the most fanciful fiction as written is very
> largely true, or we would not understand it.[20]

Although Blake and Coleridge would not have liked the
emphasis here on memory, John Livingston Lowes's *The Road
to Xanadu: A Study in the Ways of the Imagination* (1927) long ago
demonstrated its importance in the creative process.

What may we say, then, that is useful about Blake's theories
of perception? First, when he claims that he *sees* everything that
he paints in his 'World of imagination & Vision' and that
'Nature is Imagination' (BL, 30), we must believe him. His
pictorial art is witness to the truth of these words written to
Trusler in 1799. Further, the magnificently successful marriage

of the pictorial and the poetic in his illuminated books should persuade us that he also visualized the characters in his poems, along with their actions and settings. This being true, it follows that portrait painting, with the subject always sitting before the painter, his purpose to produce a realistic and recognizable likeness, 'is Idolatry & destroys the Soul' in the same way that the worship of idols destroys the soul by denying the One unseen God, unseen except in the mind's eye. The reason is that 'Nature [realistically conceived] & Fancy [the imagination] are Two Things & can Never be joined'.[21] It is literally impossible to join them, Blake means, for 'Mental Things are alone Real' or capable of existing in his mind (BPP, 555).

Finally, it is useful to understand something of Blake's 'fourfold vision', subject of a poem that is part of a second letter written to Butts on 22 November 1802 (BL, 60–2). Symbolic numbers, like other symbols, are defined by their context, and we make no attempt here to collect and examine every reference to Blake's four kinds of vision. Each one did not always refer to precisely same complex state of mind or being. Furthermore, a vision or way of seeing expresses itself normally in terms of a description of things seen, a fact that additionally complicates any critical analysis of Blake's perceptual theory and may tempt the critic into very strange waters indeed.

Single vision is, however, defined clearly enough in Blake's letter: it is 'Newton's sleep' (BL, l. 88), presumably the sleep of death, but also the unquestioning unimaginative acceptance of a mechanistic Newtonian world-view, seen by what the poem calls the 'outward' eye (l. 30), the vegetative eye that sees a thistle as a 'trifle' (l. 25). In painting, such single vision seems to be associated with William Gilpin's school of picturesque landscape painting and with portrait painting, both discussed by Blake in his earlier letter of the same day to Butts. The second letter is obviously a continuation of or postscript to the first. In it, Blake quotes approvingly a letter from Sir Joshua Reynolds to Gilpin: 'Perhaps Picturesque is somewhat synonymous to the word Taste, which we should think improperly applied to Homer or Milton, but very well to Prior or Pope'.[22] Whatever excellences picturesque painting may have, they are those of 'an inferior order, . . . incompatible with the Grand Style'. By contrast, Blake assures Butts, the drawings and pictures he had sent to him were the product of 'my Head & my Heart in

Unison' (BL, 58), a phrase reminiscent (perhaps fortuitously) of Wordsworth's 'sweet counsels between head and heart' (*Prelude,* XI, l. 353). Blake in the same letter apologizes for his delay in finishing his miniature of Mrs Butts: 'Portrait Painting is the direct contrary to Designing & Historical Painting in every respect. If you have not Nature before you for Every Touch, you cannot Paint Portrait; & if you have Nature before you at all, you cannot paint History; it was Michael Angelo's opinion & is Mine' (BL, 59).

When one recalls Blake's historical paintings (not to mention Michelangelo's), it is clear that they could not have been produced by single vision. Gilpin, in his *Three Essays: On Picturesque Beauty; On Picturesque Travel; and On Sketching Landscape* (1792), is equally clear concerning the necessity of having Nature before you for every touch in painting landscape: 'the *characteristic features* of a scene . . . [and] the leading ideas must be fixed on the spot: if left to the memory, they soon evaporate'. 'Written references, made on the spot', are essential if the painting cannot be completed there and if there is any possibility of confusing the several distances in the landscape.[23] Here we have the reasons for Blake's association of picturesque landscape painting and portrait painting and his low opinion of both modes of 'single vision'. Like the world of abstractions, it is a world largely without imagination. Wordsworth felt the same way about it, though somewhat less passionately: that Sir Joshua Reynolds normally painted portraits from eleven to four each day 'grieved' him 'as a sacrifice of great things to little ones'.[24]

But Blake's poem asserts – and we should recall that it is a portion of a personal letter to an intimate friend – that 'a double vision is always with me' (BL, l. 28), seen with the 'inward Eye' that transforms a thistle into 'an old Man grey' (l. 29). This double vision threatens Blake on his journey with 'endless woe' and transforms the sun into fallen 'Los the terrible' (l. 38), a condition of work without hope, of labouring in poverty night and day without ease or love. But the 'I' of the poem defies Los, and the poems ends triumphantly: 'With the bows of my Mind & the Arrows of Thought – / My bowstring fierce with Ardour breathes' (ll. 78–9). Here we have a world of conflict, the Blakean world of Experience, in which Los, the poet's presiding genius, can desert and become the enemy. The only defence is defiance and persistence in the 'intellectual War' (*The Four Zoas,* 'Night the Ninth': BPP, 392), which, however, can be won in terms of creation of the art work.

Threefold vision exists in 'soft Beulah's night' according to line 86 of the poem. We must go elsewhere for an understanding of it. Beulah's night appears again, presumably, in Blake's threefold 'Crystal Cabinet' (written in 1803), which 'opens into a World / And a little lovely Moony Night' (ll. 7–8: BPP, 479), a phrase echoed in the Beulah of *Jerusalem,* where 'every Female . . . Creates at her will a little moony night', searching 'sea & land for gratifications to the / Male Genius' (*Jerusalem* 69, 15–19: BPP, 221). 'There is from Great Eternity', we read in 'Night the First' of *The Four Zoas,* 'a mild & pleasant rest / Namd Beulah a Soft Moony Universe feminine lovely' (BPP, 299), lines that are echoed in *Milton* (30, 13–14: BPP, 128). Common to all these passages is their feminine 'moony' or moonstruck quality: Beulah, which derives from Isaiah and means 'married', is a place of mind for 'romantic' love and rest from the arduous pursuits of the 'Male Genius', a place where woman, her female hypocritical will no longer dominant and limiting man's desires and binding him, may find her true place or function – to serve him in love and thus fulfil herself.

But the poetic genius cannot sleep or love his life away if he is to achieve the 'supreme delight' of 'fourfold vision', otherwise unexplained in the poem sent to Butts on 22 November 1802. However, we learn from *Milton* that Blake's fourfold vision is the vision of Eden, which is 'created . . . In the great Wars of Eternity, in fury of Poetic Inspiration, / To build the Universe stupendous: Mental forms Creating' (30, ll. 15, 19–20: BPP, 128). The Saviour in *Jerusalem* explains further the nature of these wars: 'Our wars are wars of life, & wounds of love, / With intellectual spears, & long winged arrows of thought. / . . . We live as One man' (34 [38], 14–17: BPP, 178).

This is perhaps all we need to know. The man of fourfold vision is an active creative thinker and artist, deeply involved in life and spiritual love, who lives in utter selflessness in a community of artists like himself. This communal existence is a totally ethical existence of such intensity that it rises to the level of religious ecstasy in mystical union with deity:

for contracting our infinite senses
We behold multitude; or expanding: we behold as one,
As One Man all the Universal Family; and that One Man
We call Jesus the Christ: and he in us, and we in him,
Live in perfect harmony in Eden the land of life,
Giving, recieving, and forgiving each others trespasses.
(34 [38], 17–23: BPP, 178)

The last lines are the most important. Blake's Eden, 'the garden
of God', is 'the land of life' – *this* life, where men still trespass
against one another but forgive each other daily.[25] The highest
form of imaginative vision, the fourfold vision of the artist, is
also the highest ethical vision. That the other major Romantic
poets similarly identified the creative and the ethical imagination is a point we need not labour at this time.

But Blake's Eden is no more guaranteed than the reign of
Shelley's Prometheus. It must be guarded. '*Now* I a fourfold
vision see' (italics added), Blake writes in the poem sent to
Butts, which closes with the rhyme words of the child's nightly
prayer, 'Now I lay me down to sleep; I pray the Lord my soul
to keep.' Blake's prayer is equally fearful of the sleep of death:
'May God us keep / From Single vision & Newton's sleep!'
Thus Blake builds a well-guarded city in the land of Ulro: 'And
fourfold, / The great City of Golgonooza' (*Jerusalem* 12, 45–6:
BPP, 154). 'And every part of the City is fourfold; & every
inhabitant, fourfold. . . . And every house, fourfold' (13, ll. 20,
22: 155). Presumably all those who live in these houses and
labour to build this city have fourfold vision. For it is a city built
not only by men but out of men, out of the best that is in them.
'The stones are pity, and the bricks, well wrought affections: /
Enameld with love & kindness' (12, 30–1: 154). This city is built
by 'golden builders' (l. 25) in the place most distantly removed
from Eden. But both the city and the garden are completely
humanized, and both are places of the actively creative human
mind. Although the city of art is designed to protect and defend
the garden, their similarities are more interesting than their differences. For 'every Generated Body in its inward form, / Is a
garden of delight & a building of magnificence, / Built by the
Sons of Los' (*Milton* 26, 31–3: BPP, 122), as they labour in or
around Golgonooza creating truly human people. The

'stupendous ruins / Arches & pyramids & porches colonades & domes' (38, 21–2: 138) call to mind Wordsworth's 'mighty city' of heavenly glory in *The Excursion* (Bk II, l. 827ff.), Coleridge's 'stately pleasure dome', Byron's Rome with its treasures of the Vatican and St. Peter's, the architectural splendours of Shelley's *Prometheus Unbound* and of Keats's Hyperion poems.

A poet such as Blake could only have a low opinion of the more decorous Augustans as he contemplated, sometimes exuberantly and sometimes satirically, the new spirit of the age. Hazlitt wrote a book on the subject and M. H. Abrams has discussed it authoritatively in his essay 'English Romanticism: The Spirit of the Age', the chief focus of which is political.[26] It was an age conscious of great and revolutionary changes, and those who lived through them felt intensely and emotionally involved. Although Blake in *The Marriage* is commonly satirical, he is hopeful when he writes, 'a new heaven is begun' (BPP, 34), a phrase reminiscent of Revelation's 'new heaven and a new earth'.[27] Wordsworth and Coleridge thought for a time that it had come to France, and, despite the failure of the French Revolution, Keats believed in 1816 that 'Great spirits now on earth are sojourning.' Shelley in 1821 at the end of his *Defence of Poetry* paid noble tribute to the poets of his own time but thought that their achievement was due 'less [to] their spirit than the spirit of the age'. By the time Blake wrote his Preface to *Milton* (1807–9?), a New Age in his opinion was struggling to be born, although forces of the old repressive order were still powerful. Blake called upon the 'Young Men of the New Age', himself among them, to reject classical 'Models' 'set up by artifice' and be 'true to our own Imaginations'. With the full maturity of the New Age, it would appear, 'the Daughters of Memory shall become the Daughters of Inspiration' (BPP, 94). For Blake, Memory is concerned with things past and of no concern to the Spirit of Prophecy, which expresses a divinely inspired vision of things to be or that should be.

The most interesting aspect of Blake's Preface to *Milton* is not his main purpose, to celebrate the Bible and the freed artistic imagination, but the means or assumption that he employs to achieve that purpose. Clearly for the poet, Pope's directive in *An Essay on Criticism* is no longer valid: 'Learn hence for Ancient *Rules* a just Esteem: / To copy *Nature* is to copy *Them*' (ll.

139–40). In Blake's vocabulary ancient rules have become ancient rooted error; nature has become 'this Vegetable Glass of Nature' (BPP, 545), a delusive goddess, and to copy is merely to imitate surfaces, as if holding up a mirror to life, to produce a picturesque sketch or portrait. Such passive imitation is at odds with the sublime inspiration of the biblical prophets, poets like Milton, and the true Poetic Genius of 'All Religions are One'. The old honoured words have thus become dirty words, and the last thing Blake wished to hear was 'how learn'd *Greece* her useful Rules indites, / When to repress, and when indulge our Flights' (*Essay on Criticism,* ll. 92–3). For him, for whom originality of vision was everything, the word 'copy' has become associated with 'dis-arranged imitations', which has itself become synonymous with 'plagiarism, and bungling' ('A Descriptive Catalogue': BPP, 540). Pope's poetry has become 'Popes Metaphysical Jargon of Rhyming'.[28] 'He who copies does not Execute he only Imitates what is already Executed'.[29] Such an artist lacks 'the Poetic or Prophetic character'; he is 'at the ratio of all things, & stand[s] still unable to do other than repeat the same dull round over again' (BPP, 1). He is incapable of true 'Invention', for 'Execution is only the result of Invention' (565), a term that has almost disappeared from twentieth-century criticism.[30] Blake uses the word to refer to an original discovery of the imagination. 'To Engrave after another Painter', he had written to Trusler, 'is infinitely more laborious than to Engrave one's own Inventions' (BL, 30). In 1817, in a letter of 8 October to Benjamin Bailey, Keats uses the word in the same sense. *Endymion,* he says, will be 'a trial of my Powers of Imagination and chiefly of my invention which is a rare thing indeed – by which I must make 4000 Lines of one bare circumstance and fill them with Poetry'.[31]

A true imaginative invention then is quite different from the memory's imitation or copy. Memory produces allegory, but allegory and 'Vision' are 'Two Distinct Things', for 'Vision or Imagination is a Representation of what Eternally Exists' ('A Vision of the Last Judgment': BPP, 544). Memory recalls what the 'perishing mortal eye can see' (532), but the imagination sees 'Visions of . . . eternal principles or characters of human life' (527), that is, visions of 'spiritual existences', unchanging attributes of *human nature* (like those represented in statues of the

Greek gods), for 'Spirits are organized men'.[32] Thus allegory
compared with visionary poetry is 'a totally distinct & inferior
kind of Poetry'.[33]

Poetry of the 'Visionary Fancy or Imagination' (BPP, 544) is
superior then for the reason that it concerns itself with permanent, unchanging truths about human experience. Such truths
are born of the highest human faculty: 'the Imaginative Image
returns ⟨by⟩ the seed of Contemplative Thought' (BPP, 545),
of a kind illustrated by the writings of the biblical prophets.
'Contemplative Thought', for Blake, is not unlike Wordsworth's 'Reason in her most exalted mood' (*Prelude*, XIV,
l. 192), which cannot exist apart from imagination and spiritual
or intellectual love. Such 'Thought' is the product of the whole
mind of man functioning at its highest and fullest or most comprehensive capacity, at which point it becomes not merely
human but divine, 'the True Vine of Eternity', echoing the
Christ of John 15:1, 'The Human Imagination' (BPP, 545). Men
are admitted into Blake's heaven, where they can see, along
with Christ, 'the Permanent Realities of Every Thing which we
see reflected in this Vegetable Glass of Nature' (545), 'not
because they have ⟨curbed &⟩ governed their Passions or have
No Passions but because they have Cultivated their Under-
standings. The Treasures of Heaven are not Negations of
Passion but Realities of Intellect from which All the Passions
Emanate' (553–4). Those not admitted are those who have
'no Passions of their own because No Intellect' (554). Blake
is here close to Coleridge, who wrote to Thomas Poole on
23 March 1801, 'deep Thinking is attainable only by a man of
deep Feeling, and . . . all Truth is a species of Revelation'.[34]
In the year following, Coleridge can say of Bowles that 'he
has no native Passion, because he is not a Thinker'.[35]

In Blake's vocabulary, the terms 'Contemplative Thought',
'The Human Imagination', 'the Understanding', 'Intellect' (from
which the passions emanate), are closely associated and may be
used synonymously. The ideas that a man holds in his mind
with true faith or passionate conviction will be deeply entwined
with the element of feeling and they will be expressed with
Blakean energy. But for Blake, as for Shelley (and Berkeley),
'Mental Things are alone Real' (BPP, 555). 'Existence Out of
Mind or Thought' is only in 'the Mind of a Fool', not in Blake's
mind, and is created, not eternal. Therefore, 'Error or Creation',

man's erroneous, Urizenic conception of himself and his world, will cease to exist, will be 'Burned Up the Moment Men cease to behold it'. This apocalyptic moment Blake calls 'The Last Judgment' when 'Bad Art & Science' will be overwhelmed.[36] It is also true that because mental things are alone real to the eyes of the man of imagination, 'Nature is Imagination itself', as Blake informed Trusler. 'This World is all One continued Vision of Fancy or Imagination' (BL, 30). Blake had not made, as noted earlier, Coleridge's distinction between the two latter terms.

We must not think, however, despite Blake's emphasis on the enduring, unchanging, or eternal elements of existence, that he championed any Johnsonian variety of doctrine that would elevate the general over the particular. Dr Johnson said in his life of Cowley, 'Great thoughts are always general', and he went on to attack the 'laboured particularities' of the metaphysical poets. Imlac in *Rasselas* understood very clearly that 'the business of a poet . . . is to examine, not the individual, but the species; to remark general properties and large appearances' (ch. 10). But Blake wrote, 'General Knowledge is Remote Knowledge[;] it is in Particulars that Wisdom consists & Happiness Too' (BPP, 550). Or, when annotating Reynolds's *Discourses:* 'To Generalize is to be an Idiot[.] To Particularize is the Alone Distinction of Merit' (630). Blake had more than one reason for vehemently preferring the specific and particular; perhaps the chief reason was his passionate concern for the uniqueness of each human individual. But the consequences for his aesthetics are clear: 'General Masses are as Much Art as a Pasteboard Man is Human.' It therefore follows that 'not a line [should be] drawn without intention & that most discriminate & particular . . . Poetry admits not a Letter that is Insignificant' (550), for 'Every Poem must necessarily be a perfect Unity'.[37] Coleridge could not have said it better.

That Blake was a skilled poetic craftsman and most knowledgeable aesthetician must not obscure the further fact that for him literary theory or criticism is a branch of the study of the soul's or personality's salvation. Nothing is more serious or further removed from any variety of art-for-art's-sake doctrine. The true poetic genius, exemplified by the purified Milton, must annihilate self or 'selfhood' to achieve a state of being not unlike those 'enthralments far / More self-destroying' described by Keats in *Endymion* but essentially synonymous with the loss of personal identity (I, ll. 798–9), a state of being also described by Coleridge in 'Religious Musings' as 'all self-annihilated' (ll. 43–4). In short, the poetic imagination cannot exist unless it is an ethical imagination – that is, a visionary, spiritual, redeemed imagination. The expanded consciousness that results produces a new, redeemed, integrated or unified being whose visionary ideal is of a brotherhood of man, a deep care and concern for all suffering humanity, and a burning faith in the possibilities of the future. And the process of expansiveness seems to begin (and may end) in the eye. But the power that redeems the eye and allows it to see the beauty, the infinite in all things, is not always clearly identified. Sometimes it appears to be a form of divine grace, sometimes it appears without explanation; always it is mysterious, beyond the power of the conscious will. Aesthetics, for Blake, is finally a branch of eschatology, and in *Milton* Satan is the enemy of art and the artist.

If Eden is unity, Satan, the Tempter, is alienation or isolation: a fragmentation of the several aspects of the individual psyche or alienation of individuals from one another, from that which is greater than self, from the unity or community of man, or from the unity of all created things. It is a fragmentation of some larger, greater, earlier unity, In this condition, the self asserts itself against other selves, imposing its own will to repress or to destroy others; or the calculating reason attempts to suppress the other faculties of man and tyrannize over them.

Inverting the Romantic and apocalyptic or biblical metaphor of marriage, Blake describes Satan in *Milton* as the negation of the bride of the Lamb, she who is also a great city, the new Jerusalem of Revelation. In 'Satans bosom', very different from Abraham's, Blake beholds 'a ruind Man: a ruind building of God not made with hands', his place a place of 'ruind palaces & cities & mighty works', in which dwells 'Mystery Babylon', the whore of Revelation 17:5 (38, 15ff.: BPP, 138). Thus Blake defines the ultimate evil in terms of fallen art.

But architecture, the most social of all the arts, does not exist in isolation, and Blake does not limit his definition of Satan to the metaphor of a building in ruins. Satan is also associated with or made the symbolic equivalent of the churches of Urizen, teaching 'fear, terror, *constriction*; abject *selfishness* (l. 39; BPP, 138; italics added), and with 'the Idol Virtues of the Natural

Heart [prudence, justice, temperance and fortitude, i.e., the four chief or cardinal virtues] & Satans Seat . . . in all its Selfish Natural Virtue' (ll. 46–7). Thus Blake defines Satan the enemy of man in the broadest, most inclusive terms: bad art, bad religion and bad ethics or morality. In short, his name in Blake is also legion, and when two hundred or so lines later he returns to the subject, Satan is associated with the abstracting 'Reasoning Power in Man', 'Rational Demonstration', Bacon, Locke and Newton – Blake's symbols of bad science and philosophy, bad logic, psychology and physics. However, the emphasis in this passage is also heavily aesthetic, as Milton 'in terrible majesty' comes 'to cast off the rotten rags of Memory by Inspiration' and denounce 'the tame high finisher of paltry Blots, / Indefinite, or paltry Rhymes', those 'who pretend to Poetry that they may destroy Imagination; / By imitation of Natures Images drawn from Remembrance' (41, 3ff.: BPP, 144). Blake's seeming differences with Wordsworth on the natural man, on accuracy of description, recollection and imagination in poetry we consider in the next chapter.[38] We may recall here, however, that Coleridge in the *Biographia* denounced the 'natural' man as 'selfish, sensual, gross, and hard-hearted' (II, 32) and that Shelley in his 'Speculations on Morals' denied the power of sympathy (the basis of his ethics) to the 'infant', the 'savage', and the 'solitary beast' (SP, 188).

If for Blake the Last Judgment is an overwhelming of bad art, it follows logically that the true Christianity of the Gospel, the religion of Jesus, is the 'liberty both of body & mind to exercise the Divine Arts of Imagination' (*Jerusalem,* 'To the Christians': BPP, 229). Thus the Divine Spirit, the Holy Ghost, becomes 'an Intellectual Fountain', the 'Treasures of Heaven' 'Mental Studies & Performances', and 'the Life of Man . . . Art & Science' (ibid.). The 'Pains of Hell [are] Ignorance' and 'the labours of Art & Science . . . alone are the labours of the Gospel' (229–30). It is little exaggeration to conclude, then, that Blake's religion and aesthetics are essentially one. Such a poet will inevitably conceive his function to be that of healing 'the sick of spiritual disease', to 'teach them True Happiness' (230, 231). This humanistic and therapeutic purpose is also basically that of the other major Romantic poets.

3 Wordsworth: the Blakean Response

We probably do not sufficiently emphasize today that Wordsworth was reared and educated from the first in the doctrines
of the Anglican faith. The headmaster of the Hawkshead
Grammar School, so beloved by him, was an Anglican clergyman. His uncle William Cookson, himself a clergyman, des-
tined him for the Anglican clergy, and as late as May 1792 the
poet could write, 'it is at present my intention to take orders in
the approaching winter or spring. My Uncle the Clergyman
will furnish me with a title.'[1] In Wordsworth's time at St. John's
College, Cambridge, chapel attendance was mandatory; Roman
Catholics and Nonconformists were still excluded, although in
the early nineteenth century a wave of evangelicalism swept
over the university. Most of Wordsworth's acquaintances at St.
John's became Anglican clergymen, including his best friend,
Robert Jones, who was his companion at the time of the important experiences described in Book VI of *The Prelude* (going over
the Simplon Pass) and at the opening of Book XIV (climbing
Snowdon).

In the course of his long life, Wordsworth never escaped far
from the faith of his childhood and youth. The penultimate line
of 'Resolution and Independence', written in May–July 1802, in
all its starkly unqualified and undefined simplicity, suggests a
quite orthodox deity: ' "God", said I, "be my help and stay
secure." '[2] The meeting with the old leech-gatherer, the poem
tells us, may have come about as a result of 'peculiar grace, / A
leading from above, a something given' (ll. 50–1). In a letter to
Sara Hutchinson of 14 June 1802, written while the poem was
still in process of composition, Wordsworth explains, 'I consider the manner in which I was rescued from my dejection and
despair almost as an interposition of Providence' (WL, I, 366).
The letter goes on to assert, not very surprisingly, 'I believe

God has given me a strong imagination.' Perhaps even more convincingly orthodox is the diction of 'Ode to Duty', written in early 1804, with its reference to 'the Godhead's most benignant grace' (l. 50). The closing paragraph of the 1805 *Prelude* refers to the joint function of Wordsworth and Coleridge as that of bringing about the 'redemption' of mankind '(should Providence such grace to us vouchsafe)'. In 1822 he completed 102 Ecclesiastical Sonnets, reflecting his doctrinal orthodoxy, on the history of the Church of England; by 1845 their number had increased to 145.

Even at the height of his revolutionary fervour, when writing his letter to the Bishop of Llandaff in 1793, Wordsworth had no illusions about the corruption of the human heart, and nowhere in the letter do we find the least hint of the heretical doctrine of the innate goodness of man: Wordsworth's 'grand objection to monarchy . . . is drawn from the eternal nature of man. The office of king is a trial to which human virtue is not equal.' In other words, no man is good enough to be king. His flawed human nature will inevitably affect his acts, however well-intentioned. Other passages in the letter support this position. Earlier in it Wordsworth had pointed out that, given 'the natural tendency of power to corrupt the heart of man, a sensible republican will think it essential that the office of legislator be not intrusted to the same man for a succession of years'. At another point in the letter Wordsworth writes 'that a man's past services are no sufficient security for his future character'.[3] The firm implication behind all these statements is that Wordsworth does not believe in the innate goodness of man.

It was concluded long ago, to be sure, that Wordsworth had no philosophy in him, but that he did have strong beliefs. It is also clear that strength of belief is no guarantee of either consistency or clarity of belief. Still, one must always read Wordsworth with an awareness of his Anglican background. Blake did not. He did, however, annotate the 'Preface' to Wordsworth's collected *Poems* of 1815, along with the 'Essay, Supplementary to the Preface', and Wordsworth's Preface to *The Excursion* (1814). Of the first two, Blake wrote, 'I do not know who wrote these Prefaces [.] they are very mischievous & direct contrary to Wordsworths own Practise.'[4] There are, evidently, substantial differences between the minds of Blake and Wordsworth, and we should not ignore them or explain them away.

Blake told Henry Crabb Robinson that reading Wordsworth's 'Prospectus' to *The Recluse* 'caused him a bowel complaint which nearly killed him'.[5] But Blake took Wordsworth seriously enough to copy in a four-page transcript, made in 1826, all 107 lines of the 'Prospectus' as well as the last paragraph of the prose Preface. The differences between the two poets should not obscure their sympathies. Because of the fragmentary nature of the available documentation (Wordsworth had almost nothing to say about Blake), it has seemed best to plumb the two poets chiefly on subjects where they touch: for example, on the marriage of mind and nature, on memory and imagination, and on the reconciliation of opposites.[6]

Blake objected first to Wordsworth's statement in the Preface to the 1815 *Poems* that 'the powers requisite for the production of poetry are: first, those of Observation and Description, . . . whether the things depicted be actually present to the senses, or have a place only in the memory. . . . 2ndly, Sensibility' (WPW, II, 431–2). Upon this Blake commented, 'One Power alone makes a Poet. – Imagination The Divine Vision' (BPP, 654). But Wordsworth in the same Preface of 1815 had defined imagination in terms that Blake should have found quite acceptable: it has nothing to do with making 'a faithful copy' of 'external objects', but, instead, 'is a word of higher import, denoting operations of the mind upon those objects, and processes of *creation*' (WPW, II, 436; italics added). The result is to make the object 're-act upon the mind . . . like a new existence' (II, 438). Imagination for Wordsworth and Blake (as well as for Coleridge) 'shapes and *creates*' (ibid.). This activity proceeds from and is governed by the 'almost divine powers' of the soul (II, 439). Blake finally found his own 'Imagination The Divine Vision' in the last paragraph of Wordsworth's Essay Supplementary, the 'Vision and the Faculty Divine', a quotation from *The Excursion* (I, l. 79) that Blake copied approvingly in the margin. But before that late point Blake had read that the muse of Milton is a 'heavenly Muse' (WPW, II, 439), and both Blake and Wordsworth aspired to rival Milton. Blake was aware of Wordsworth's ambition, but Wordsworth had never seen Blake's *Milton A Poem in 2 Books To Justify the Ways of God to Men,* which exists today in only four copies. The position of the two poets is so close that Blake may well have felt some degree of competitive jealousy when reading Wordsworth's volumes. 'The grand storehouses of... poetical... Imagination', Wordsworth wrote, 'are the prophetic and lyrical parts of the Holy Scriptures, and the works of Milton' (II, 439). Blake would have agreed, as also with Wordsworth's rejection of the anthropomorphism of the Greek and Roman poets. Despite the many classical allusions in Milton's poetry, he remained, for Wordsworth, 'a Hebrew in soul' (II, 440). Blake would also have subscribed to Wordsworth's Coleridgean account (although Wordsworth quotes Charles Lamb) of the important unifying function of the imagination: to consolidate 'numbers into unity' and to draw ' "all things to one . . . and serve to one effect" ' (II, 439).

Blake and Wordsworth, sharing an equally elevated view of the nature and origin of poetry (poetry for the Wordsworth of the 1800 Preface has a 'divine origin' [WPW, II, 411]), inevitably held in contempt mere fashion in poetry and the merely popular.[7] The two poets, however, would seem at first to be basically at odds in their theories concerning the relation between Nature and imagination, the world of the senses and the visionary world, external and inner reality. On these subjects, Blake suffered from the great disadvantage of never having read *The Prelude,* and he objected violently to Wordsworth's title for one poem in the 1815 edition: 'Influence of Natural Objects in calling forth and strengthening the Imagination *in Boyhood and early Youth'* (italics added). Although Blake had read or would read stanza nine of the Intimations Ode, he wrote, presumably ignoring the italicized qualifying phrase: 'Natural Objects always did & now do Weaken deaden & obliterate Imagination in Me [.] Wordsworth must know that what he writes Valuable is Not to be found in Nature [.] Read Michael Angelos [second] Sonnet vol 2 p. 179' (BPP, 655), lines 5–8 of which in Wordsworth's translation Blake had memorized, transposing lines 6 and 7 as he wrote them in an autograph album belonging to William Upcott:

> Heaven born the Soul a Heavenward Course must hold
> For what delights the Sense is False & Weak
> Beyond the Visible World she soars to Seek
> Ideal Form, The Universal Mold.   (BPP, 675)

First to be noticed is Blake's contention that Wordsworth's theory and practice do not always agree: several of Wordsworth's poems incorporate assumptions acceptable to Blake as 'Valuable', and Blake singled out for particular commendation Wordsworth's poem 'To H.C. Six Years Old', which he described as 'in the highest degree Imaginative' (BPP, 654). Like Michelangelo's sonnet, it too draws a contrast between 'the soiling earth' (l. 29) and a better and higher world.

In addition, Wordsworth knew as well as Blake that natural objects could 'deaden & obliterate Imagination'. This insight, the result of his own experience, he recorded in *The Prelude* in his account of the 'tyranny' of the eye, the 'most despotic of our senses', descriptive of that period when he was in bondage to the picturesque tradition, its 'rules of mimic art transferred / To things above all art' (XII, ll. 129, 111–12). (Even his idea in the 1800 Preface of poetry originating in 'emotion recollected in tranquillity' is a means of avoiding the 'tyranny of the eye'.) In *The Prelude* a 'mind so far / Perverted' becomes concerned with surfaces, superficial things, 'a comparison of scene with scene', 'to the moral power . . . and the spirit of the place, / Insensible' (XII, ll. 88–9, 115, 119–21). In this perverted or fallen state, another aspect of his period of Godwinian rationalism, culminating in despair, Wordsworth 'rejoiced / To lay the inner faculties asleep' (XII, ll. 146–7). This is the 'sleep / Of Death' of the 'Prospectus' to *The Recluse* (ll. 60–1). But Wordsworth recovered:

> I had known
> Too forcibly, too early in my life,
> Visitings of imaginative power
> For this to last: I shook the habit off
> Entirely and for ever, and again
> In Nature's presence stood, as now I stand,
> A sensitive being, a *creative* soul.
>
> (*Prelude,* XII, ll. 201–7)

Such 'a *creative* soul' will make the new 'creation (by no lower name / Can it be called)', described in Wordsworth's 'Prospectus' (ll. 69–70). He had no higher opinion of the picturesque than Blake, and he understood as clearly as Blake the moral danger of submitting himself to the rule of 'passive taste', this 'degradation' (XII, ll. 154, 193). Wordsworth, obviously, is not a landscape poet in the eighteenth-century tradition any more than is Blake. His typical concern is, as he described it in 'Elegiac Stanzas Suggested by a Picture of Peele Castle', to 'add the gleam, / The light that never was, on sea or land, / The consecration, and the Poet's dream' (ll. 14–16). On the last paragraph of Wordsworth's Essay Supplementary Blake observes: 'It. . . Was writ by another hand & mind from the rest of these Prefaces. Perhaps they are the opinions of a Portrait or Landscape Painter' (BPP, 655). In this last paragraph Wordsworth had quoted Milton, referred to the 'vision and the Faculty Divine', and attacked the vulgar reading public. Here Blake either fundamentally misunderstands Wordsworth or he approves of what Wordsworth says and suggests facetiously, as he had earlier, that someone else – 'a Portrait or Landscape Painter' – had written the rest of the essay.

Let us juxtapose Blake's statement in his letter to Trusler of 23 August 1799 that 'Nature is Imagination', which he then defines as 'Spiritual Sensation' (BL, 30), with Wordsworth's description of his ascent of Mount Snowdon in Book XIV of *The Prelude*, where the scene ('that vision') is transformed by the imagination to become 'the type / Of a majestic intellect', 'the emblem of a mind / That feeds upon infinity, that broods / Over the dark abyss' (ll. 66–7, 70–2). That is, it becomes a symbol of the creative imagination itself, which like the God of Creation in Genesis 1:2 brooded over the face of the chaotic waters, or like the Holy Spirit of *Paradise Lost* 'dovelike sat'st brooding on the vast abyss, / And mad'st it pregnant' (I, ll. 21–2). For such a mind as that described by Wordsworth, then, 'Nature is Imagination' not only in the sense that it symbolizes imagination: nature is actually recreated by imagination in the poet's mind. Such minds, 'by sensible impressions not enthralled, . . . hold fit converse with the spiritual world, . . . till Time shall be no more' (*Prelude,* XIV, ll. 106–11), as in the Book of Revelation. Thus it is that the creative imagination transforms nature into an image of itself and at the same time provides an escape from the bondage of sense or 'sensible impressions'. 'Such minds are truly from the Deity' (*Prelude,* XIV, l. 112). As Blake knew when he annotated Wordsworth's *Poems,* 'Imagination is the Divine Vision not of The World nor of Man . . . as he is a Natural Man but only as he is a Spiritual

Man' (BPP, 655). In the 1805 *Prelude* Mount Snowdon was 'the perfect image of a mighty Mind, / . . . That is exalted by an under-presence, / The sense of God, or whatsoe'er is dim / Or vast in its own [spiritual] being' (XIII, ll. 70–4). We have here nature as an image of God as opposed to nature as an image of the mind's awareness of God or of its own sublime vastness. Blake would surely have approved.

If for Blake the creative imagination is 'Spiritual Sensation', transforming the sun into a heavenly host of angels singing 'Holy Holy Holy is the Lord God Almighty' (BPP, 555), poetry for Wordsworth, although 'ethereal and transcendent', is 'yet incapable to sustain her existence without sensuous incarnation' or embodiment (WPW, II, 412). It is the function of poetry not to describe the sun as it exists in itself but as it appears, as it seems 'to exist to the *senses*' (II, 410). These are the redeemed or purified senses of such poets as Milton and Wordsworth – and Blake.[8] We read a page or so after, as Blake had read, 'Poetry is most just to its own divine origin when it administers the comforts and breathes the spirit of religion' (WPW, II, 411). And this religion is not that haughty, sectarian religion that, 'being from the calculating understanding, is cold and formal'. It is true 'Christianity, the religion of humility' (412). The enemy here is clearly the proud and angelic 'systematic reasoning' of Blake's *Marriage* (BPP, 41); and although Blake detested false humility ('Humble to God Haughty to Man' [511]), he believed that 'Forgiveness of Sins . . . alone is the Gospel' (792). Such daily forgiving is impossible for the proud man and cannot exist without a Blakean self-annihilation, an act of humility. Readers of poetry, Wordsworth explained, 'are to be humbled and humanised, in order that they may be purified and exalted' (WPW, II, 426).

Additional views expressed in Wordsworth's Essay Supplementary of 1815 with which Blake could sympathize exist in some variety. Wordsworth deplored the French aversion to Shakespeare as well as the English misunderstanding of his genius as 'wild' and 'irregular', the 'slow progress' of the fame of *Paradise Lost,* the popularity of Pope, and Dr Johnson's *Lives of the Poets,* beginning as it did with Cowley and omitting Chaucer, Spenser and other Elizabethans. Blake would also have agreed with Wordsworth that the job of the poet is to break 'the bonds of custom', overcome 'the prejudices of false refinement', and divest 'the reader of the pride that induces him to dwell upon those points wherein men differ from each other, to the exclusion of those in which all men are alike'.[9] The poet must concern himself with generic man or mankind, a concern that stresses the spiritual kinship of all men as well as their common social and political community.

The Wordsworthian mark of poetic genius is also Blakean. Genius, as Wordsworth said, 'is the introduction of a new element into the intellectual universe' (WPW, II, 428). This is new invention, not imitation or copy. Such new poetry, the implication is, will necessarily be difficult poetry and will require that the reader 'exert himself' intellectually in high degree. The reader is not to be 'amused without the trouble of thought' (II, 429). All this sounds very modern. 'Make it new', Pound urged. Eliot proclaimed that a literary work that is not 'new' is 'therefore not . . . a work of art' at all.[10]

And yet to the extent that a poet writes out of a tradition of orthodox Christianity, there will appear in his poetry assumptions or beliefs that are by no means new, so old indeed that they may seem startlingly novel, even exotic, to a modern reader whose religion is merely nominal. Such a belief is that in the fallen state of nature, so prominent in Blake's annotations of Wordsworth's 'Prospectus'. For Blake, we have seen, nature is fallen not absolutely but only in the eye or mind of the beholder. 'Every body does not see alike', he claimed in the letter to Trusler (BL, 30), and he himself could see the sun not as a round disk somewhat like a guinea but as a heavenly host of choiring angels. In *The Marriage,* once the cherub with his flaming sword left his guard at the tree of life, everything would appear as it is, 'infinite and holy' (BPP, 38). Similarly, Wordsworth in his 'Prospectus' announces that he would teach all men to find 'Paradise', the condition of Eden, as 'a simple produce of the common day' (l. 55).

Blake appears finally not to have understood all the 107 lines of the 'Prospectus' that he copied out. Upon lines 63–8[11] he commented, 'You shall not bring me down to believe such fitting & fitted[.] I know better'; and upon lines 72–82,[12] underlining the words 'Humanity in fields and groves / Pipe solitary anguish', he wrote, 'does not this Fit & is it not Fitting most Exquisitely too but to what [?] not to Mind but to the Vile Body only & to its Laws of Good & Evil & its Enmities against

Mind' (BPP, 656). We know, however, that 'the Vile Body' could also be, for Blake, 'the human form divine', in which in the world of *Innocence* 'God is dwelling too' ('The Divine Image'). Blake did not annotate the 'Paradise' regained in the simple light of 'common day' that would result from Wordsworth's wedding of man and nature, the marriage between the 'discerning' or perceiving 'intellect of man' and 'this goodly universe' (ll. 52–3). The Miltonic context of the 'Prospectus' demands a redeemed mankind, 'the sensual' aroused 'from their sleep / Of Death' (ll. 60–1), as in Psalms 13:3 and echoing Milton's 'universe of death' in *Paradise Lost* ;[13] but primarily a mankind redeemed from bondage to the tyranny of 'the bodily eye, . . . most despotic of our senses', when Wordsworth 'rejoiced / To lay the inner faculties asleep' (*Prelude,* XII, ll. 128–9, 146–7).

Wordsworth's marriage of the two great contraries – the I and the world – will produce a new awakening, as in Revelation, and also a new 'creation (by no lower name / Can it be called)' – a new heaven and a new earth, as again in Revelation as well as in Blake, consequent upon the marriage of Christ and his bride, the New Jerusalem, the city that is also a woman. In aesthetic terms, however, the best gloss upon the Wordsworthian new creation is to be found in chapter XIII of the *Biographia,* in the famous definition of the primary and secondary imagination. The former is 'a repetition in the finite mind of the eternal act of creation in the infinite I AM'. The latter 'dissolves, diffuses, dissipates' (i.e., *creates* chaos) in order to make the universe anew ('re-create') (I, 202).

Wordsworth's 'Prospectus' will recreate the world, that is, the way in which it is perceived, by means of this marriage. It follows of necessity that earth or nature must be humanized, and so it is in Wordsworth's 'human Soul of universal earth' (l. 84), in which Blake might have recognized his own 'Tharmas humanizing' all nature in 'Night the Ninth' of *The Four Zoas* (BPP, 386). But for Wordsworth it is the 'prophetic Spirit! that inspir'st / The human Soul of universal earth', the 'dread Power! / Whose gracious favour is the primal source / Of all illumination' (ll. 83–4, 99–101). This is Wordsworth's muse, as it were, in one sense, but it is also his own imagination that he implores to 'descend' upon him and grant to him the 'gift of genuine insight' (l. 88). This sounds very like Coleridge's 'echo' of the 'Prime Agent of all human Perception' (*Biographia*, I, 202). However this may be, the faculty that humanizes or redeems nature so that it becomes exquisitely fitted to be married to the mind of man is the faculty of the poetic imagination.

The marriage ceremony is an act or expression or faith, faith in things unseen. In the Anglican ceremony, the man marrying the woman is compared to Christ married to the Church, which must obey Him. For these terms, Wordsworth has substituted the marriage of man's discerning mind and a humanized, not deified, nature, to which the imagination has the most direct access, the 'Vision and the Faculty divine' (WPW, II, 430). Such a marriage based on religious faith is accompanied by (or produced by) 'natural piety' in the sense that such visionary faith is nurtured amid natural scenes, has nothing to do with the organized religion of the churches, and is potentially available to 'the whole species' of man (l. 65). The 'Prospectus' makes perfectly clear Wordsworth's awareness of the 'solitary anguish' of fallen man and opposes to it the Wordsworthian sacrament of holy marriage. Blake commented, 'There is no such Thing as Natural Piety Because The Natural Man is at Enmity with God' (BPP, 654), misreading as an expression of deism or natural religion the famous lines prefixed as epigraph to the Intimations Ode. But Blake knew at another time, when reading Lavater's *Aphorisms on Man,* that 'creation is. God descending . . . & every thing on earth is the word of God & in its essence is God' (BPP, 589). Wordsworth in his greatest poetry is less self-contradictory than Blake, who frequently fails to define the context of his remarks, as when he refers, in one of his last letters, to 'the Delusive Goddess Nature & her Laws' (BL, 163), that same goddess in which Wordsworth found comfort and support. [14]

A most important point of disagreement between the two poets was upon the relation between imagination and memory. Blake's last marginal note to Wordsworth's 1815 *Poems* was, 'Imagination has nothing to do with Memory'. This statement may be less profound and exclusive than it appears, for it may refer to nothing more – however important and interesting this may be – than to the different ways in which the two men thought that they composed and the different forms that their visions took. Wordsworth's muse was largely retrospective, making poetry out of past events 'recollected in tranquillity'.

But memory for Wordsworth could be, and usually was, creative. In *The Prelude* he imagines himself as one gliding in a boat over 'a still water', looking down and

> solacing himself
> With such discoveries as his eye can make
> Beneath him in the bottom of the deep,

and seeing 'many beauteous sights'. 'Such pleasant office', he concludes, 'have we long pursued / Incumbent o'er the surface of past time / With like success' (*Prelude,* IV, ll. 258–61, 271–3).

Blake described his visions – his pictures in the mind – in verbal terms, and these pictures, in one sense, are not usually pictures of anything Blake had seen with his vegetative eye. But as Richard Gregory has explained, even active theories of perception place great emphasis upon the brain's memory banks, and the most ordinary perceptions are understood to be 'imaginative constructions – fictions – based (as indeed is science fiction also) more on the stored past than on the present. . . . Even the most fanciful fiction as written is very largely true, or we would not understand it. . . . Science fiction characters may have green hair and an exoskeleton – but is this novelty not a mere reshuffling of the pack of our [remembered] experiences?'[15] We may never have seen a mitred bishop with bat wings or another with crosier and scales, as Blake drew them, but our memory somehow tells us that we have seen mitres, men, bats, crosiers and scales.

With some time and thought and with the aid of memory, we can understand Blake's illuminations. They are not so wholly of the imagination that their meaning remains private to William Blake. Both poets, in fact and theory, use and emphasize the imagination. Blake's use is less restrained and produces pictures and poems that are fantastic or effectively grotesque, like gargoyles. But Wordsworth, clearly, also transformed nature in his mind, often giving to it a visionary splendour. An important source of their disagreement over memory and imagination is, in fact, their differing subjects. Wordsworth typically transforms the seemingly natural and ordinary experience into one of wonder, exciting in the reader, as Coleridge put it in the *Biographia,* 'a feeling analogous to the supernatural' (II, 6). Blake typically domesticates experiences and states of being that seemed to be supernatural but in fact were psychological. Coleridge's description of poetic genius, which appears in the midst of his discussion of Wordsworth's genius, suggests the common ground on which they meet:

> To find no contradiction in the union of old and new; to contemplate the ANCIENT of days and all his works with feelings as fresh, as if all had then sprang forth at the first creative fiat; characterizes the mind that feels the riddle of the world, and may help to unravel it. To carry on the feelings of childhood into the powers of manhood; to combine the child's sense of wonder and novelty with the appearances, which every day for perhaps forty years had rendered familiar;
>
> > 'With sun and moon and stars throughout the year
> > And man and woman;'
>
> this the character and privilege of genius *(Biographia,* I, 59).

Although this passage appeared originally in *The Friend* (1809–10), it anticipates Coleridge's doctrine, developed in the *Biographia,* of the union, 'balance or reconciliation of opposite or discordant qualities' (II, 12), to reproduce finally a sense of *'multëity in unity'*, Coleridge's definition of beauty. *'The sense of beauty'*, he writes, *'subsists in simultaneous intuition of the relation of parts, each to each, and of all to a whole.'*[16] The parts, or our awareness of them, thus retain their separate identity in the unity of the whole. In this light we may consider Wordsworth's discussion of metre in terms of excitement and order, the irregular and the regular or ordered, and the 'perception of similitude in dissimilitude' (WPW, II, 400).

These passages in both Wordsworth and Coleridge imply a marriage of contraries in which a true unity or harmony is achieved without loss of identity by either element or partner, male or female. This is the essence of Blake's doctrine. Wordsworth argues, 'The end of Poetry is to produce excitement in co-existence with an overbalance of pleasure', but such excitement 'is an unusual and irregular state of mind' and therefore requires 'the co-presence of something regular', metre, if the excitement is not to become painful and 'overbalance' the sense of pleasure (WPW, II, 399). The 'irregular' and the 'regular',

then, must be kept in a state of balance or harmony. As Coleridge expressed it, there must be a 'balance or reconciliation of
. . . a more than usual state of emotion, with more than usual
order' (*Biographia*, II, 12). Similarly, for Wordsworth 'the pleasure received from metrical language' derives chiefly from 'the
perception of similitude in dissimilitude. This principle is the
great spring of the activity of our minds' (WPW, II, 400) – and
also the principle of metaphor as well as Coleridge's definition
of beauty, unity or sameness in multeity. Wordsworth continues, in a statement open to diverse interpretation, 'From this
principle the direction of the sexual appetite, and all the passions
connected with it, take their origin.' Surely this is one of the most
startling (and uncharacteristic) statements Wordsworth ever
made. What can he mean? He has said, it would appear, that the
sex drive, expressing itself in the attraction or union of opposites, originates in the perception of similitude or sameness of
male and female. Here then is not the metaphor but the idea of
marriage. Polarities, perceiving the similitude, attract and come
together.

Blake's 'Eternal Men . . . at the golden feast' of 'Night the
Ninth' 'shudderd at the horrible thing' – 'the female form now
separate' (BPP, 386). In *The Book of Urizen* 'Eternity shudderd'
for the same reason and in the same words: 'at sight / Of the
first female now separate' (plate 18, ll. 9–10: BPP, 77).
Enitharmon, with a will of her own, split off from Los. Blake
is not here proposing as an ideal the hermaphrodite: he is echoing Genesis 2, 'And the Lord God said, It is not good that the
man should be alone' (verse 18). Thus the creation of Eve and
the institution of marriage in which the man and the woman,
forsaking all others, 'shall be one flesh' (verse 24). Genesis 2
describes prelapsarian Eden, which is symbolic of Blake's highest state. But fallen man, as one of the Eternals in 'Night the
Ninth' explains, 'is a Worm wearied with joy [.] he seeks the
caves of sleep / Among the Flowers of Beulah in his Selfish cold
repose / Forsaking Brotherhood & Universal Love' (BPP, 386).
There is then a higher union, embracing all mankind, just as
there is for Shelley. In the famous words of his *Defence of Poetry*:
'The great secret of morals is love, or a going out of our own
nature and an identification of ourselves' with that which is 'not
our own'.[17] This requires an act of perception or, as Shelley calls
it, imagination, the 'great instrument of moral good'. But it is

also a Wordsworthian perception of similitude in dissimilitude. Shelley's virtuous man 'must put himself in the place of another and of many others; the pains and pleasures of his species must become his own' (SP, 283). To do this he must perceive imaginatively the similitude of all the infinite varieties of men.

So also with Wordsworth: 'upon the accuracy with which similitude in dissimilitude, and dissimilitude in similitude are perceived, depend our taste and our moral feelings' (WPW, II, 400). Although he does not elaborate, what is involved here is a Coleridgean perception of the many become one, *'multëity in unity'*, as well as a Blakean marriage of contraries, in which a poor beclouded or benighted angel, believing that all men are 'fools, sinners, & nothings', can be transformed and arise as Elijah in *The Marriage of Heaven and Hell*, once he has come to understand that 'the worship of God is. Honouring his gifts in *other* men' (BPP, 42; italics added). But Wordsworth's linking of aesthetics and ethics, 'taste' and 'moral feelings', most clearly anticipates Shelley's thought in the *Defence*.

Blake expressed the same idea in 'All Religions are One': 'As all men are alike (tho' infinitely various) So all Religions & . . . all similars have one source. The true Man is the source he being the Poetic Genius' (BPP, 3). Blake's final attitude toward the Wordsworth he often misunderstood may be suggested by his remark to Crabb Robinson that Wordsworth was 'a Pagan' but nevertheless 'the greatest poet of the age'.[18] Blake had not read Wordsworth's letter to Lady Beaumont of 21 May 1807, in which Wordsworth wrote that 'to be incapable of a feeling of Poetry in my sense of the word is to be without love of human nature and reverence for God. . . . For this multitude of unhappy, and misguided, and misguiding beings, an entire *regeneration* must be produced.'[19]

Wordsworth's discussion of similitude and dissimilitude in the 1800 Preface is followed immediately by his most famous definition of poetry and its origins. It is an artful weaving together of contraries, which unites in a single sentence such opposite or discordant elements as 'spontaneous overflow' and tranquil recollection, 'powerful feelings' and contemplation, 'emotion' and 'tranquillity', memory of past emotion and creation in the poet's mind of present emotion 'kindred' to it (WPW, II, 400). 'In this mood successful composition generally begins.' It is a very complex mood indeed, holding in suspension or balance a number of contrary qualities or states. These are sometimes ignored, to the peril of the reader or critic, in order to emphasize the first of these several elements, 'the spontaneous overflow of powerful feelings', a phrase that had earlier appeared in the sixth paragraph of the Preface (WPW, II, 387). There, in the same sentence, he limits himself to only two contrary states, thus insisting upon the balanced state of tension in which they exist. The true poet is 'possessed of more than usual organic sensibility', but he has also 'thought long and deeply'. Many years afterward, in a letter of 24 September 1827, Wordsworth could stress the latter quality at the expense of the former:

> The logical faculty has infinitely more to do with Poetry than the Young and the inexperienced, whether writer or critic, ever dreams of. Indeed, as the materials upon which that faculty is exercised in Poetry are so subtle, so plastic, so complex, the application of it requires an adroitness which can proceed from nothing but practice, a discernment, which emotion is so far from bestowing that at first it is ever in the way of it.[20]

Similarly, still later, on 16 April 1834, Wordsworth could reverse the great emphasis upon the natural and spontaneous in the 1800 Preface: 'Poetry is infinitely more of an art than the world is disposed to believe'.[21] This we might believe from the poet who revised *The Prelude* over a period of nearly four decades, but we have concerned ourselves here, not with his later reconsiderations, but with his thought in its period of greatest strength and originality.

4 The Unity of Coleridge's Critical Theory

The remarkable fact about Coleridge the critic, often regarded as the father of modern criticism, is not that many of his ideas are so highly derivative as sometimes to amount to plagiarism, nor that his most famous critical work, *Biographia Literaria,* is also one of the most disorderly books ever to be published in English, nor even that parts of it are written in a style almost unreadable. (Byron compared him in the Dedication to *Don Juan* to a hunting hawk released for flight with his hood still upon him, 'Explaining Metaphysics to the nation – / I wish he would explain his Explanation.' For Shelley in *Letter to Maria Gisborne* Coleridge was a 'hooded eagle', his mind 'with its own internal lightning blind' [ll. 208, 205].) No, the miracle of Coleridge's critical theory lies in the small number of his seminal ideas, the internal consistency of those ideas, the remarkable flexibility with which they may be restated in numerous and quite different contexts, the extent to which the theory may be translated into practical criticism of such a poet as Wordsworth, and the firm philosophical and psychological base upon which all this rests.

In considering the mature critical theories of Coleridge, we begin with an account of them in *Biographia Literaria,* stressing first their internal consistency and then the consistency of their application to the theory and poetry of Wordsworth. Next, we examine some of Coleridge's other writings, early and late, to determine the general consistency of his mature views. Finally, we study the philosophical or psychological foundation upon

which the entire homogeneous structure rests. For however
often the agonized mind of Coleridge got off the track, it
always returned unerringly.

Coleridge owed much to the fearsome Reverend James
Bowyer, Head Master of the Grammar School of Christ's Hospital, who flogged him once for expressing sentiments of an
atheistical inclination. The young Coleridge had been reading
Voltaire and Erasmus Darwin. But his taste for such writers
must surely have been a fleeting one. Charles Lamb in 'Christ's
Hospital Five and Thirty Years Ago' remembered Coleridge at
this early time unfolding in the cloisters to some passer-by 'the
mysteries of Jamblichus, or Plotinus'. And Coleridge informed
Thomas Poole in a letter of 16 October 1797 that even in childhood his 'mind had been habituated *to the Vast* – I never regarded
my senses in any way as the criteria of my belief. I regulated all
my creeds by my conceptions not by my *sight* – even at that
age.'[1] Coleridge, who says he was eight years old at the time,
credits this habit of mind to his 'early reading of Fairy Tales &
Genii &c &c', including romances, and insists he knows 'no
other way of giving his mind a love of "the Great", & "the
Whole"'. Others, he continues, 'contemplate nothing but *parts* –
and all *parts* are necessarily little – and the Universe to them is
but a mass of *little things*' (ibid.). Such persons, *'rationally* educated, as it is styled', call 'the want of imagination Judgment'
(ibid., 354–5). We perceive much of the mature Coleridge in
these sentences, most notably his habit of contemplating the
activities of his own mind, its synthesizing power and thrust, its
quest for unity in all things, a quest that, like some great thirst,
had to be satisfied with regularity again and again.

This at Christ's Hospital Bowyer in large part did. If we can
believe what we read in chapter 1 of the *Biographia,* the foundations of Coleridge's literary theory were laid before he entered
Cambridge in 1791. Through Bowyer's efforts, he tells us, he
came to understand the total internal consistency and the absolute verbal unity of the truly great poem. 'I learnt from him,
that Poetry, even that of the loftiest and, seemingly, that of the
wildest odes, had a logic of its own, as severe as that of science;
and more difficult, because more subtle, more complex, and
dependent on more, and more fugitive causes. In the truly great
poets, he would say, there is a reason assignable, not only for
every word, but for the position of every word' (*Biographia*, I,

4). Bowyer made the boys in his class show why various Homeric synonyms would be inferior to the words Homer chose 'and *wherein* consisted the peculiar fitness of the word in the original text' (I, 5). Although Bowyer would not have scored very high on one of today's student evaluations of professors, he taught Coleridge something else of great value: to prefer plain English when possible. 'In our own English compositions . . . he showed no mercy to phrase, metaphor, or image, unsupported by a sound sense, or where the same sense might have been conveyed with equal force and dignity in plainer words' (ibid.). (This lesson Coleridge remembered when writing *The Ancient Mariner* and the conversation poems, indeed all his great poems, as well as when discussing with Wordsworth the Preface to *Lyrical Ballads*. But he forgot it when writing a good many pages of the *Biographia*.)

Before he left school, presumably, Coleridge had 'abstracted two critical aphorisms, deeming them to comprise the conditions and criteria of poetic style' (*Biographia*, I, 14). The second of these, reflecting his interest over many years in 'the true nature of poetic diction' (I, 1), one of the chief subjects of the *Biographia,* restates Bowyer's principle and classroom teaching:

> whatever [poetic] lines can be translated into other words of the same language, without diminution of their significance, . . . are so far vicious in their diction. . . . I was wont bold[l]y to affirm, that it would be scarcely more difficult to push a stone out from the pyramids with the bare hand, than to alter a word, or the position of a word, in Milton or Shakespeare, (in their most important works at least,) without making the author say something else, or something worse, than he does say (I, 14–15).

Here, then, we have the concept of the great poem as not only a work of absolute verbal integrity, the individual words unalterably fused into a single unity, but also a work of absolute perfection, a finished creation that one alters only to its detriment.

Coleridge's other critical aphorism logically proceeds from his concept of the complete fusion of the smallest parts of a great poem, the individual words of it: 'not the poem which we have *read*, but that to which we *return*, with the greatest pleasure, possesses the genuine power, and claims the name of *essen-*

tial poetry' (Biographia, I, 14). This is a way of saying that the great poem cannot be read, it can only be reread. Coleridge in chapter 1 does not discuss the nature of the 'pleasure' he refers to; later, however, he will reveal it to consist in important part in the pleasure the reader experiences when he *perceives* the relations of the parts to the whole of the poem.

Applying these principles to the poetry of Pope's epigrammatic couplets, whether in *The Rape of the Lock,* the *Essay on Man,* or the translation of the *Iliad,* Coleridge objected to their lack of fusion: 'a *point* was looked for at the end of each second line, and the whole was as it were a sorites [a heap of syllogisms], or , if I may exchange a logical for a grammatical metaphor, a *conjunction disjunctive,* of epigrams' (*Biographia,* I, 11). Bowles's sonnets, by contrast, reconciled a number of opposite or discordant qualities: the 'tender' with the 'manly', the 'natural and real' with the 'dignified and harmonious' (I, 10). Bowles and Cowper, he concluded, were 'the first who combined natural thoughts with natural diction; the first who *reconciled* the heart with the head', two of Coleridge's great psychological polarities (I, 16; italics added). By contrast, 'our faulty elder poets sacrificed the passion and passionate flow of poetry, to the subtleties of intellect' (I, 15). Opposites are not balanced or reconciled. The faulty modern poets sacrificed 'to the glare and glitter of a perpetual, yet broken and heterogeneous imagery, or rather to an amphibious something, made up, half of image, and half of abstract meaning' (ibid.). In neither is there fusion.

We need no more than suggest here the long persistence of these ideas. In the *Table Talk* for 3 July 1833 we read, 'but the great thing in poetry is, *quocunque modo,* to effect a unity of impression upon the whole; and a too great fullness and profusion of point in the parts will prevent this. Who can read with pleasure more than a hundred lines or so of Hudibras at one time? Each couplet or quatrain is so whole in itself, that you can't connect them. There is no fusion – just as it is in Seneca.'[2] At an even later date (23 June 1834), again recorded in the *Table Talk,* he returned to *Hudibras* and described its style as the product of the fancy, which 'brings together images which have no connection natural or moral, but are yoked together by the poet by means of some accidental coincidence' (ibid., 518). By contrast, 'the Imagination modifies images, and gives unity to variety; it sees all things in one, *il più nell' uno*' (ibid.). That

Coleridge was himself aware of the coherence of his critical theory over the years we may deduce from a statement he made in a note to chapter 2 of the *Biographia:* 'I had derived peculiar advantages from my school discipline, and . . . my *general* theory of poetry was the same then as now', a now not clearly defined.[3]

Not, however, until Coleridge made his first acquaintance with Wordsworth's poems did he distinguish sharply between the fancy and the imagination. Whether this distinction took shape after reading *Descriptive Sketches* during his last year at Cambridge, 1794, or after meeting Wordsworth in 1795 and hearing him recite several of his unpublished poems, the *Biographia* does not make quite clear. But whatever the poems may have been, Coleridge recognized in them, he says, a most impressive 'union' of opposite or discordant qualities.

> It was the union of deep feeling with profound thought; the fine balance of truth in observing, with the imaginative faculty in modifying the objects observed; and above all the original gift of spreading the tone, the *atmosphere,* and with it the depth and height of the ideal world around forms, incidents, and situations, of which, for the common view, custom had bedimmed all the lustre, had dried up the sparkle and the dew drops (I, 59).

He then decided that 'fancy and imagination were two distinct and widely different faculties' (I, 60). Five chapters later he coined the word *'esemplastic',* from the Greek meaning 'to shape into one', and defined imagination as the *'plastic power'* (I, 107). The earliest date of writing, it appears, on which Coleridge clearly distinguished imagination and fancy was 10 September 1802, in a letter to William Sotheby. Of this distinction we hear no more in chapter 10, but near the end of it he described the long poem he planned in 1797, 'The Brook', which must have interested Wordsworth. Coleridge 'sought for a subject, that should give equal room and freedom for description, incident, and impassioned reflections on men, nature, and society, yet supply in itself a natural connection to the parts, and unity to the whole' (I, 129). He thought he had found this 'natural connection' in tracing the course of a stream in Somerset from its source to the point where it emptied into the sea. But it was Wordsworth who described his *Recluse,* intended to include *The*

Excursion as one of its parts, as 'a philosophical poem, containing views of Man, Nature, and Society',[4] there achieving a union of polarities somewhat different from that imagined by Coleridge.

Wordsworth continued over the years to stimulate Coleridge's thinking about the imagination. In 1812 Coleridge contributed to Southey's *Omniana* an article, later incorporated into the *Biographia,* in which he defined the imagination as the 'shaping and modifying power' and the fancy as 'the aggregative and associative power' *(Biographia,* I, 193), dependent upon the association of ideas by means of the memory. Wordsworth replied to this in the Preface to his collected *Poems* of 1815, where two of the classifications he used, 'Poems of the Fancy' and 'Poems of the Imagination', would seem to indicate the importance the concepts had for him. They are of course no less important to Coleridge, who replied directly to Wordsworth in chapters 4 and 12 of the *Biographia*.[5] Their disagreement, however, is not over fundamentals. In respect to Coleridge's definition of the fancy, Wordsworth wrote, 'my objection is only that the definition is too general';[6] of the imagination he asserted that 'it recoils from everything but the plastic', which is to say that it is the 'plastic power', as Coleridge called it. Wordsworth continued: 'Fancy is given to quicken and to beguile the temporal part of our nature, Imagination to incite and to support the eternal' (WPW, II, 442). Coleridge would agree with the latter statement (so would Blake) and wrote of Wordsworth, 'I am disposed to conjecture, that he has mistaken the co-presence of fancy with imagination for the operation of the latter singly. A man may work with two very different tools at the same moment; . . . but the work effected by each is distinct and different' *(Biographia*, I, 194). Toward the end of the 1815 Preface Wordsworth illustrated his understanding of both concepts by quoting two lines by Jeremy Taylor and two by Milton. Revealingly and quite characteristically, Coleridge closed his chapter 12 with a very different kind of quotation from Bishop Taylor: 'he to whom all things are one, who draweth all things to one, and seeth all things in one, may enjoy true peace and rest of spirit' (ibid.).

Coleridge entitled his next chapter 'On the imagination, or esemplastic power', and in it appears the famous distinction between the primary and the secondary imagination, along with the contrasted definition of the fancy. He conceived the function of both varieties of imagination in typically Romantic terms of divine creation, of life, of vitality. The central emphasis upon the act of true creation presupposes an organic fusion of parts resulting in a genuine unity. The very act of 'all human Perception' is a creative act in the sense that man perceiving actually creates the world in which he lives. (As Shelley wrote, remembering Berkeley's 'esse est percipi', 'Nothing exists but as it is perceived';[7] but Blake, along with Wordsworth and Coleridge, knew that all men do not see alike.) Fancy, on the other hand, uses what Coleridge calls 'counters' (from the Latin *computare,* to reckon or compute) and is the equivalent of one of Blake's unredeemed daughters of memory. As Coleridge said in the *Biographia:* 'Equally with the ordinary memory the Fancy must receive all its materials ready made [hence unoriginal or conventional] from the [mechanical, uncreative] law of association' of ideas (I, 202).

The implications of these distinctions Coleridge developed in the closely reasoned chapter 14, climactic in his discussion of critical theory, which opens with an account of the speculative origins of *Lyrical Ballads* and defines each of the two sorts of poems to be provided by the two poets in terms of a reconciliation of opposites. Coleridge's poems were to domesticate or humanize the 'supernatural, or at least romantic', by means of producing in the reader 'that willing suspension of disbelief for the moment, which constitutes poetic faith' (*Biographia,* II, 6). Wordsworth's object was the converse of this: to transform or make new the 'things of every day, and to excite a feeling analogous to the supernatural, by awakening the mind's attention from the lethargy of custom'. One poet then set out to naturalize the supernatural, the other to supernaturalize the natural. Both poets proposed to alter basically the reader's mode of perception: an alteration and purification as fundamental to them as to Blake. Coleridge's four contributions to the volume of 1798 were 'The Rime of the Ancyent Marinere', 'The Foster-Mother's Tale', 'The Nightingale, a Conversational Poem' (which replaced 'Lewti'), and 'The Dungeon'.

But Coleridge felt the public need to clarify the critical points of agreement and difference between his own views and those set forth in Wordsworth's several prefaces. As a preliminary to this discussion in the *Biographia,* he defines the poem, poetry and poetic genius finally in terms of the imagination, which 'reveals itself', in the famous words, 'in the balance or reconciliation of opposite or discordant qualities' (II, 12). The true poetry of imagination is thus a poetry of inclusion, of broad inclusiveness on many levels, not a poetry of exclusion. But first the end product of the poetic imagination, the poem, must be distinguished, in terms of purpose, from works of science and history (whose immediate purpose is *not* to produce pleasure), and from novels and prose romances even if metre were superadded (for they would lack organic unity). The poem is then defined in terms of 'such delight from the *whole,* as is compatible with a distinct gratification from each component *part*' (II, 10). Here the emphasis on pleasure is equal to that in Wordsworth's 1798 Advertisement to the *Lyrical Ballads* and in the 1800 Preface.

Coleridge then proceeds to define the '*legitimate* poem' in terms of organic unity or harmony of parts with the whole: 'it must be one, the parts of which mutually support and explain each other; all in their proportion harmonizing with, and supporting the purpose [pleasure] and known influences of metrical arrangement' (ibid.). Right-minded critics of all ages, Coleridge says, deny 'the praises of a just poem . . . to a series of striking lines of distiches, each of which, absorbing the whole attention of the reader to itself, disjoins it from its context, and makes it a separate whole, instead of an harmonizing part' (ibid.). Too great perfection of the part then will work against the illusion of organic unity in the whole. Here Coleridge has restated as a general principle the criticism of Pope's couplets that he made in chapter 1, where he says he is describing the critical opinions of his years at Christ's Hospital and Cambridge. Coleridge's last remarks in chapter 14 before moving on to define the larger term poetry, as distinct from the poem, clarify the nature of aesthetic pleasure as well as the structure of the legitimate poem. The reader should not be 'carried forward . . . merely or chiefly by the mechanical impulse of curiosity, or by a restless desire to arrive at the final solution; but by the pleasurable activity of mind excited by the attractions of the journey itself' (II, 11). This statement denies to the versified novel (of Coleridge's day) the name of poem more persuasively than his earlier remarks.

Chapter 14 ends with the famous definition of poetry in terms of the mind of the poet, especially the poet's imagination. As Coleridge, typically contemplating his own thought processes from above, knew: 'My own conclusions on the nature of poetry, in the strictest use of the word, have been in part anticipated in the preceding disquisition on the fancy and imagination' (*Biographia*, II, 12). But that disquisition, as we have seen, was anticipated, if we may believe the *Biographia,* in important respects at Christ's Hospital and Cambridge. There he first thought through his ideas on the total internal consistency and unified perfection of the great poem, its absolute verbal unity, its smallest parts fused unalterably into a genuine whole that would combine and reconcile opposite or discordant qualities, as in the poetry of Milton and Shakespeare and, among moderns working at their best, of Cowper and Bowles.[8]

The famous penultimate paragraph of chapter 14 so describes the functions of the imagination. Here we also encounter certain favourite Romantic words: 'blends', *'fuses'*, 'harmonizes'. The unity implied or described in this paragraph may be called organic or natural in the sense that the imagination that creates it 'subordinates art to nature'. This of course is merely the illusion of naturalness. For Coleridge clearly understood that art is artifical: in 1818 he delivered a lecture entitled 'On Poesy or Art', in which he stated that 'Art . . . is the mediatress between, and reconciler of, nature and man. It is, therefore, the power of humanizing nature, of infusing the thoughts and passions of man into every thing which is the object of his contemplation . . .and it stamps them into unity in the mould of a moral idea.'[9] Blake expressed a similar idea in *The Marriage of Heaven and Hell:* 'Where man is not nature is barren' (BPP, 37).

In the *Biographia* Coleridge attacked at length Wordsworth's emphasis on nature and the natural, including Wordsworth's supposed use of the natural diction of real men in his poetry. He objected to Wordsworth's 'insertion of accidental circumstances. . . . as contravening the essence of poetry, . . . the most intense, weighty and philosophical product of human art' (II, 101). Art has no place for *'accidentality'*: the *'mistress of poets . . . hath not her existence in matter, but in reason'* (II, 102).

makes art 2ⁿᵈ ony to Nature,

And in the famous definition at the end of chapter 14, we learn
that the imagination is 'first put in action by the will and understanding, and retained under their irremissive . . . control'
(II, 12). The very act of balancing or reconciling opposite
or discordant qualities or ideas would seem to be an act of the
understanding, 'the regulative, substantiating and realizing
power', if not of the speculative reason itself, 'the power by
which we produce or aim to produce unity, necessity, and
universality in all our knowledge by means of principles
a priori' (I, 193). In either event, the reason or the understanding appears to be (to recall Blake's *Marriage*) 'the bound or
outward circumference' or imagination's energy.

In Coleridge's examples of opposite or discordant qualities
that are balanced or reconciled, we find large numbers of abstractions: sameness, difference, the general, the representative,
order, judgment, art and the artificial. In fact, there is 'a more
than usual state of emotion, with more than usual order;
judgement ever awake and steady self-possession. . . . Finally,
GOOD SENSE is the BODY of poetic genius' *(Biographia,* II,
12, 13), although imagination is the soul within, bounded by the
body of good sense. 'No man was ever yet a great poet, without
being at the same time a profound philosopher', Coleridge
asserts, using Shakespeare as example, in a discussion of the
'characteristics of original poetic genius in general' (II, 19, 14).
Further, the functions or faculties of poet and philosopher cannot, for him, exist in fragmented isolation from each other; each
is necessary to the other. Finally, these forces – 'the creative
power and the intellectual energy' – must be 'reconciled',
neither one losing any part of its identity, even though 'each in
its excess of strength seems to threaten the extinction of the
other' (II, 19). But in Coleridge's metaphor, once 'reconciled',
they 'fought each with its shield before the breast of the other'.
Or changing the metaphor to one of marriage and birth, he
writes that Shakespeare 'first studied patiently, meditated deeply, understood minutely, till knowledge, become habitual and
intuitive, wedded itself to his habitual feelings, and at length
gave birth to that stupendous power' that placed him at the
head of English drama (II, 19–20). These polar faculties thus
richly wedded, Shakespeare empathetically 'darts himself
forth, and passes into the forms of human character and passion.
. . . SHAKESPEARE becomes all things, yet forever remaining

himself' (II, 20). The empathy so described looks forward remarkably to that claimed for Shakespeare by Keats in elaborating his notion of the 'poetical Character'.

Another one of the 'characteristics of original poetic genius in general' is 'the power of reducing multitude into unity of effect' (*Biographia*, II, 14), a power that may express itself in many forms, one of these being the unified cluster of various poetic images. They become a mark of the true poetic genius when 'they have the effect of reducing multitude to unity' (II, 16). There is more art than nature at work here, presumably; for by contrast we learn that the artless 'intercourse of uneducated men, is distinguished from the diction of their superiors in knowledge and power, by the greater *disjunction* and *separation* in the component parts' of their conversation (II, 44). They lack the ability to 'subordinate and arrange the different parts' so as to convey their meaning 'as an organized whole' (ibid.). Coleridge dealt with this subject also in *The Friend*, in an essay that opens with a discussion of the qualities distinguishing the speech of educated men. There we learn that the educated man has 'the habit of foreseeing, in each integral part, or . . . in every sentence, the whole that he then intends to communicate', whereas in the conversation of 'an ignorant man . . . memory alone is called into action' (I, 449). There is no fusion of the parts; the accidental and multitudinous have not been reduced to unity. In the speech of an ignorant man, 'the "*and then*", the "*and there*", and the still less significant, "*and so*" . . . constitute . . . all his connections'. Obviously, the quality of organic unity is not to be found in the speech of natural man; in such unity there is more art than nature, although one of its chief effects is to create the illusion of naturalness. Yeats put the matter thus in 'Adam's Curse':

> A line will take us hours maybe;
> Yet if it does not seem a moment's thought,
> Our stitching and unstitching has been naught.
>
> (ll. 4–6)

Coleridge even describes metre in terms of a 'balance of antagonists', a reconciliation, 'a union' of opposite or polar qualities (*Biographia,* II, 50). He traces its origin 'to the balance in the [poet's] mind effected by that spontaneous effort which strives to *hold in check* the workings of *passion*' (II, 49, italics added). This 'balance of antagonists became organized into *metre* . . . by a supervening act of the will and judgement', although 'the *elements* of metre owe their existence to a state of increased excitement'. But 'as these elements are formed into metre *artificially,* by a *voluntary* act', the critic has the right to expect that in the poem 'these two conditions [will] be reconciled and co-present. There must be not only a partnership, but a union; an interpenetration of passion and of will, of *spontaneous* impulse and of *voluntary* purpose' (II, 50).

This principle, however, is merely a particularized expression of a much more general principle of human nature. Art here imitates nature. There is a

> high spiritual instinct of the human being impelling us to seek unity by harmonious adjustment, and thus establishing the principle, that *all* the parts of an organized whole must be assimilated to the more *important* and *essential* parts. . . . The composition of a poem . . . consists either in the interfusion of the SAME throughout the radically DIFFERENT, or of the different throughout a base radically the same (*Biographia,* II, 56).

Poetry is one of the '*imitative* arts', totally different from 'copying'; that is, poetry imitates life or the principle of life. What that is will be discussed shortly and in some detail.

If the imagination is in essence the power to shape into one and the poem one of its highest creations, the broader, more inclusive and abstract product of the imagination is beauty. Coleridge defines it in Pythagorean terms of '*multëity in unity*'.[10] 'The safest definition, then, of Beauty, as well as the oldest, is that of Pythagoras: THE REDUCTION OF MANY TO ONE. . . . *The sense of beauty subsists in simultaneous intuition of the relation of parts, each to each, and of all to a whole*' (*Biographia,* II, 238, 239). Coleridge implies that intimate familiarity is an essential element in the intuition of beauty: the great poem must be reread, made the reader's own, if he is to achieve a '*simultaneous intuition of the relation of parts*'.

Multeity in unity: here we have the very principle of life itself. Poetic form imitates this principle, and our sense or awareness of the beautiful depends upon and is called to consciousness by our awareness of formal relationship in the several elements of the art work. In his essay entitled 'Hints Towards the Formation of a More Comprehensive Theory of Life', Coleridge, concluding a complex argument, writes that 'Life, then, we consider as the copula, or the unity of thesis and antithesis, position and counterposition. . . . Thus, in the identity of the two counter-powers, Life *sub*sists; in their strife it *con*sists: and in their reconciliation it at once dies and is born again into a new form.'[11] More specifically, 'the two counteracting tendencies of nature [are], namely, that of *detachment* from the universal life . . . and that of *attachment* or reduction into it' (CCW, I, 389). Most basically, then, 'the idea of polarity, which has been given as the universal law of Life' (392), expresses itself in terms of attraction and repulsion, which, as Blake says in *The Marriage,* 'are necessary to Human existence' (BPP, 34). 'Whoever tries to reconcile them seeks to destroy existence' (39), Blake adds, by destroying the polar principle of existence.

For Coleridge, as for Blake, man is above nature, created by God, who unassisted by nature 'made Man in His own image' (CCW, I, 411). For Coleridge the 'reconciliation' of nature's polarities in man does *not* destroy the basis of human existence. But this seeming difference between Blake and Coleridge is largely semantic.[12] In Blake's parable of the Prolific and the Devourer the term 'reconcile' means something like 'erase the differences' between these two principal forces (BPP, 39). In Coleridgean man, in whom the natural and the supernatural meet, there has been achieved 'the highest realization and reconciliation of both her [nature's] tendencies, that of the most perfect detachment with the greatest possible union'.[13] The principle of polar opposites in man, through God, expresses itself in terms social, political, intellectual; in terms of liberty and restraint, independence and submission, originality of genius and resignation to the natural world.

In Man the centripetal and individualizing tendency of all Nature is itself concentred and individualized – he is a revelation of Nature! Henceforward, . . . he who stands the most on himself, and stands the firmest, is the truest, because the most

individual, Man. In social and political life this acme is interdependence: in moral life it is independence: in intellectual life
it is genius. Nor does the form of polarity, which has accompanied the law of individuation up its whole ascent, desert it
here. As the height, so the depth. The intensities must be at
once opposite and equal. As the liberty, so must be the reverence for law. As the independence, so must be the service and
the submission to the Supreme Will! As the ideal genius and
the originality, in the same proportion must be the resignation to the real world, the sympathy and the intercommunion with Nature. In the conciliating mid-point, or
equator, does the Man live, and only by its equal presence in
both its poles can that life be manifested! (CCW, I, 412)

Attraction and repulsion, expansion and compression or limita-
tion, stability or permanence and change, liberty and restraint:
in the opposing demands of such polarities as these does human
life at its best consist, reconciling these polarities both within
the individual and within society. Thus 'Life itself is not a *thing*
. . . but an *act* and *process*' (416), and the essence of that process is
conflict, strife, tension between polar opposites.

Because art as a whole is an imitation, in Coleridge's special
sense of the word, of life, so must it be with poetry, painting,
and the novel. And in the drama, which should be 'not *a copy* of
nature; but . . . an imitation. This is the universal principle of the
fine arts. . . . that ever-varying balance, or balancing, of images,
notions, or feelings . . . conceived as in opposition to each other;
in short, the perception of identity and contrariety.'[14] The great
merit of Sir Walter Scott's novels, Coleridge explains in a letter
of 8 April 1820, lies in the nature of the subject:

the contrast between the Loyalists & their opponents can
never be *obsolete,* for it is the contest between the two great
moving Principles of social Humanity – religious adherence
to the Past and the Ancient, the Desire & the admiration of
Permanence, on the one hand; and the Passion for increase of
Knowledge, for Truth as the offspring of Reason, in short,
the mighty Instincts of *Progression* and *Free-agency*, on the
other. In all subjects of deep and lasting Interest, you will
detect a struggle between two opposites, two polar Forces,
both of which are alike necessary to our human Well-being,

& necessary each to the continued existence of the other –
Well therefore may we contemplate with intense feelings
those whirlwinds which are, for free-agents, the appointed
means & only possible condition of that *equi-librium,* in which
our moral Being subsists: while the disturbance of the same
constitutes our sense of Life. Thus in the ancient Tragedy the
lofty Struggle between irresistible Fate & unconquerable Free
Will, which founds it's equilibrium in the Providence & the
Future Retribution [recompense] of Christianity–.[15]

Similarly for painting: 'In Raphael's admirable Galatea . . . is the
balance, the perfect reconciliation, effected between these two
conflicting principles of the FREE LIFE, and of the confining
FORM! How entirely is the stiffness that would have resulted
from the obvious regularity of the latter, *fused* and . . . almost
volatilized by the interpenetration . . . of the former' (*Biographia,*
II, 234–5).

Coleridge's differences with Wordsworth's theory, chiefly as
set forth in the 1800 Preface, have in large part been anticipated
in the preceding sketch of Coleridge's own critical theory. In
Coleridge's words, Wordsworth contended that 'the proper
diction for poetry in general consists altogether in a language
taken, with due exceptions, from the mouths of men in real
[low and rustic] life, a language which actually constitutes the
natural conversation of [such] men under the influence of
natural feelings' (*Biographia,* II, 29). Coleridge objected that such
language was unimaginative or unpoetic: the great *'disjunction
and separation* in the component parts' of it precluded any
reconciliation of opposite or discordant elements (II, 44). In his
conversation

the rustic . . . aims almost solely to convey *insulated* facts; . . .
while the educated man chiefly seeks to discover and express
those *connections* of things, or those relative *bearings* of fact to
fact, from which some more or less general law is deducible.
For *facts* are valuable to a wise man, chiefly as they lead to the
discovery of the indwelling *law* [of opposites], which is the
true *being* of things, the sole solution of their modes of exis-

tence, and in the knowledge of which consists our dignity and our power (II, 39).

Poetry, concerned with generic man, is 'essentially *ideal, . . . it* avoids and excludes all *accident*' (II, 33). Thus in a poem it is not possible to imitate truly a dull and garrulous discourser, without repeating the effects of dullness and garrulity' (II, 36), and with deadly effect Coleridge quotes from 'The Thorn', which Wordsworth consequently revised. Coleridge would not be convinced that the best part of language is formed from the rural objects with which the rustic is daily concerned.[16] Rather, it 'is derived from reflection on the acts of the mind itself. It is formed by a voluntary appropriation of fixed symbols to internal acts, to processes and results of imagination' (II, 39–40). In short, it is poets who make the language, not farmers or shepherds. Once again, the '*mistress of poets . . . hath not her existence in matter, but in reason*' (II, 102).

In dealing with Wordsworth's contention in the 1800 Preface that no '*essential* difference' exists 'between the language of prose and metrical composition',[17] Coleridge uses a pragmatic strategy similar to that he had employed in disposing of rustic language as the language of poetry. He demonstrates that poetry that uses the language of prose is prosaic or inferior poetry, and he appeals to three stanzas from Samuel Daniel's interminable *Civil Wars between the Two Houses of Lancaster and York,* which are written chiefly in the language of abstraction and low intensity (*Biographia,* II, 60–1). Similarly, he shows that the closer the metre of poetry approximates the movement of prose, the more prosaic and the less poetic it becomes. This he does by most unkindly printing in the form of prose some five lines from Wordsworth's *The Brothers,* changing only the unnatural position of the word 'there' in two instances (II, 62–3). Earlier in chapter 18, as we have seen, Coleridge had established the general principle that metre reconciles basic human opposites by combining spontaneous impulse and voluntary purpose, a reconciliation that the poet ignores or fails to achieve at his great peril.

Coleridge conceives his magnificent climactic discussion in chapter 22 of the characteristic defects and excellences of Wordsworth's poetry chiefly in terms, explicit or implicit, of its failure or success in reconciling opposites. Thus he observes, first, that a number of Wordsworth's poems reveal an inconstancy, a disharmony, or an incongruity of style, in which lines of 'peculiar felicity' may be followed by lines 'not only unimpassioned but undistinguished', lines that use language 'only proper in prose' and so are incapable of achieving a union or reconciliation of polar opposites or the intensity that may result from the perfect fusion of all the parts of a poem (*Biographia,* II, 97).

Second, the *'matter-of-factness'* evident in certain of Wordsworth's poems may take the form of 'a laborious minuteness and fidelity in the representation of objects' (*Biographia,* II, 101). The act of reading such a description is like fitting the pieces of a jig-saw puzzle together. 'We first look at one part, and then at another, then join and dove-tail them; and when the successive acts of attention have been completed, there is a retrogressive effort of mind to behold it as a whole. The poet should paint to the imagination, not to the fancy' (II, 102). In short, no act of genuine creation has taken place in the poet's mind: the shaping, modifying and unifying powers of the imagination have not been at work.

When the Wordsworthian matter-of-factness takes the form of 'the insertion of accidental circumstances, in order to the full explanation of his . . . characters' (*Biographia,* II, 101), it ignores the principle of the reader's 'willing suspension of disbelief . . . which constitutes poetic faith' (II, 6) and also contravenes the philosophic 'essence of poetry', which, unlike history, does not admit of accidentality. Granting the praiseworthiness of Wordsworth's democratic and Christian emphasis on generic man in his choice of characters from low life, Coleridge objects nevertheless to his *'biographical* attention to probability, and an *anxiety* of explanation' (II, 103). This is placing truth before pleasure, which is the immediate object of poetry and distinguishes it from the sermon, the moral essay, philosophy and prose generally. Such accidentality is admissible in biography and in certain kinds of novels, like those of Defoe, 'meant to pass for histories', but it can never be 'legitimately introduced in a *poem,* the characters of which, amid the strongest individualization, must still remain representative' (II, 106–7).

Coleridge's discussion of the remaining three characteristic defects of Wordsworth's poems focuses on their occasional lack of dramatic propriety or appropriateness. In brief, these defects are 'undue predilection for the dramatic form', disproportionate 'intensity of feeling', and 'thoughts and images too great for the subject' (*Biographia,* II, 109). Unlike Shakespeare, Wordsworth is not a 'Spinozistic deity – an omnipresent creativeness',[18] permeating and empathetically entering into all his characters, his own character or identity absorbed beyond recognition in a dramatic creation of perfect internal unity. Certain of Wordsworth's dramatic poems reveal a fundamental failure of dramatic fusion. The 'thoughts and diction' of dramatic characters presumably speaking for the poet may be different from those of the poet as first-person persona, thereby producing 'an incongruity of style' (*Biographia,* II, 109). Or the thoughts and diction are the same, which creates 'a species of ventriloquism'. To such a sameness with dramatic difference or variety of characters the reader cannot give a willing suspension of disbelief. Coleridge's 'fourth class of defects' is closely related to the third (ibid.); it is an undramatic or inappropriate 'intensity of feeling', as in 'Anecdote for Fathers'. Fifth, in some poems Coleridge finds an undramatic presence of 'thoughts and images too great for the subject' (ibid.) He objected to the six-year-old 'Mighty Prophet! Seer blest!' of the Intimations Ode (II, 111–12).

Coleridge phrases his discussion of the characteristic excellences of Wordsworth's poems almost wholly in terms of a perfect fused unity or a perfect unifying reconciliation of opposites. The 'infallible test of a blameless style [is] its *untranslatableness* in words of the same language without injury to the meaning' (*Biographia,* II, 115). This 'austere purity of language', this 'perfect appropriateness of the words to the meaning', Wordsworth has, and in discussing it Coleridge recalled his boyhood training under Bowyer.

Wordsworth's second characteristic excellence is essentially that of original genius, with all that this implies. His best poems are genuine imaginative creations – not copies of the fancy. Their thoughts and sentiments 'are *fresh* and have the dew upon them' (*Biographia,* II, 118), a figure that Coleridge had used earlier in chapter 4. The great example here is (despite the 'best Philosopher') the Intimations Ode, addressed to readers who are 'accustomed to watch the flux and reflux of their inmost nature, to venture at times into the twilight realms of consciousness, and to feel a deep interest in modes of inmost being, to which they know that the attributes of time and space are inapplicable and alien, but which yet can not be conveyed save in symbols of time and space' (II, 120). Such readers, one feels rather certain, would relish *The Ancient Mariner* as well as Blake's prophetic poems.

The remainder of Coleridge's discussion of Wordsworth develops the specific attributes of original genius. There is a 'perfect truth of nature in his images and descriptions'; but the imagination transforms this truth so as to bring 'out many a vein and many a tint, which escapes the eye of common observation' and thus brightens the way of 'the traveller on the dusty high road of custom' (*Biographia,* II, 121) – in short, teaches him to see with his imaginative eye. Indeed, in what remains of chapter 22, Coleridge describes Wordsworth as essentially an imaginative seer, whose poems achieve 'a union of deep and subtle thought with sensibility; a sympathy with man as man' (II, 122). Such an imaginative seer can perceive beneath all 'disguise the human face divine' (II, 123), like Blake himself, whom Coleridge, after reading 'The Divine Image' where 'the human form divine' appears, would pronounce to be 'a man of Genius'.[19] Wordsworth understands, with love or sympathy, man's most fundamental polarities, the union in him of the fallen creature and of the divine Creator. 'The superscription and the image of the Creator still remain legible to *him* under the dark lines, with which guilt or calamity had cancelled or cross-barred it' (II, 123). As an example of 'the blending, *fusing* power of Imagination' that makes possible the poetic expression of such insight, Coleridge (somewhat oddly) quotes the passage from Wordsworth's 'The Mad Mother' in which the mother nurses her infant. Wordsworth has, then,

> the gift of IMAGINATION in the highest and strictest sense of the word. . . . To employ his own words [in 'Elegiac Stanzas', ll. 14–16], which are at once an instance and an illustration, he does indeed to all thoughts and to all objects

> > add the gleam,
> > The light that never was, on sea or land,
> > The consecration, and the poet's dream.
> >
> > (II, 124)

All things and all thoughts, in short, Wordsworth's poems place in a new and holy light, consecrating them, making them, for the reader, sacred.

Deriving from the central and controlling position of Coleridge's concept of the imagination as that creative power of mind that marries polar opposites, thus transforming or redeeming them and fusing them in the single poem – the remarkable consistency of his critical theory and his practical criticism is sufficiently obvious not to require added summary here. That his poetic imagination is also an ethical imagination that recognizes the sameness and kinship of all men, of whatever rank or station, while wishing to preserve in the poem their infinite variety and individuality, is equally clear. To the extent that Coleridge is correct, Wordsworth also incorporates into his poetry, often implicitly, these same doctrines. Wordsworth's muse consecrates all things and all thoughts, even the lowliest, whereas Los's spectre, the anti-poet, curses all things and thoughts.

> He curses Heaven & Earth, Day & Night, Sun and Moon
> He curses Forest Spring & River, Desart & sandy Waste
> Cities & Nations, Families & Peoples, Tongues & Laws
> (Jerusalem 10, 25–7: BPP, 152)

The 'dread Spectres' make a curse of man's life and all that he perceives by taking

> the Two Contraries which are calld Qualities, with which
> Every Substance is clothed, they name them Good & Evil
> From them they make an abstract, which is a Negation
>   . . . it is the Reasoning Power
> An Abstract objecting power, that Negatives every thing
> This is the Spectre of Man . . .
> Therefore Los stands in London building Golgonooza,
> (Ibid., 5, ll. 8–10, 13–15, 17: BPP, 151)

the city of art that is truly human, Blake's magnificent outpost in Ulro against the triumph of ultimate evil.

When one considers the exalted position in the hierarchy of poetry that Coleridge (along with Blake and Wordsworth) accorded to *Paradise Lost,* when one recalls his overwhelming feelings of personal guilt going back even into childhood and described in his autobiographical letters of 1797–8 to Thomas Poole, when one contemplates the implications of his Anglican schooling, not to mention the fact that his father was a vicar in the church – it seems probable that during the greater part of Coleridge's life he took the doctrine of man as a fallen creature very seriously, despite a period of religious perplexity. No one of his great poems is inconsistent with such doctrine. In his 'Confessio Fidei', dated 3 November 1816, he wrote, 'I BELIEVE, and hold it as the fundamental article of Christianity, that I am a fallen creature. . . . I receive with full and grateful faith the assurance of revelation, that the Word, which is from all eternity with God, and is God, assumed our human nature in order to redeem me, and all mankind from this our connate corruption.'[20] Such belief is consistent with Coleridge's other thought: in Christ are reconciled human and divine, finite and infinite, word or spirit and flesh. But He came to redeem fallen man, and it is only because of Him that we call Adam's fall fortunate. Christ is unnecessary to the man who believes in the essential goodness or benevolence of man – and we have little evidence that Coleridge could so believe for long. In a letter of March 1798 he wrote, 'I believe most steadfastly in original Sin. . . . And for this inherent depravity, I believe, that the *Spirit* of the Gospel is the sole cure.'[21]

In the verse and notes of 'Religious Musings', published in *Poems on Various Subjects* (1796) and subtitled 'A Desultory Poem, Written on the Christmas Eve of 1794', we read of the first millennium of a thousand years followed by a universal redemption of all sinful men, who, we learn in the notes, 'in the first age . . . were innocent from ignorance of Vice; they fell, that by the knowledge of consequences they might attain intellectual security, i.e. Virtue, which is a wise and strong–nerv'd Innocence'.[22] We find much of the essential Coleridge in this early poem, along with much of the Book of Revelation and a Blakean higher innocence. It is the Crucifixion, contemplated by 'the thought-benighted Sceptic', that leads the soul of the persona, through 'perfect Love', to become 'absorbed'.

> Till by exclusive consciousness of God
> All self-annihilated it shall make
> God its Identity: God all in all!
>
> (ll. 41–3)

Here then, already in Coleridge's first volume of poems, appears the Romantic experience, the annihilation of self, the loss of the sense of personal identity by absorption or union or reconciliation with some great opposite – in this instance not Nature but God, who is, however, 'Nature's essence, mind, and energy!' (l. 49). This experience might seem pantheistic if Coleridge's prose argument to the poem did not focus so explicitly on the 'Person of Christ'. The problem inherent in fallen man's ability to love such a creation would seem to be a problem of perception, here solved in theological terms. For it is 'the Elect, regenerate through faith, . . . Enrobed with Light, and naturalised in Heaven' (ll. 88, 93), who find the natural world exquisitely fitted to the Mind, as Wordsworth said it was in his 'Prospectus'. Coleridge illuminates the nature of his heavenly 'Light' by means of the simile of a shepherd creeping through a 'thick fog', his eye fixed darkling on the road immediately before him; then, miraculously, the sun bursts through 'the black vapour. . . . And wide around the landscape streams with glory.' The character of the light has changed.

Similarly, when a man has nourished his soul upon the 'one Mind, one omnipresent Mind, / Omnific', whose 'most holy name is Love'.

> He from his small particular orbit flies
> With blest outstarting! From himself he flies,
> Stands in the sun, and with no partial gaze
> Views all creation; and he loves it all,
> And blesses it, and calls it very good!
>
> (ll. 109–13)

He 'calls it very good' even as on the sixth day 'God saw everything that he had made, and, behold, *it was* very good' (Genesis 1:31). The act of loving perception here described is then an act of creation parallel to the Divine Creation and to that extent anticipates Coleridge's later thought on the imagination, his central concern with the relation of parts to whole. In 'Religious

Musings', however, he expresses it explicitly in religious and ethical terms.

> 'Tis the sublime of man,
> Our noontide Majesty, to know ourselves
> Parts and proportions of one wondrous whole!
> This fraternises man. . . .
> But 'tis God
> Diffused through all, that doth make all one whole.
>
> (ll. 126–31)

This knowledge or perception of parts in relation to the whole seems to be limited to the pure in spirit, the Elect. For,

> Made blind by lusts, disherited of soul,
> No common centre Man, no common sire
> Knoweth! A sordid solitary thing,
> Mid countless brethren with a lonely heart
> Through courts and cities the smooth savage roams
> Feeling himself, his own low self the whole;
> When he by sacred sympathy might make
> The whole one Self! Self, that no alien knows!
> Self, far diffused as Fancy's wing can travel![23]

Here is Coleridge's dream, early and late, of union, communion, community, to be achieved in this poem by sympathetic, imaginative identification of self with all mankind.

There then follows a Miltonic history of 'Good through Evil', 'wide-wasting ills! yet each the immediate source / Of mightier good' (ll. 195, 217–18). From avarice, luxury and war sprang science, freedom, philosophers and bards, who, 'enamoured with the charms of order, hate / The unseemly disproportion' (ll. 230–1). Such as these, on the fated day, in their 'rage' for order in a chaotic world, will

> Then o'er the wild and wavy chaos rush
> And tame the outrageous mass, with plastic might
> Moulding Confusion to such perfect forms,
> As erst were wont, – bright visions of the day! –
> To float before them.
>
> (ll. 245–9)

Once again Coleridge describes the act of poetic composition by 'eloquent men' (l. 240), men who are at the same time visionaries possessed of 'plastic might' not unlike the 'esemplastic power' and who in the creative act of reducing chaos to cosmos depict not the world's confusion but the 'bright visions' of their own imaginations.

At this date, however, Coleridge's poem gives its perfect faith not to poetry but to the 'dear Saviour of Mankind! / Thee, Lamb of God!' (ll. 168–9). The 'wretched Many', because they are 'far removed . . . / From all that softens or ennobles Man', cannot understand poetry (ll. 262, 260–1). In their wretchedness they must await the Day of Judgment for their 'day of Retribution', which however is 'nigh' (l. 303) and which Coleridge describes in terms vivid enough but only superficially Blakean. The Last Judgment is not for Coleridge, as it sometimes was for Blake, 'an overwhelming of Bad Art & Science'.[24] Even so, at the end of the poem, Coleridge makes implicit the close association of the creative poet and the creative, form-imposing forces of the universe, as he addresses those 'Spirits . . . of plastic power, that interfused / Roll through the grosser and material mass / In organizing surge! Holies of God! / (And what if Monads of the infinite mind?)' (ll. 402, 405–8). This last line, echoed in lines 44–5 of 'The Eolian Harp', is not far removed from the doctrine announced in a letter of 1802 that 'every Thing has a Life of it's own, . . . we are all *one Life*'.[25] Each of Leibnitz's monads reflected the universe in itself, and in his hierarchy the highest place was given to those monads that most clearly reflected the universe. Are Coleridge's monads poets 'of plastic power', not only reflecting but 'organizing' our perception of the universe?

In 'The Eolian Harp' Coleridge asked:

> And what if all of animated nature
> Be but organic Harps diversely fram'd,
> That tremble into thought, as o'er them sweeps
> Plastic and vast, one intellectual breeze,
> At once the Soul of each, and God of all?[26]

All Nature sings, in short, and turns into thought when a plastic or shaping and creative 'intellectual breeze' sweeps over it. The breeze is the soul of each aspect of animated nature; it is thus the soul that is the ultimate source of the music in a natural world innately harmonious. This is pantheistic, whether atheistic or not the poem does not tell us, but either way the poem's Sara reproves the persona, who at once acknowledges her as a 'Meek Daughter in the family of Christ!' Recognizing himself as 'a sinful and most miserable man', he renounces 'these shapings of the unregenerate mind'.

Of all the Romantic poets, Coleridge felt the greatest hunger after community and had the greatest need to persuade himself that he (as well as all others) was a true part of some much greater whole. If all nature sings, *poetic* man also participates in this great harmony of 'the one Life within us and abroad' (l. 26). His soul can also tremble into thought and sing: it is 'plastic and vast'.

These two early poems, 'Religious Musings' and 'The Eolian Harp', published when Coleridge was twenty-four and which for some years he thought most highly of, underline the essential unity of his thought despite its fluctuations and his several recantations. In both poems, the blessed vision of creation as 'very good', the great symphony of all Nature's harmony, is denied to wretched, fallen men. In one, only the Elect can see it; in the other, 'the unregenerate mind', the persona now persuaded that he is a 'sinful and most miserable man', cannot bear it. Coleridge would give much of his later thought to the problems poeticized thus early. Men must be taught to see and to hear, those men who, as he wrote in the *Biographia,* 'have eyes, yet see not, ears that hear not, and hearts that neither feel nor understand' (II, 6). Nature, rightly understood, must come home to men's bosoms if man is to see all creation as very good and to hear the 'organic Harps' of all nature 'tremble into thought'. The 'mystery of genius in the Fine Arts', Coleridge stated in 1818, is 'to make the external internal, . . . to make nature thought'.[27] Coleridge solved the mystery most succinctly, perhaps, in his lecture 'On Poesy or Art'. But the idea was central to his thought and he gave to it many expressions, explicit and implicit. Indeed, when one takes a final and random sampling of his more interesting thought, its internal consistency becomes even more startling, as we observe some idea on the periphery of his thought leading straight to the centre, or some central idea taking us by implication all the way out to a point on the periphery.[28]

In order to make nature thought, to make the external internal, Coleridge finds it necessary to solve the epistemological problem of I and the World, Subject and Object, mind and matter, Man and Nature. How can we know anything that is outside ourselves? This question becomes one of the central concerns of the *Biographia*. In chapter 8 Coleridge states the problem as Descartes understood it: 'To the best of my knowledge Des Cartes was the first philosopher, who introduced the absolute and essential heterogeneity of the soul as intelligence, and the body as matter', defined as 'a *space-filling* substance. Yet . . . the law of causality holds only between homogeneous things, i.e. things having some common property; and cannot extend from one world into another, its opposite' (I, 88–9).

Coleridge examined and solved the problem in detail as early as his essays on method in *The Friend,* but his most succinct solution appears in his essay 'On Life', where he defines 'a THING as the synthesis of opposing energies'.[29] This is not only the principle of the imagination, the mind's most creative power; it is also the very principle of life, which is a 'copula' of forces (CCW, I, 392). Further, 'Life, *as* Life, supposes a positive or universal principle in Nature, with a negative principle in every particular animal, the latter, or limitative power, constantly acting to individualize, and, as it were, *figure* the former. *Thus*, then, Life itself is not a *thing* – a self-subsistent *hypostasis* – but an *act* and *process*' (I, 416). So also is the primary imagination an 'act', and it is this that makes possible perception in all men, for it is 'a repetition in the finite mind of the eternal act of creation in the infinite I AM'. Thus act speaks to act, process to process. The 'first and simplest *differential* act of Nature, . . . like every other power in Nature, is designated by its opposite poles, and must be represented as the magnetic axis, the northern pole of which signifies rest, attraction, fixity, coherence, or hardness; . . . while the southern pole, as its antithesis, represents mobility, repulsion, incoherence, and fusibility' (I, 401–2). As Blake says in *The Marriage,* 'Opposition is true Friendship' (BPP, 41).

It therefore follows, for Coleridge as for Blake, that 'nothing real does or can exist corresponding to either pole *exclusively*' (CCW, I, 402). In Blake's words, again in *The Marriage*, 'Attraction and Repulsion . . . are necessary to Human existence' (BPP, 34). Thus it is that mind and nature find their common ground of being in energy. They have ceased to be heterogeneous, and mind can now extend itself from its world into that other world and make the external internal and nature thought. The 'productive power, which is in nature as nature, is essentially one (i.e., of one kind) with the intelligence, which is in the human mind above nature' (*The Friend*, I, 402). On 23 June 1829 Coleridge felt the need to clarify the obscurity of this sentence in a note: 'the productive Power, = vis natur*ans* . . . is essentially [one] &c. – In other words, Idea and Law are the Subjective and Objective *Poles* of the same magnet – i.e. of the same living and energizing Reason. What is an idea in the Subject, i.e. in the Mind, is a Law in the Object, i.e. in Nature' (497). This is *natura naturans,* the informing spirit within nature, to be clearly distinguished from the teeming *natura naturata* of the 'sensible World', the nature always about to be born and about to die.

Coleridge makes two further points about man and nature. God created

> the material world . . . for the sake of man, at once the high-priest and representative of the Creator, *as far as* he partakes of that [divine] reason in which the essences of all things co-exist in all their distinctions yet as one and indivisible. But I speak of man in his idea, and as subsumed in the divine humanity, in whom alone God loved the world. (*The Friend*, I, 516)

Bluntly stated, God made the world for the Elect (to use a term from 'Religious Musings'), not for fallen man. Nevertheless, as man makes efforts to understand nature, 'he is inevitably tempted to misinterpret a constant precedence [in nature] into positive causation, and thus to break and scatter the one divine and invisible life of nature into countless idols of the sense; and falling prostrate before lifeless images, the creatures of his own abstraction, is himself sensualized' (I, 518). Such a man, Blake would say, is in bondage to 'the Delusive Goddess Nature & her

Laws',[30] viewing the world's wonders through his vegetative eye only. This is the peculiar temptation of the materialistic scientist classifying the forms of *natura naturata,* viewing 'objects (*as* objects) . . . essentially fixed and dead' (*Biographia,* I, 202). Neither the primary nor the secondary imagination is at work here. But even the poet may be subject to this temptation; if he succumbs, he ceases to be a poet and becomes a pedant. As Coleridge said of Wordsworth in 1803: 'always to look at the superficies of Objects for the purpose of taking Delight in their Beauty . . . is . . . deleterious to the Health & manhood of Intellect'.[31] (Wordsworth, we may note, understood this distinction as well as Coleridge.) By the time that Coleridge wrote *The Friend,* its effects had become much more deleterious: it could lead to a form of pantheism that was '*practically* atheistic', confounding 'the Creator with the Aggregate of his Creatures', with *natura naturata* (I, 523, 522).

The 'contemplation of reason . . . [is] that intuition of things which arises when we possess ourselves, as one with the whole' (*The Friend,* I, 520). Such contemplation is quite different from 'abstract knowledge, or the science of the mere understanding', a 'science of delusion' (I, 520–1). Abstract knowledge 'presents itself when transferring reality to the negations of reality, to the ever-varying framework of the uniform life'. It leads us to 'think of ourselves as separated beings, and place nature in antithesis to the mind, as object to subject, thing to thought, death to life' (I, 520). It is, however, by means of the higher reason that we know that existence or the life-principle 'is an eternal and infinite self-rejoicing, self-loving, with a joy unfathomable, with a love all-comprehensive' (I, 521). Coleridge never claimed that all men possess this reason or that any man possesses its full powers at all times.

> But we can not force any man into an insight or intuitive possession of the true philosophy, because we cannot give him . . . intellectual intuition, or constructive imagination; because we can not organize for him an eye that can see, an ear that can listen to, or a heart that can feel, the harmonies of Nature, or recognize in her endless forms, the thousandfold realization of those simple and majestic laws, which yet in their absoluteness can be discovered only in the recesses of his own spirit, – not by that man, therefore, whose imaginative

powers have been *ossified* by the continual reaction and assimilating influences of mere *objects* on his mind, and who is a prisoner to his eye and its reflex, the passive fancy! – not by him in whom an unbroken familiarity with the organic world, as if it were mechanical, with the sensitive, but as if it were insensate, has engendered the coarse and hard spirit of a sorcerer.[32]

One is tempted to discover in this magnificently Coleridgean and somewhat incoherent sentence all the essentials of Coleridge's philosophy. Here we have the reconciliation of intellect and intuition in a single phrase; of imagination and the senses; the concept of Nature as harmony; the distinction between *natura naturata* and *natura naturans*; the identity of man and nature in the identity of idea and law; the horror of nature viewed as a conglomeration of dead and lifeless objects; the viewer subject to the tyranny of the eye (referred to in the same paragraph as 'habitual slavery to the eye'),[33] victim of the passive fancy; the film of familiarity and a mechanical philosophy; man living in a world of dead things, his spirit coarse and hard, in league with evil spirits. The man described has 'paralyzed his imaginative powers'.[34] For such men, according to Coleridge, did Wordsworth write his poems in *Lyrical Ballads*, addressing readers dead to 'the loveliness and the wonders of the world . . . ; an inexhaustible treasure, but for which, in consequence of the film of familiarity and selfish solicitude', they cannot see with their eyes nor hear with their ears; their 'hearts neither feel nor understand' (*Biographia*, II, 6).

Nature exists then in the eye of the beholder, where it acquires its meaning. Not every man will be improved by country living, as Coleridge reminds us in the *Biographia*. The 'organs of spirit . . . are not developed in all alike', but are distinct from 'the organs of sense', which 'are framed for a corresponding world of sense' (I, 167). The organs of spirit resolve themselves finally into 'the philosophic imagination, the sacred power of *self*-intuition', which only those can acquire 'who *within themselves* can interpret and understand the symbol, that the wings of the air-sylph are forming within the skin of the caterpillar; those only, who feel *in their own spirits* the same instinct' (ibid., italics added). The 'act of contemplation makes the thing contemplated; . . . I . . . simply contemplating, the representative forms of things rise up into existence' (I, 173). Even natural philosophy or science, beginning with a concept of nature in 'its passive and material sense' (I, 174), is potentially capable of transcending *natura naturata*.

> The highest perfection of natural philosophy would consist in the perfect spiritualization of all the laws of nature into laws of intuition and intellect. The phaenomena (*the material*) must wholly disappear, and the laws alone (*the formal*) must remain. Thence it comes, that in nature itself the more the principle of law breaks forth, the more does the *husk* drop off, the phaenomena themselves become more spiritual and at length cease altogether in our consciousness (I, 175–6).

In this sense only is there 'a more perfect language than that of words – the language of God himself, as uttered by Nature'.[35]

But such a language the uneducated man of unphilosophic mind cannot understand, nor can any other man of rather ordinary unColeridgean mind. Hence at the end of *The Prelude* Wordsworth says we 'will teach them' – through art, which in its educative capacity brings out in a man the best that lies latent within him, draws out of the depths of him a new man, leads him literally out of the prison of himself into a bright new world with which he can feel at one, no longer at enmity with nature. In this capacity, art becomes 'the mediatress between, and reconciler of, nature and man',[36] for art imitates life and, like life, reconciles all the great polar energies, the pattern of which is life. Art 'is, therefore, the power of humanizing nature, of infusing the thoughts and passions of man into every thing which is the object of his contemplation' (ibid.). A genuine infusion of man into nature must take place. When it does *not,* inferior poetry or unpoetry is the result, as Coleridge understood as early as 1802. 'A Poet's *Heart & Intellect* should be *combined, intimately* combined & *unified*, with the great appearances in Nature – & not merely held in solution & loose mixture with them, in the shape of formal Similes', as in the poems of Bowles.[37] Therefore, it follows, 'if the artist copies the mere nature, the *natura naturata*, what idle rivalry!'[38] To do so is to 'produce masks only, not forms breathing life' ('On Poesy and Art', *Biographia*, I, 258).

Life, and the essence of life as a pattern of polar energies: Coleridge returns again and again to the idea. For this reason the artist 'must master the essence, the *natura naturans,* which presupposes a bond between nature in the higher sense and the soul of man' ('On Poesy and Art', *Biographia,* I, 257). He 'must imitate that which is within the thing, that which is active . . . , and discourses to us by symbols' (I, 259), the only means of true communication and the enemy of abstraction. Man's mind, for Coleridge, is made in 'God's image, & that too in the sublimest sense – the Image of the *Creator'.*[39] It is man's awesome duty, therefore, to be actively creative and to make metaphors or symbols. Thus Coleridge plans a work to demonstrate that the reputations of Locke, Hobbes and Hume are 'wholly unmerited'.[40] And he attacks Newton as 'a mere materialist' in whose system '*Mind* . . . is always passive – a very lazy Looker-on on an external World'.[41] Wordsworth, he thought, would in *The Excursion* remove 'the sandy Sophisms of Locke, and Mechanic Dogmatists' and substitute the principle of 'Life, and Intelligence . . . for the philosophy of mechanism which . . . strikes *Death* and . . . demands Conceptions'.[42] This is Coleridge's mere understanding, Blake's abstracting faculty Urizen, under attack, the equivalent of what Coleridge calls elsewhere 'notions, the depthless abstractions of fleeting *phaenomena,* the shadows of sailing vapors', which create no images.[43] These notions are very different from what one finds in the Scriptures, whose histories

> are the living educts of the imagination; of that reconciling and mediatory power, which incorporating the reason in images of the senses, and organizing (as it were) the flux of the senses by the permanence and self-circling energies of the reason, gives birth to a system of symbols, harmonious in themselves, and consubstantial with the truths of which they are the conductors (ibid., 436).

This sentence offers, one is tempted to say, a rather accurate account of Blake's achievement. The Scriptures give 'birth to a system of symbols'; the symbol itself organizes God and nature, the eternal and the temporal, to make them intelligible to man.

5 Blake, Wordsworth and Coleridge: A Preliminary Synthesis

The literary and related assumptions shared by Blake, Wordsworth and Coleridge illustrate delightfully, under nearly perfect laboratory conditions, the true existence and the nature of a genuine *Zeitgeist*, for Coleridge did not know of Blake until 1818 and Wordsworth does not mention him at all in his letters.[1] Conversely, no two major poets of the period discussed poetry more often or at greater length than Wordsworth and Coleridge, each stimulating the other to new creative efforts and conclusions.

One of the most obvious and remarkable sympathies that binds together all three poets is their enthusiasm for the Bible and *Paradise Lost* as great poetic repositories.[2] For Blake, in 1799, these two books owe their greatness to the fact that 'they are addressed to the Imagination, which is Spiritual Sensation' or experience.[3] He subtitled his *Milton* 'a Poem in 2 Books . . . To Justify the Ways of God to Men'. Wordsworth in his 'Prospectus' sought for his blank verse, like Milton, 'fit audience . . . though few' (l. 23), a phrase he adapted from the opening lines of Book VII of *Paradise Lost*. He wrote in 1815 that 'the grand store-houses of enthusiastic and meditative Imagination . . . are the prophetic and lyrical parts of the Holy Scriptures'. For him, Milton 'was a Hebrew in soul'.[4] Coleridge repeatedly compared the Scriptures and *Paradise Lost* as examples of the highest form of poetry, equally sublime. He had concluded as early as 1802 that 'the Hebrew Poets' 'possessed beyond all others' the quality

of '*Imagination*, or the *modifying*, and *co-adunating* Faculty',
which he contrasts with the fancy, 'the aggregative Faculty of
the mind'.[5] In the *Biographia* we are told, 'the poet should paint
to the imagination, not to the fancy. . . . Masterpieces of the
former mode . . . abound in the writings of Milton', and Coleridge quotes as illustration a passage from the ninth book of
Paradise Lost (*Biographia*, II, 102–3). For him, Milton is a poetic
'deity' equal to Shakespeare, though quite different.[6]

Even more interesting than the fact of this shared enthusiasm
for *Paradise Lost* and the Bible, however similar in phrasing, are
the implications, in terms of belief, of this enthusiasm. As T. S.
Eliot has (reluctantly) taught us, 'Actually, one probably has
more pleasure in the poetry when one shares the beliefs of the
poet.' Eliot confessed his own inability, 'in practice, wholly [to]
separate my poetic appreciation from my personal beliefs'.[7]
Neither, we soon discover, could Blake, Wordsworth or Coleridge. Blake wrote his own version of the biblical books of
Genesis and Revelation, as well as his *Milton*. Wordsworth's
'Prospectus' was Miltonically 'intent to weigh / The good and
evil of our mortal state' (ll. 8–9). The 1805 *Prelude* closed with a
poetic manifesto that looks forward to no less than the very
'redemption' of Wordsworth's (and Coleridge's) readers (XIII,
l. 441). The *Ancient Mariner* is as dependent upon the Bible as
'Religious Musings', and the *Biographia* closes with a statement
of the author's belief 'concerning the true evidences of
Christianity' and an assertion that the 'Object' of the
book and the author's only 'Defence' in writing it are 'to kindle
young minds . . . by showing that the Scheme of Christianity
. . . though not discoverable by human Reason, is yet in
accordance with it'.[8]

In important part we have here the grounds for the first
generation of Romantics' violent opposition to deism and the
coldly rationalistic world of abstractions, supported by Newtonian and other science, associated with it. These poets could
neither worship an absentee-God nor live in a world-machine.
Thus Blake in 1788 wrote 'There is No Natural Religion'; later,
he created Urizen and wrote address 'To the Deists' in *Jerusalem*.
Blake recognized the fallen state of man, denounced Rousseau,
identified ignorance with Hell, and the Arts and Sciences with
Gospel. In 1798 Wordsworth 'felt. . . a sense sublime / Of something . . . deeply interfused' in both man and nature, thus link-

ing them together: it was, in Coleridgean idiom, 'A motion and a spirit, that impels / All thinking things, all objects of all thought, / And rolls through all things' ('Tintern Abbey', ll. 95–102). In these early lines Wordsworth solved the epistemological problem so central in the *Biographia* and for the other Romantic poets, including Byron.[9] By the end of 'Tintern Abbey' the persona has earned the right to call himself 'a worshipper of Nature' (l. 152). Coleridge, as we have seen, thought that Wordsworth's *Excursion* was to have begun 'by removing the sandy sophisms of Locke, and the Mechanic Dogmatists' and to have ended by substituting the principle of the one 'Life' in all things, for 'the philosophy of mechanism which in every thing that is most worthy of the human Intellect strikes *Death*'.[10] One form of such death is the death of poetry, Coleridge implied in the *Biographia*, for 'the mechanical system of philosophy which has needlessly infected our theological opinions, . . . teaching us to consider the world in its relation to God, as of a building to its mason, leaves the idea of omnipresence a mere abstract notion in the state-room of our reason' (II, 59).

Instead of a 'mere abstract notion . . . of our reason', Blake might have written 'your reason'. We need not consider again these poets' common abhorrence of 'the calculating understanding, . . . cold and formal', as Wordsworth described it.[11] They objected to and rejected all forms of a mechanistic world-view, whether primarily religiously oriented, like deism, or scientifically oriented, like Newtonian physics. The great crisis of *The Prelude*, when Wordsworth 'yielded up moral questions in despair', was brought on by the pride of 'Reason's naked self' in and of itself to answer all questions (XI, ll. 305, 234). The paradoxical 'crisis of that strong disease' occurred when Wordsworth 'drooped, / Deeming our blessed reason of least use / Where wanted most' (XI, ll. 306–9). The cure came when he was 'led . . . back . . . / To those sweet counsels between head and heart' (XI, ll. 352–3), productive of true knowledge and a peace of mind that sustained him even at the crowning of Napoleon, when it seemed as if the sun, which had risen in splendour 'and moved / In exultation among living clouds', had 'turned into a geegaw, a machine' and set 'like an opera phantom' (1805 *Prelude*, X, ll. 936–41). The imagery of the machine is never far distant, for Wordsworth, from the world of disaster and the sleep of death. For Coleridge, 'abstract knowledge, or the science of the mere understanding', is 'a science of delusion' that transfers 'reality to the negations of reality', much in the same way that Blake's 'delusive Goddess Nature & her Laws', product of 'the Reasoning Power, / An Abstract objecting power . . . the Spectre of Man', reduces the living contraries of all things to a lifeless 'abstract, which is a Negation'.[12] A mankind capable of inventing such science and such laws is in some sense fallen, and so Blake, Wordsworth and Coleridge viewed it, as *Paradise Lost* and the Bible had viewed it.

Surely one of the most perverse misrepresentations of Romanticism is that which denies to it a reasonable and realistic view of human nature compatible with the historical record of man's actions. And such a view has been denied to Romanticism by some of the most influential critics of the twentieth century, academic and otherwise – by Douglas Bush and Hoxie Neale Fairchild, for example, and, earlier, by T. E. Hulme and T. S. Eliot.[13] In 1916, when Eliot delivered a series of Oxford University Extension Lectures on Modern French Literature, his syllabus found in Rousseau the 'germs' of all that was deplorable in the modern period; for among Rousseau's 'main tendencies' was 'Humanitarianism: belief in the fundamental goodness of human nature'. This was Lecture I. Lecture II, entitled 'THE REACTION AGAINST ROMANTICISM', asserted, 'The beginning of the twentieth century has witnessed a return to the ideals of classicism. . . . The classicist point of view has been defined as essentially a belief in Original Sin – the necessity for austere discipline.'[14]

Unfortunately for this argument, the facts do not support it, any more than they support the closely associated cluster of primitivistic ideas in any form that are frequently attributed to Romanticism. Blake and Coleridge are quite orthodox in their insistence upon man's inherently sinful nature. Blake's address 'To the Deists' in *Jerusalem* asserts, 'Man is born a Spectre or Satan & is altogether an Evil, & . . . must continually be changed into his direct Contrary'. The view that 'teaches that Man is Righteous in his Vegetated Spectre [is] an Opinion of fatal & accursed consequence' (BPP, 198). Coleridge wrote in a letter of 1 March 1798, 'I believe most stedfastly in original Sin . . . this inherent depravity'.[15] His position here is, as we have seen, entirely consistent with that in his 'Confessio Fidei' of 1816.

More elusive is the orthodoxy of the early Wordsworth, but his letter to the Bishop of Llandaff, already examined, indicates that on the question of man's innate corruption he was perfectly orthodox.

The existence of any scheme of redemption implies, in the mind of its author, the need for it. Thus all three poets identified the poetic voice with the prophetic voice and the seer's vision. They elevated the distinguishing faculty of the poet, the imagination, to the very highest of man's intellectual faculties, and conversely distrusted the powers of Urizen, the analytic reason, that reduces the world of things (nature) to a world of death. One may recall again the last verse paragraph of the 1805 *Prelude*, with its 'redemption, surely yet to come', to be accomplished by the two 'Prophets of Nature', for 'man's estate [was] by doom of Nature yoked / With toil' (XIII, ll. 441, 442; XII, ll. 175–6). Wordsworth here clearly alludes to Genesis 3:17: 'cursed is the ground for thy sake'. He finally accepted the fallen state of (higher) man following his traumatic rationalistic period, and he found redeemed man in lower, humbler man (*Prelude*, XIII, ll. 60–106). But on 21 May 1807 the 'entire regeneration' that Wordsworth called for was still waiting to 'be produced', for 'nineteen out of twenty' worldlings are incapable of 'any genuine enjoyment of Poetry', a terrifying truth, 'because to be incapable of a feeling of Poetry in my sense of the word is to be without love of human nature and reverence for God'.[16] Yet, paradoxically, of the three poets Wordsworth sings the most often of natural goodness and virtue.

Most men, then, were still in need of redemption; and poetry for Blake, Wordsworth and Coleridge was to be the agent or means of it. Poetry becomes an instrument of the soul's salvation, its truths operative truths, the poetic imagination an ethical imagination. For these poets, further, man as a fallen creature perceives nature as fallen. But nature is fallen only in the eye of the beholder. As Blake knew, once the negating cherub in *The Marriage* leaves

> his guard at [Eden's] tree of life . . . , the whole creation will be consumed and appear infinite and holy whereas it now appears finite & corrupt. This will come to pass by an improvement of sensual enjoyment. . . . If the doors of

perception were cleansed every thing would appear to man as it is, infinite. For man has closed himself up, till he sees all things thro' narrow chinks of his cavern (BPP, 38, 39).

Twenty or so years later, in 'A Vision of the Last Judgment' (1810), Blake was still saying the same thing: 'Error or Creation . . . is Burned Up the Moment Men cease to behold it' (BPP, 555). (A last judgment, then, an apocalyptic revelation, can come at any time in the life of an individual.) Similarly, Wordsworth's 'Prospectus' will teach men to find 'Paradise' the 'simple produce of the common day', rousing 'the sensual from their sleep / Of death' (ll. 47, 55, 60–1), the tyranny of the bodily eye, a visual despotism strong or seductive enough to lead even Wordsworth at one period to rejoice as he laid his 'inner faculties asleep' (*Prelude*, XII, ll. 147). The redeemed man, however, the 'majestic intellect' suggested by Mount Snowdon, lives 'in a world of life . . . , / By sensible impressions *not* enthralled' (XIV, ll. 67, 105–6, italics added). Coleridge was also aware of the 'habitual slavery to the eye' of the man of no imagination, 'a prisoner to his own eye, and its reflex, the passive fancy!'[17] Although Coleridge asserted that it was impossible to 'organize' for such a man 'an eye that can see, an ear that can listen to, or a heart that can feel, the harmonies of Nature' (ibid.), it was this very man, according to Coleridge, whom Wordsworth addressed in *Lyrical Ballads*. Wordsworth was

to excite a feeling analogous to the supernatural, by awakening the mind's attention from the lethargy of custom, and directing it to the loveliness and the wonders of the world before us; an inexhaustible treasure, but for which, in consequence of the film of familiarity and selfish soliticitude [i.e., Blake's sin of selfhood] we have eyes, yet see not, ears and hear not, and hearts that neither feel nor understand. (*Biographia*, II, 6)

These sightless eyes and deaf ears appear in a number of passages in the Bible, in Psalm 115 for example, descriptive of heathen idols; but it is more probable that Coleridge was remembering and echoing I Corinthians 2:9: 'Eye hath not seen, nor ear heard, neither have entered into the heart of man, the things which God hath prepared for them that love him.' It would seem, then, that Coleridge was announcing a new St Paul – Wordsworth himself.[18]

The central doctrine preached by Wordsworth as well as by Coleridge and Blake was the ancient Christian doctrine of man as a fallen creature who was also capable of redemption and who thus possessed extra-human or divine potentialities (Coleridge also referred Miltonically to the 'human face divine' appearing in *Paradise Lost*.)[19] Redemption can be achieved by means of the power of the imagination, which will permit man to escape from the sin of selfhood, isolation, involution. All three poets assert the possibility of a community of humanity that will stress men's similarities, not their differences. Eden, in short, can be now.[20]

The ability to perceive similarities or similitudes is also the ability to create metaphors, reconciling or fusing apparent differences. As Wordsworth puts it in *The Prelude*,

> Dust as we are, the immortal spirit grows
> Like harmony in music; there is a dark
> Inscrutable workmanship that reconciles
> Discordant elements, makes them cling together
> In one society.
>
> (I, ll. 340–4)

Here life imitates art, for the several faculties of the human personality, like the members of a commonwealth, must function finally in harmonious union. This is not to deny that each of these poets had periods of political revolution, but increasingly the political struggle became internalized, focused primarily upon the individual, not the state. This transformation had the most important implications for the poems each wrote.

All three poets, furthermore, departed from the reverential, eighteenth-century use of the Greek and, particularly, the Roman classics as models, preferring the imaginative symbols of the Bible and of *Paradise Lost*. 'The anthropomorphitism [sic] of the Pagan religion', Wordsworth wrote, 'subjected the minds of the greatest poets in those countries too much to the bondage of definite form; from which the Hebrews were preserved by their abhorrence of idolatry'.[21] Although the first generation of Romantic poets sensed 'Permanent Realities . . . reflected in this Vegetable Glass of Nature',[22] they understood also that Nature must be transformed in the mind of man by the imagination. To imitate the classics or to use them as models, then, would be to imitate an imitation of an image in a mirror. Thus Blake and Coleridge held portrait painting in low esteem, and Wordsworth took essentially the same position in terms of the tyranny of the eye and the picturesque tradition. Coleridge deplored the detailed minutiae of Dutch paintings trying to trick the eye by creating an illusion of actuality, a confusion of art and 'reality'. Poetry is 'ideal', he argued in an 1811 lecture and again in the *Biographia*.[23]

Although Wordsworth in his theory seems to give great importance to memory, by memory he does not mean us to conceive a precise, exact visual image, as in a casual snapshot, but memory transformed imaginatively, transcending the actuality of the past or any simple recollection of it, and given present (and future) significance. All this is evident from *The Prelude*, in the poet's account of his crossing – unknowingly – the high point of the Alps (VI, l. 592ff.). In short, Wordsworth had an 'imaginative memory', a faculty denied by Coleridge to Hazlitt as a portrait painter for the reason that 'the Object must be *before* him' while he paints.[24] Here one recalls Blake's confession that one cannot paint portraits 'without the original sitting before you for Every touch, all likenesses from memory being necessarily very very defective; but Nature & Fancy are Two Things & can Never be joined; neither ought any one to attempt it, for it is Idolatry & destroys the Soul'.[25] All three poets held in low esteem the 'Daughters of Memory', memory in its simple state, if such is possible, a passive faculty, and they contrasted it with imagination. All three, even Wordsworth, are essentially concerned not merely with remembrance of things past but with 'something evermore about to be' (*Prelude*, VI, l. 609), a prophetic sense of what may be or must be achieved in the future.

Such poets of visionary futures, of aspiration and change and growth, have nothing to do with mechanic as distinct from organic form. Wordsworth asked in *The Prelude*, 'But who shall parcel out / His intellect by geometric rules? . . . Who knows the individual hour in which / His habits were first sown, even as a seed?' He refers to the flowing, ever changing 'river of my mind' (II, l. 203ff.), the latter a metaphor for mind that also appears in Shelley's 'Mont Blanc' and in 'Speculations on Morals'.[26] To the extent that Wordsworth's poetry is a poetry of sincerity, concerned with his reaction to the world external to his own mind, he like Blake and Coleridge will in theory reject 'artifice' and the 'artificial', however conscious and skilful all three were themselves as artificers and craftsmen. Wordsworth attacks personification as 'a mechanical device of style',[27] and his whole argument in favour of using in poetry the real language spoken by men constitutes a rejection of the artificial diction of eighteenth-century verse. Coleridge, denouncing those who confound 'mechanical regularity with organic form', defines the difference: 'The form is mechanic when on any given material we impress a pre-determined form. . . . The organic . . . is innate; it shapes as it develops itself from within.'[28] Overlooking the difficulty that every well-planned poem, in whose beginning is its end, foreseen by the poet, has a 'pre-determined form' and then a mechanic form, we might argue that Byron's *Don Juan* is the greatest poetic example of organic form produced in the Romantic period. Of it Byron said that although he had 'materials' he had no 'plan',[29] and indeed the poem stopped growing only when the death of its author intervened.

Fallen Urizen, the great measurer and divider, with his compass and his Newtonian single vision, is Blake's chief exponent of artificial, mechanic form, whose sins are compounded by his wish to dominate all the other faculties of man. This is the primary sin of selfhood. Blake knew, along with Wordsworth and Coleridge, that these faculties must exist in a state of harmonious union (productive tension) within the individual. Wordsworth approvingly observed that Coleridge was 'no officious slave . . . of that false secondary power / By which we multiply distinctions' but, instead, one to whom 'the unity of all hath been revealed' (*Prelude*, II, ll. 215–16, 221). All three poets recognized the necessary interdependence of the chief faculties, the essential importance of 'those sweet counsels between head and heart' (*Prelude*, XI, l. 353), between reason and emotion, with imagination uniting the two. As sound as this psychology may be in explaining the origins of peace of mind, the union of 'head and heart' must surely have been a contemporary cliché. Blake closes a letter of 23 December 1796, 'Yours in head &

heart' (BL, 27), and on 22 November 1802 he assured Butts that 'there is not one touch in those Drawings & Pictures but what came from my Head & my Heart in Unison' (58). For Coleridge, in the most Blakean style, the imagination *incorporates* 'the reason in images of the sense[s]' and *organizes* 'the flux of the senses by the permanence and self-circling energies of the reason'.[30] A quarter of a century earlier, Blake had understood that 'Reason is the bound or outward circumference of Energy', which is itself 'Eternal Delight' (BPP, 34). The senses, when cleansed or purified, become the Gates to Eternity. The total unity of the human personality is a central Blakean doctrine.

Most of the images of the senses are visual. All three poets utilize and emphasize the imagery of sight, seeing, vision. One thinks of Blake's fourfold vision (which of course involves the other senses as well); of Wordsworth's 'Elegiac Stanzas' with its 'light that never was, on sea or land'; or his Intimations Ode, where though far inland we *see* the children playing by the shore (and also hear the mighty waters rolling). Coleridge's Dejection Ode laments the loss of that power within that envelops the earth with 'a light, a glory, a fair luminous cloud' and permits the poet to create a visionary 'new Earth and new Heaven' (ll. 54, 69), as in the biblical Revelation. When looking at objects of nature, Coleridge sought 'a symbolical language for something within me that already and forever exists'.[31] Blake understood that such 'Imaginative Image[s]' of mortal 'Generative Nature' live on forever in the writings of the poets or prophets who created them (BPP, 545).

Such a visionary faculty, when functioning properly, will *see* a unity, experience a single unified vision. Thus all three poets insist upon the absolute unity of the work of art. Blake wrote, 'As Poetry admits not a Letter that is Insignificant so Painting admits not a Grain of Sand or a Blade of Grass much less an Insignificant Blur or Mark' (BL, 55). Coleridge objected at various times to the disjointed couplets of Samuel Butler and Pope, each complete and entire in itself, but lacking 'fusion'.[32] (For Blake, Pope's poetry, with Prior's, belonged to an inferior order associated with the word 'Taste', a word 'which we should think improperly applied to Homer or Milton', masters of 'the Grand Style'.[33]) Coleridge's definition of beauty is the reduction of multeity to unity; for Wordsworth the poetic imagination consolidates 'numbers into unity' and, quoting Charles Lamb on Hogarth, 'draws all things to one'.[34] Even the pleasure we receive from 'metrical language' derives, for Wordsworth, 'from the perception of similitude in dissimilitude'.[35]

Such unity, however, may be immensely enriched by the symbolic implications of the poem. Blake's 'Vision or Imagination', which he distinguishes clearly (and violently) from allegory, is essentially synonymous with Coleridge's 'symbol', which he also distinguishes from allegory. Blake's 'Vision or Imagination is a Representation of what Eternally Exists' (BPP, 544), as in the Hebrew Bible; Coleridge's symbol 'is characterized . . . above all by the translucence of the eternal through and in the temporal', illustrated by the wheels that Ezekiel beheld.[36] Coleridge's allegory is associated with the fancy, which is a 'mode of Memory';[37] Blake's allegory is in fact 'formed by the daughters of Memory' (BPP, 544).

Wordsworth seems less explicit. In the 1800 Preface he 'at all times endeavoured to look steadily at my subject',[38] as Byron also did, in an effort to avoid falsehood of description. But in practice, it appears, Wordsworth assumed that the essence of the universal would be expressed in terms of the particular, which would function as a 'symbol'. Thus Mount Snowdon becomes the type of a mighty human mind. In the 1800 Preface Wordsworth also agrees with Aristotle that poetry is more philosophic than history because its final 'object is truth, not individual and local, but general, and operative' (ibid., 394). He chooses incidents from common life not because they were inherently interesting, but because such incidents, by no means common in the lives of his readers, allowed him to trace 'the *primary* laws of our nature . . . the *essential* passions of the heart' (ibid., 386, italics added). Wordsworth therefore agrees with Blake that 'it is in Particulars that Wisdom consists' (BPP, 550). But these particulars are symbolic of universal and eternal principles. As Blake observed in 'A Descriptive Catalogue', 'Visions of these eternal principles or characters of human life appear to poets, in all ages' (BPP, 527).

Thus again in the thinking of these three poets are polar opposites united and reconciled. Equally essential for the three is the union of intellect and passion or strong feeling. For Blake the passions emanate from the intellect; a man of no intellect can have no passions (BPP, 553–4). For Wordsworth the poet must have 'more than usual organic sensibility' (in order to write poetry that is an expression of powerful feelings), but he must also have 'thought long and deeply'.[39] In Coleridge's opinion, writing to Sotheby, Bowles 'has no native Passion, because he is not a Thinker'.[40] To the extent that all three poets believed in the transformative, creative and redemptive power of the imagination, 'Error' or the 'Corporeal Vegetative' creation, as Blake would call it in 'A Vision of the Last Judgment' (BPP, 555, 552), witnessed by eyes that see not, ears that hear not, ceases to exist when men cease thus to behold it.[41]

In the same remarkable letter to Sotheby in which Coleridge made for the first time his famous distinction between the fancy and the imagination, he also observed:

> Nature has her proper interest; & he will know what it is, who believes & feels, that every Thing has a Life of it's own, & that we are all *one Life*. A poet's *Heart & Intellect* should be *combined, intimately* combined & *unified*, with the great appearances in Nature – & not merely held in solution & loose mixture with them, in the shape of formal Similies.[42]

Thus do man and nature become coadunate, the latter modified or humanized by the power of the imagination. And so, for Coleridge, are the two greatest of all the opposites reconciled. Similarly in the Wordsworthian process of interaction between man and nature, the latter is transformed utterly as it is recreated in the mind: the term *imagination* denotes 'the operations of the mind upon [external] objects, and processes of creation'.[43] Thus for Wordsworth 'Imagination . . . has no reference to images that are merely a faithful copy . . . but is a word of higher import' (ibid.). Thus also for Coleridge: poetry is 'not the mere copy of things, but the contemplation of mind upon things'.[44]

For all three poets, the term *copy* or *imitation* in any literal sense is a dirty word. Blake more consistently and extravagantly than either Wordsworth or Coleridge humanized nature. The greatest poetry, he believed, is 'address'd to the Intellectual powers, while it is altogether hidden from the Corporeal Understanding'.[45] Coleridge made a comparable distinction: the Understanding apprehends and retains as a mode of memory the mere notices of Experience, the surfaces of things, *natura naturata* or Blake's 'delusive Goddess Nature'.[46] 'But to the Eyes of the Man of Imagination, Nature is Imagination itself' (ibid., 30). Similarly, the Coleridgean imagination is 'the power of humanizing nature'.[47] For all these poets, beyond the world of appearances is a world of universal laws or principles, the concern of poetry, and these are apprehended by the higher Reason. For Wordsworth's similar interest we go to *The Prelude*: Reason in her most exalted mood is identified in Book XIV with spiritual love and imagination. This is very different from the 'Reason's naked self' that became the object of Wordsworth's fervour during his disastrous rationalistic period.

To recapitulate: Blake, Wordsworth and Coleridge, however unorthodox, are deeply Christian, soaked in the two great literary sources, the Bible and *Paradise Lost*, both of which books describe a personal deity actively concerned with man's spiritual well-being. For this reason, all three poets opposed deism and the whole world of abstractions in poetry, even though they all used abstract language in their prose, Coleridge's being the most consistently abstract. Further, as in the Bible and *Paradise Lost*, they viewed man as a fallen creature who must be redeemed. Fallen himself, he perceives nature as fallen. But nature is fallen only in the eye of the beholder, for the mind does not passively mirror a reality external to itself: it is active and engages in *acts* of perception or in intellectual activities. Thus an act of perception or a state of consciousness relying primarily upon *passive* memory is not a true act, not a creative state, nor is one relying primarily upon the passive fallen senses, reporting or describing the mere surfaces of things, a true act. It is the faculty of imagination that is truly active and creative, and its distinguishing characteristic is originality, which it achieves basically by reconciling apparent opposites. It 'imitates' but never copies nature. Instead, it transforms nature by humanizing it, rendering the external internal, thus ending the war between individual man and nature and reconciling, by means of art, the great polar opposites.

Such imaginative perception on the aesthetic level is not always clearly distinguished from religious experience and may lead directly to it, as in the *Ancient Mariner*, where the Mariner learns to communicate with God by prayer as a result of his perception of beauty.[48] The imagination, then, is also an ethical imagination, reconciling individual to individual (or to individuals). In this kind of reconciliation of opposites or discordants, the antithetical self is annihilated, the fragmented personality achieves harmonious unity, and a condition of community is realized in this world. The poet of such an apocalypse preserves in the great love expressed in his poems the uniqueness of individual man even in the act of describing generic man, the enduring human qualities that all men share and that bind men together. Thus polar opposites are again brought into meaningful relationship, for the contraries are 'necessary to Human existence':[49] this is the very principle of life. It manifests itself in the creation of poetry primarily in the 'reconciliation' of reason and imagination, feeling and thought. The result is a poem of perfect unity, most typically bound together by metaphors and symbols (not allegory), expressive of the very act of poetic perception, for nothing exists except as it is perceived. To perceive is to create. When in *The Marriage* Blake's friend, the Angel, ran away frightened at the sight of the monstrous Leviathan that his own 'metaphysics' had created, the poet, miraculously, is left 'sitting on a pleasant bank beside a river by moon light hearing a harper who sung to the harp' (BPP, 41). Just as miraculously, Leviathan, 'a monstrous serpent' with 'two globes of crimson fire' upon its crest, had disappeared along with the Angel.

6 Byron as a Romantic Poet

Even when we try to forget Byron's letters and think only of his miscellaneous prose, we feel his sense of the immediacy of life pressing down hard upon us – life as the word is commonly or vulgarly used, a thing distinct from literature. Relatively, and by contrast with the red blood of this life, Byron's purely literary judgments may seem pale indeed. After looking over the audience at Covent Garden one evening and seeing there 'the most distinguished old and young Babylonians of quality', he burst out laughing and concluded that 'the house had been divided between your public and your *understood* courtesans; – but the Intriguantes much outnumbered the regular mercenaries'. This he recorded in his journal for 17 and 18 December 1813. 'How I do delight in observing life as it really is!' he continued, '– and myself, after all, the worst of any. But no matter – I must avoid egotism.'[1] Here, we suggest, is the authentic Byron. No other of the major Romantic poets possessed the knowledge or the gusto or the voice necessary to write these lines, and they explain much about the difficulty that innumerable literary critics have experienced in their efforts to fit Byron into a general theory of Romanticism.

In some ways Byron lived as vividly and vitally outside literary tradition as in it. Compared with his observation on the audience at Covent Garden, his review of Wordsworth's *Poems* of 1807 is shocking in its cool lack of enthusiasm and in its clearly expressed sense of superiority to the poetry, especially when one recalls some of the great poems published in these two volumes – 'Resolution and Independence', 'The Solitary Reaper', 'She was a phantom of delight', 'Elegiac Stanzas', and the Intimations Ode.[2] He did not even know, presumably, the correct title of Wordsworth's *Lyrical Ballads*, calling it 'Lyric

Ballads' (LJ, I, 341). That Byron was only nineteen when he wrote hardly excuses him. Less than a year later, after reading the *Edinburgh's* review of his *Hours of Idleness*, he came near to blowing his brains out. Literature was important to him. No less important was the opinion of critics and common readers. And yet his commitment to this art and his serious involvement in the world of ideas was unequal to or different in its character from the commitment of Blake, for example, or the involvement of Coleridge. Byron was not a visionary and he was not an intellectual. Serious ideas of complexity located on the frontiers of knowledge did not constitute the area of existence that most passionately interested him. There seems to have been a tendency native within him to translate the analysis of ideas into rhetoric, literary criticism into controversy, poetry into poets and their non-literary lives.

That Byron's first speech in the House of Lords, on the frame-workers bill, a bill that asked for the death penalty, should employ all the traditional, emotional appeals of persuasive parliamentary rhetoric should not surprise us; but that he, barely turned twenty-one, could employ these with such success is a matter of some interest, for here one senses at least one ingredient of the genuine Byronic essence. The last paragraph of the speech is especially impressive, the last sentence most impressive of all, with its one hundred and fifty words, with the hammer-blows of its fourfold parallel imperatives ('suppose this man'), and with its inflammatory diction: 'suppose one of these men, as I have seen them, – meagre with famine, sullen with despair, careless of a life which your Lordships are perhaps about to value at something less than the price of a stocking-frame; – suppose this man surrounded by the children for whom he is unable to procure bread'.[3] Byron had 'seen' them, even as he had *seen* the audience at Covent Garden, and the visual and emotional element has wholly displaced the intellectual.

One may repeatedly observe elsewhere such Byronic displacement of the intellectual element. In his speech of 21 April 1812 supporting Catholic emancipation, a subject lending itself, presumably, somewhat more to intellectual analysis than the frame-workers bill, rhetorical *ad hominem* appeals to the emotions are even more prominent and the reduction of analysis to inflammatory anecdote occurs repeatedly. However, it is startling to find this same belligerent tone, these same strategies, present in Byron's 'Reply to Blackwood's *Edinburgh Magazine*', dated 15 March 1820, which pretends in part to be literary criticism. But here one learns remarkably little, in fact, about Byron's literary principles, although much about his literary prejudices. This essay is not criticism but controversy, aimed against the other version (*Blackwood's* in this case), contradicting it, and the tone is quite properly belligerent: Byron the man of action is engaged in an act of combative will almost military in its deliberate strategy and disciplined thrust.[4] The essay, in short, is not an exploration of an idea or a poem, followed wherever the journey may lead, looking for something, for anything interesting. Instead, the 'Reply to Blackwood's' is a defence, a defence of certain cultural monuments like Pope, and finally a very personal defence of self. Byron was little interested in theoretical discussion with broad and abstract implications. After Leigh Hunt told him that the style of *The Story of Rimini* had been formed *'upon system'*, Byron concluded, 'when a man talks of system, his case is hopeless'.[5] He entertained his own detested Urizen, of course, and he felt essentially the same contempt for Wordsworth's 1800 Preface and the *Biographia* that he did for Hunt's 'system'.[6]

And yet Byron did write an astonishing quantity of poetry, as of prose. He has told us why, more than once, and most melodramatically: to allow himself to forget, to escape his feelings of guilt, to save himself from going mad. There was another and truer reason: Byron was the most melancholy and lonesome of men. He was an author but not an intellectual. He alone among the major Romantic poets could write, 'I liked the Dandies – they were always very civil to *me* – though in general they disliked literary people'; or, 'in general I do not draw well with Literary men . . . I never know what to say to them after I have praised their last publication. – There are several exceptions to be sure – but they have either been men of the world – such as Scott – & Moore &c. or visionaries out of it – such as Shelley &c.'[7]

To begin, it is hard to take seriously the two etceteras in Byron's last sentence. There were no other important authorial exceptions in his life, but not even these three exceptional men could have filled for long the aching void within him, the egotistical emptiness that left him alone in his life with the self that did not satisfy him. Although we may grant to Moore a magnificent intuitive understanding of Byron's complex nature – his proud and shy reserve in society, his schoolboy gaiety with a few intimates, and the deep melancholy or uneasiniess underlying both – granting this, the number of hours that Moore spent in Byron's company should not be exaggerated. For Moore's usual place of residence during Byron's London years was not London but elsewhere: chiefly in the village of Kegworth, Leicestershire, and after June 1813, near Ashbourne, Derbyshire, a drive of twenty-four hours from London. · Byron's acquaintance with Scott was even more limited. Scott first met Byron on 7 April 1815 in John Murray's drawing room, and had a number of conversations with him; but Scott left London on the following 10th of June, and after returning briefly to the city saw Byron for the last time on 13 September 1815.[8] As for Shelley, his temperament was far distant from that of Byron. Nor were his relations with Byron wholly satisfying to him in the summer of 1816, when the two poets first met, or later. During the initial period of intimacy Shelley completed for eventual publication only two rather short poems, 'Hymn to Intellectual Beauty' and 'Mont Blanc'.[9] To be sure, they are crucial poems, signalling a breakthrough, but Byron (as well as Mary Shelley) was much more productive at this time. Altogether, between 1816 and 1822 the two poets saw each other on intimate terms, at various places, for a total of about twelve months. During Byron's years of exile abroad, the last eight years of his life, Shelley was the *only* literary friend and intellectual equal that he had.

In short, Byron wrote not out of fullness but out of emptiness, a loneliness that was otherwise unbearable, his own mind supplying itself with occupation, activity, ideas, adventures, dialogue, speech, people, creating all these to suit best or to please himself, as he invented himself (and other characters) time and again in his poems or his letters, many of the latter written nominally to Murray but actually to Murray's group of literary advisors, his 'Senate'.[10]

One not very well acquainted with William Blake might be surprised to discover his description of himself in the album of William Upcott as a man 'who is very much delighted with being in good Company'. Blake's continuation might seem more characteristic: 'Born 28 Novr in London & has died several times since.'[11] But surely it is even more surprising to come upon Byron's expressions of his own total need at times to live in privacy.[12] To his journal of 10 April 1814 he confessed, 'I do not know that I am happiest when alone; but this I am sure of, that I never am long in the society even of *her* [Augusta?] I love . . . without a yearning for the company of my lamp and my utterly confused and tumbled-over library . . . I have not stirred out of these rooms for these four days past.' But he had 'boxed one hour' (with Gentleman Jackson), 'written an ode to Napoleon Buonaparte – copied it . . . redde away the rest of my time – besides giving poor [James Wedderburn Webster?] a world of advice about this mistress of his'.[13] He also penned at least four letters.

Byron wrote then, it appears, in order to achieve the most meaningful and satisfying relationship with himself, writing partly out of boredom, partly out of loneliness, partly in order to feed an ever hungry ego – if these three are not one.[14] Such a temperament, discontented with the society in which it found itself, expressing itself in its own chosen lifestyle, acutely and sensitively aware of itself, is not often likely to assume the role of poet–prophet, with all that it implied for Blake, Wordsworth and Coleridge.[15] There are, then, important differences between these poets and Byron, born the year Blake etched 'There is No Natural Religion' and 'All Religions are One'. One of the most interesting of these is Byron's elevation toward the end of his life of the tone (and ideal) of the gentleman as a major and determining criterion of literary merit. Although this gentle-manliness is not enough by itself to make either poem or poet, 'neither poet nor poem will ever be good for any thing with-out it'.[16] Vulgarity or the 'shabby-genteel', not coarseness or blackguardism, is the negation of gentlemanliness and is the 'grand distinction' of the cockney school, in which Byron placed Keats, the master of the school being Leigh Hunt. 'Burns is often coarse, but never *vulgar*. Chatterton is never vulgar, nor Wordsworth, nor the higher of the Lake School, though they treat of low life in all its branches' (LJ, V, 591). Vulgarity depends upon neither 'low themes' nor 'low language' and is far worse than blackguardism, which 'comprehends wit, humour, and strong sense at times', qualities not to be found, it would seem, in the vulgar cockney poets. By contrast, 'you see the man of education, the gentlemen, and the scholar [but not the pedant], sporting with his subject, – its master, not its slave' (592).

Pope is such a writer. But to the extent that Wordsworth and Coleridge are neither vulgar nor cockney, they too, presumably, possess the quality of 'gentlemanliness' as poets, if not as men. For Byron's taste, when it was not influenced or determined by his temper, his politics or his personal grudges, could be very sure. He could also be very honest. 'My indignation', he wrote, 'at Mr. Keats' depreciation of Pope has hardly permitted me to do justice to his own genius. . . . His fragment of *Hyperion* seems actually inspired by the Titans, and is as sublime as Æschylus.'[17] Keats, he wrote in *Don Juan*, 'without Greek / Contrived to talk about the gods of late, / Much as they might have been supposed to speak' (XI, st. 60). Byron, champion of the poetry of Pope and the criticism of Dr Johnson, master himself of the high conversational style and the satiric mode, paid highest tribute of all to the great epic master of the sublime, Milton, admitting even in his 'Letter on Bowles's Strictures on Pope', 'I shall not presume to say that Pope is as high a poet as Shakespeare and Milton'.[18] In this judgment, Byron stands with all the other great poets of his age, as also in his judgment of 'the sublime of sacred poetry',[19] the Old Testament, his example chosen from the book of Isaiah, one of the prophets with whom Blake dined in *The Marriage of Heaven and Hell*.

Indeed, despite all, Byron was a more typical Romantic poet than many modern critics are prepared to admit. M. H. Abrams in *Natural Supernaturalism* omits discussion of him altogether 'because in his greatest work he speaks with an ironic countervoice and deliberately opens a satirical perspective on the vatic stance of his Romantic contemporaries'.[20] But to the extent that 'central Romantic ideas and forms of imagination were', as Abrams asserts, 'secularized versions of traditional theological concepts, imagery, and design', Byron, it may be argued, was the most purely Romantic of them all.

He was as genuinely convinced as Blake, for example, of the fallen state of man and is the only one of the major Romantic poets who wrote a full-length play that explicitly and centrally introduces the expulsion-from-Eden story as the chief initial motivating force of the narrative. This is *Cain*. Moreover, his *Heaven and Earth*, like so many important poems of this period, dreams of a new heaven and earth. But Japhet's prophecy of the Apocalypse and millennium (not to come in this flooded and unfinished play) is also an indictment of the divine injustice. It reminds us of Blake's postlapsarian 'holy Word' (in the 'Introduction' to *Songs of Experience*) that might do all things if it would, but does not: 'That might controll / The starry pole; / And fallen fallen light renew!' Byron's Japhet still has faith, even in the play's last scene that brings the flood:

> The eternal Will
> Shall deign to expound this dream
> Of good and evil; and redeem
> Unto himself all times, all things;
> And, gathered under his almighty wings,
> Abolish hell!
> And to the expiated Earth
> Restore the beauty of her birth,
> Her Eden in an endless paradise,
> Where man no more can fall as once he fell,
> And even the very demons shall do well!
> (Act I, sc. iii, ll. 193–203)

All this will come to pass when 'the Redeemer cometh . . . in glory' (ll. 205–6). Blake, then, is not the only one of the Romantic poets to propose a return to Eden, as he does in plate 3 of *The Marriage*.

But Byron more than any other of the Romantic poets raises the problem of the nature of belief, for his beliefs were in certain ways the least rigidly structured and the most viable or organic of those held by any of these poets who lived long enough – beyond their twenties – to permit them to establish a pattern of contradiction.[21] As he said of his journal on 6 December 1813, 'God knows what contradictions it may contain. If I am sincere with myself (but I fear one lies more to one's self than to any one else), every page should confute, refute, and utterly abjure its predecessor.'[22] And so, in his honest inconsistency, true to his self of the day, he contradicted himself, sometimes on the most important matters. Concerning the immortality of the soul for example, he wrote on 3 September 1811 to Francis Hodgson, who was about to take holy orders: 'I will have nothing to do

with your immortality.'[23] Ten years later he observed in his
'Detached Thoughts': 'Of the Immortality of the Soul – it
appears to me that there can be little doubt.' The reason for his
certainty he finds in the 'perpetual activity' of the mind: 'It acts
also so very independent of body – in dreams for instance
incoherently and madly.[24] In the same year, about eight months
earlier, on 27 February 1821, he described a fit of indigestion he
had had as a result of eating cockles: 'I suffered horribly. . . . I
remarked in my illness the complete inertion, inaction, and des-
truction of my chief mental faculties. I tried to rouse them, and
yet could not – and this is the *Soul*!!!'[25] Like Walt Whitman,
Byron could say of himself, 'I am large, I contain multitudes.'
But there is a constant element in these two contradictory
accounts: a continuing interest in the subject grounded in and
rising out of empirical observation of his own being, the most
interesting he ever knew.

He tried, but often failed, to maintain belief in Christ as
divine Saviour. In the letter to Hodgson cited above, he wrote,
'Christ came to save men',[26] although he professed not to understand why salvation could not be available to all, even those
heathen who had never heard of Christ. The divine injustices
pleased him no more than they pleased Blake, and Blake's
Nobodaddy is behind the scenes of *Cain*. Even so, in February
1821, he could publicly proclaim 'Jesus Christ the Son of God',
a fact proved by his 'miracles' as well as by his 'moral pre-
cepts'.[27]

'Forgiveness of Sins', Blake wrote in 'The Everlasting Gospel', 'This alone is the Gospel & this is the Life & Immortality
brought to light by Jesus.'[28] Similarly, Byron could not believe
in eternal damnation, even though '*man's* guilt' is very real to
him': 'I conceive He never made anything to be tortured in
another life.'[29] The freethinking heritage shared by Blake and
Byron is suggested by Blake's spirited denial of the existence of
hell: 'I do not believe there is such a thing litterally.'[30] Byron's
outrage over the divine injustice, first expressed in a letter of
1811, emerged again ten years later in *Cain*. Although the thrust
of the charge has shifted by 1821, in both expressions of it,
interestingly, the injustice involves a father–son relationship. In
September 1811 he had written to Hodgson: 'the basis of your
religion is *injustice*: the *Son of God*, the *pure*, the *immaculate*, the
innocent, is sacrificed for the *guilty*. . . . You convert Him [God]

into a Tyrant over an immaculate and injured Being [Christ].'[31] In *Cain* the chief being injured by God the Father is of course the title character. All this may tell us more about Byron's personality than about his theology.

When he thought of hell and damnation in terms less general and more personal, he could leave the impression that he believed much more literally in these than Blake,[32] although the tone of his remarks in the Preface to *Cain* is amusingly sceptical and in *The Vision of Judgment*, which allows George III to sneak into Heaven through the back door, sceptically amusing. Here is the public Byron, the Byronic theologian addressing his shocked audience.

Byron's deep conviction of fallen human nature is suggested most clearly, perhaps, by the fact that most of his autogenous heroes are guilty creatures. This fact he justified in a letter of 12 May 1821 to Hodgson, whose *Childe Harold's Monitor* (1818) presumably had just found him in Ravenna: 'I must remark from *Aristotle* and *Rymer*, that the *hero* of tragedy and (I add meo periculo) a *tragic* poem must be *guilty*, to excite "*terror and pity*", the end of tragic poetry.' Then Byron quoted from Dr Johnson's *Lives of the Poets*: ' "The pity which the poet is to labour for is *for* the criminal. . . . The said criminal, . . . if he be represented too great an offender, will *not be pitied*. . . ." Who is the hero of "*Paradise Lost*"? Why Satan.'[33] The Byronic hero is descended in part, to be sure, from the Satan of Milton, a poet to whom Byron confessed his debt in the Preface to *Cain*. But Byron's description of Cain as 'a proud man'[34] is true of all the Byronic heroes (as well as of Satan), and pride is the first of the seven deadly sins. All these guilty heroes are fallen creatures and in their bitter experience commonly retain some memory of a better world of innocence.

Byron asserted his belief in the Mosaic account of creation (implying also, presumably, his belief in the Mosaic account of Adam's fall) and found that Cuvier 'confirms it'.[35] The seriousness with which Byron read the Book of Genesis, however, is suggested even more persuasively in his 'Detached Thought', no. 101, where he begins with a consideration of the fall of Adam according to Genesis and moves on to contemplate the present 'inferior . . . state' of man and to explain it tentatively in terms suggested by Cuvier: that man as well as his world has been destroyed and created more than once and that in his present state or form he 'may be the relic of some higher material being wrecked in a former world – and degenerated'. The only certainties that emerge from this discussion, however, are, first, that if the account of 'Adam & Eve and the Apple and Serpent' were or could be disproved, some other account would have to be invented to explain the observable facts of man's nature; and, second, 'Creation must have had an Origin and a *Creator* – for a *Creator* is a more natural imagination than a fortuitous [and Lucretian] concourse of atoms.'[36] In all this there is no reference to Christ the Redeemer, a silence that suggests what may be demonstrated elsewhere: that Byron could not bring himself to believe consistently in the saving Grace of Christ. His is essentially a Christless Christianity.[37] Pope's (Catholic) deism was more to his sceptical taste.

As in Blake, so in Byron there are many references large and small to what M. H. Abrams calls the 'Biblical plot of the creation and fall of man, the history of man in the fallen world', but unlike Blake there are in Byron few convincing references to 'the coming redemption of man in a restored Eden'.[38] The diction of redemption is repeatedly secularized by Byron to drain from it all spiritual or religious connotations. In his second letter to Bowles, for example, in discussing the prevailing cant of the day, he refers to 'this moral *millen[n]ium* of expurgated editions in books, manners, and royal trials of divorce'.[39] The 'high argument' of Wordsworth's 'Prospectus' (l. 71), echoing *Paradise Lost*, becomes for Byron the equivalent of an '"entusymusy"', for lakes, and mountains, and daffodils, and buttercups'. This, he says, he can understand in 'the aquatic gentlemen of Windermere', but he would 'be glad to be apprized of the foundation of the London propensities of their imitative brethren [Leigh Hunt and Keats] to the same "high argument"'.[40]

Byron never seriously attempted in any major poem 'to justify the ways of God to man', a phrase used by Blake as the subtitle of his *Milton*. But he did – as did Blake, Wordsworth, Shelley and Keats – equate or associate 'evil with separateness' or isolation.[41] It would seem that Byron could embrace the Christian (and Blakean) concept of universal brotherhood no more closely or warmly than by imagining himself from the time he first went abroad as a citizen, significantly, of the world. The metaphor is political, not religious.

However, we are left with those passages in Byron's poetry describing a sense of union with the created universe, its spirit, or the spirit of the place. Wordsworth told Thomas Moore in 1820 that the 'feeling of natural objects' expressed in *Childe Harold* III was 'not caught by B. from nature herself, but from him [Wordsworth], and spoiled in the transmission. "Tintern Abbey" the source of it all.'[42] One feels the need also to explain Manfred's anguished cry that he 'cannot love' his 'Mother Earth' (Act I, sc. ii, ll. 9, 7), as well as Byron's own even more anguished outcry on 29 September 1816, at the end of his Journal to Augusta. There, although proclaiming himself to be 'a lover of Nature – and an Admirer of Beauty', he found that bitter memories had preyed upon him everywhere in the Alps, which he toured for two weeks with John Cam Hobhouse, 'and neither the music of the Shepherd – the crashing of the Avalanche – nor the torrent – the mountain – the Glacier – the Forest – nor the Cloud – have for one moment – lightened the weight upon my heart – nor enabled me to lose my own wretched identity in the majesty & power and the Glory – around – above – & beneath me'.[43]

This most remarkable sentence is noteworthy for several reasons. It tells us that Byron was seeking in the Alps an experience of great intensity, the equivalent somehow, in kind and emphasis, of a deeply religious experience, in which the sense of wretched self is lost in something larger, more beautiful, more meaningful, as in the tradition of the Spanish mystics, although there is no serious mention anywhere in this journal of the name of God. Byron knew, however, what he was seeking – this is clear – and he knew at the end that he had not found it. There was in him the need, as strong and great as in any other of the Romantic poets, to escape from the isolated self, to transcend it, and achieve a meaningful and deeply satisfying sense of union with the not-self. This experience, simultaneously expansive and sacrificial of self, has been called *the* Romantic experience. Rousseau gave it one of its earliest descriptions, in 1762, in *Lettres à M. de Malesherbes*, where he emphasizes an element not made explicit by Byron: 'Alors l'esprit perdu dans cette immensité, je ne pensois pas, je ne raisonnois pas, je ne philosophois pas.' In the agitation of his transports, he can cry out only 'O grand être! ô grand être!'[44] But Rousseau does in fact think and say a great deal more about the experience (the entire passage has not been quoted), and in his different way so also does Byron.

For Byron's impassioned outcry upon nature is not a thing of nature at all: it is most exquisite artifice, as a moment's examination demonstrates. The elaborate and carefully varied parallelism, the musical phrasing so artfully controlled, were not 'natural' even for Byron. The sentence is the product of a highly self-conscious artist, wholly aware of what he is making and aware too, one must believe, of the pleasure he experiences in the successful process of making it. Consider the parallel structure. The subject of the sentence is a series of seven substantives, all negatively modified and thus parallel to this degree. But Byron subtly varies this sevenfold parallelism by subdividing the seven into two, the first introduced by the word *neither*, the second by *nor*. This proportion is altered by the writer's refusal to subdivide the basic seven into series of three and four; instead, the division is into a pair (two) and a series more than twice as numerous (five). However, this imbalance is compensated for and a degree of symmetry re-achieved by assigning four major terms to the pair, both subject-nouns modified by an *of*-phrase ('the music of the Shepherd – the crashing of the Avalanche'), while leaving the series of five subject-nouns without any modifier except the definite article *the*. The somewhat simple and mechanical parallelism of this fivefold structure is then modified by repeating immediately before the last of the five items the *nor* which introduces the entire series, thus enclosing it within a parenthesis of *nor*s. This word is then echoed before the second verb of the sentence ('nor enabled me'), both these verbs being parallel of course but the first one ('have . . . lightened') acquiring its negative meaning from the *neither* and the *nor*s of the compound subject. The sentence then closes with a prepositional phrase with three parallel nouns ('in the majesty & power and the Glory'), the nouns dependent as objects upon *in* and biblically linked by *and*, followed by a final parallel series of three adverbs ('around – above – & beneath me').

We refrain from any analysis of the rhythm of this sentence, as artful as its parallel structure and dependent upon that structure. There is evidence also that Byron was equally self-conscious in the midst of his actual experiences in the Alps, acutely conscious of his own body, its fatigue, its awareness of temperature and moisture, its clumsiness climbing in the snow (he fell, despite his cane), his giddiness, his repeated recollection of past bitterness '(*whole woods of withered pines – all withered*' reminded him of his family). It is presumably no accident that the last word of the sentence analyzed above, which describes Byron's failure 'to lose [the sense of his] own wretched identity', is the word *me*.

As he looked upon the splendours of the Alps that inspired him, he said, to compose *Manfred* (with all its burden of guilt), did he formulate on the spot, with the scene directly before him, some of those magnificent and wonderful phrases that appeared on paper first in the Journal to Augusta and then in the dramatic poem that may be read for the most part as a kind of interior monologue?[45] How self-consciously verbal, in short, was his experience in the Alps? For the mystical experience is not an affair of words. And to the extent that the actual experiences were directly linked to the journal kept '*for*' Augusta and were associated with thoughts of her, then those experiences were coloured by deeply personal feelings of guilt. Byron, in the midst of magnificent 'Rocks – pines – torrents – Glaciers – Clouds – and Summits of eternal snow far above them', was prisoner still of the 'wretched identity' he sought to lose in 'forgetfulness' of self and past.

> Still round him clung invisibly a chain
> Which gall'd for ever, fettering though unseen,
> And heavy though it clank'd not; worn with pain,
> Which pined although it spoke not, and grew keen,
> Entering with every step, he took, through many a scene.
>
> (*Childe Harold*, III, st. 9)

Thus, in the latter half of September 1816 Byron's strong urge and desire to unite his spirit with the spirit of the universe was left unsatisfied. His willed attempt, extraordinary as it is, to live what Wordsworth preached had failed. And yet with Shelley at Clarens, scene of Rousseau's *Julie, or the New Héloïse*, in late June 1816 Byron had decided that 'love in its most extended and sublime capacity . . . is the great principle of the universe, . . . of which, though knowing ourselves a part, we lose our individuality, and mingle in the beauty of the whole'.[46] This note to *Childe Harold* III Byron attached to stanza 99, celebrating Clarens, where he returned with Hobhouse in September, but to no avail. At this later date he found himself quite unable to lose his sense of his individuality 'and mingle in the beauty of the whole'. Six years later Byron could write in *Don Juan* that 'some heathenish philosophers / Make Love the Main Spring of the Universe' (IX, st. 73), but presumably he no longer could – and Juan's characteristic union is sexual. If these passages truthfully and accurately express Byron's position, we may say then that his was an unsuccessful effort to believe, a failed faith – but for all that no less real. The marriage of Nature and the mind of Byron was short-lived, his 'spousal verse' sung chiefly in the summer of 1816, but the stormy intensity of the relationship has never been doubted and the poetic record of it in *Childe Harold* III and *Manfred* constitutes one of the great monuments of English poetry. Even Wordsworth had his 'Elegiac Stanzas'. How long must a marriage last before it becomes 'real'?

The Romantic expansiveness or empathy need not express itself of course in terms of union with a spiritualized Nature or even with another human being. It may take the form of a purely aesthetic experience as in Byron's description (in *Childe Harold* IV, stanzas 153–9) of St. Peter's at Rome. In this vast basilica the mind expands and grows 'colossal', with the result that it is not overwhelmed by the 'grandeur' of the place. But this experience comes only after the mind has made a series of gradual adjustments to the individual parts. At first, because 'our outward sense / Is but of gradual grasp', 'the great whole' of the edifice 'defies . . . our Nature's littleness, / Till, growing with its growth, we thus dilate / Our spirits to the size of that they contemplate' (st. 158). Before this mind or spirit expanding experience can take place, however, the mind 'piecemeal . . . must break, / To separate contemplation, the great whole' and get 'by heart / Its eloquent proportions, and unroll / In mighty graduations, part by part, / The glory' (st. 157).

With the exception of a few lines in stanza 156 Byron has not described the place itself but the efforts and actions that the mind, 'expanded' and 'dilate[d]', makes to comprehend it. Here Byron stands squarely within the eighteenth-century tradition of the sublime. Walter Jackson Bate explains that 'in almost all cases the sublime, as one writer said, "dilates and expands the mind, and puts its grasp to trial"; and it is conceded to be that which displays – and demands from the beholder the most vigorous response of imagination and feeling'.[47] But in this passage in *Childe Harold* IV we have no explicit reference to any loss of the sense of identity, as the mind mingles or merges with 'the great whole'. Even so, the absence of such reference in this passage may well indicate a greater submergence of self than in such lines as those in *Childe Harold* III: 'I live not in myself, but I become / Portion of that around me' (st. 73). By and large, the several Harolds, like Blake's Giant Forms, are, as Abrams puts it, 'mental travelers through . . . history, suffering the torment of . . . isolation, and ever recurrent conflict, in the restless quest for fantasied satisfaction'.[48]

The Byronic imagination, nevertheless, was capable of most wondrous deeds, allowing the mind to escape, however temporarily, from ordinary limits in the contemplation of nature and art, while remaining aware of the elemental harmony in both, as in *Childe Harold* III, st. 90, or IV, st. 136. In *The Prophecy of Dante*, after hymning the divinity inherent in creation, Byron even asserts that all those 'whose Intellect is an o'ermastering Power' are 'bards' (IV, ll. 21, 23). He who can express his thoughts in words may become 'the new Prometheus of new men' (IV, l. 14). Most persuasive of all perhaps are Byron's songs of escape from the self in the act of poetic composition, as he recreates in the mind's eye the things of nature and art that he has earlier viewed and contemplated, as in *Childe Harold* III, st. 5 and 6. At such times the mind finds 'refuge in lone caves, . . . rife / With airy images, and shapes which dwell / *Still unimpair'd*, though old, in the soul's haunted cell' (italics added). As the poet writes and gives 'form' to his 'fancy', he gains as he gives the life he images, becoming a 'being more intense' than his own. Like Cain, who cries out 'Alas! I am nothing' (Act II, scene ii, l. 420), the first-person narrator feels himself to be 'Nothing; but not so art thou, / Soul of my thought! with whom I traverse earth, . . . / Mix'd with thy spirit, blended with thy birth, / And feeling still with thee in my crush'd feeling's dearth.' The third canto at this point has become, with impeccable appropriateness, a true or genuine interior monologue, as the voice of the pilgrim-poet addresses the 'soul' or 'spirit' of his own creative thought and blends with its birth. Thus 'blended', the poet can achieve in the act of composition a daily renewal or rebirth.

However, Byron often uses the word 'blend', as a glance at a concordance demonstrates, in reference to some kind of romantic or sexual union between man and woman. Keats uses the word in this sense in *Endymion* and there supplies us with a synonym for it, 'mingle', to suggest that the 'self-destroying' experience described (I, l. 799) is basically identical with the typically Romantic union of man and nature. Keats writes of love: 'Melting into its radiance, we blend, / Mingle, and so become a part of it' (I, ll. 810–11). This seems almost like an echo of *Childe Harold* III, st. 72, which also describes Keats's 'sort of oneness' (I, l. 796). Byron writes, 'I become / Portion of that around me', and he can 'with the sky, the peak, the heaving plain / Of ocean, or the stars, mingle.' The Byronic poet can then mingle with aspects of the natural scene or mix or blend with his own characters as he creates them, or they can themselves blend, man and woman, with each other in the narrative. Despite his asserted lack of identification with his own characters as he creates them, however, Byron is 'in every line' of his poetry, as Coleridge said of Milton, contrasting him with Shakespeare. 'Shakespeare's poetry is characterless', Coleridge affirmed, in the sense that 'it does not reflect the individual Shakespeare'.[49]

That Byron lacked dramatic genius has become a cliché. He did not identify himself with his characters, as Shakespeare presumably did; he imposed himself or his sense of himself upon them. He lacked dramatic genius because he lacked a genuinely Keatsian empathy. Keats's chameleon poet 'has no Identity – he is continually . . . filling some other Body', his own identity annihilated.[50] Although this condition was alien to the solitary Byron as he wrote Romantic poems to, for, and of himself, the social (and satiric) form of this expansiveness and consequent annihilation of the sense of self is to be found in the Byronic *mobilité*, defined as 'an excessive susceptibility of immediate impressions' made upon the individual by other persons.[51] *Mobilité* makes possible and demands multiple role-playing, the role reflecting as in a mirror the character of the person 'nearest', thus requiring the power of imaginative identification with others – a chameleon quality like that of Keats's poet. Lady Blessington, who observed this quality in Byron, described him as 'a perfect chameleon' and noted that his 'chameleon-like character or manner . . . renders it difficult to portray him'.[52] Shelley found this quality in the 'language' of the fifth canto of *Don Juan*, which struck him as 'as sort of cameleon under the changing sky of the spirit that kindles it'.[53] This canto transports Juan into the harem, but Shelley's observation is equally true of the medley style of any of the other cantos and perfectly explains the psychological origins of that style, which is the 'natural' manner only of the chameleon personality.

It is also the style of Byron's letters. In this sense, Keats's chameleon poet and Byron's man of *mobilité* (with his 'chameleon' style) are very similar, for the one has no more true 'self', 'character', or 'identity' than the other. For this same reason, both these sorts of the poetical character are also clearly 'distinguished from the wordsworthian or egotistical sublime', as Keats speaks of his own chameleon nature.[54] Byron writes of the quality or characteristic of *mobilité* (attributed significantly to Adeline in her role as hostess at Norman Abbey) that it is possessed by 'actors, artists, and romancers, . . . speakers, bards, diplomatists, and dancers' (XVI, st. 97). All these, it would seem, Byron thought of as entertainers, intent on pleasing and securing the good will or approval of an audience; thus is selfhood transformed, if not temporarily annihilated. *Mobilité* is found, however, 'seldom' in heroes, 'never' in sages, and in 'very few financiers' – each group intent not on entertaining or pleasing others but seeking glory, truth, and money, respectively.

Keats's letter on the poetical character also helps to explain other aspects of the social, satiric, and epistolary genius of Byron. Like Keats's 'poetical character', this genius also

> enjoys light and shade; it lives in gusto, be it foul or fair, high or low, rich or poor, mean or elevated – It has as much delight in conceiving an Iago as an Imogen. What shocks the virtuous philosop[h]er, delights the camelion Poet. It does no harm from its relish of the dark side of things any more than from its taste for the bright one; because they both end in speculation.[55]

It is unnecessary and would indeed be tedious here to describe the remarkable stylistic and substantial range of Byron's *ottava rima* poems (or that of his letters and journals), their gusto, their relish for all aspects of life, high and low, their repeated delight in hedonistic, sceptical, or agnostic speculation, worldly-wise and cosmopolitan, never puritanical or narrowly moralistic. More startling, perhaps, is the central place that the problem of sincerity and the associated problem of consistency of belief have in Keats's theory. For no word of the Keatsian poet of no identity 'can be taken for granted as an opinion growing out of [his] identical nature'; he has 'no nature' or identity. Thus it is that 'no dependence is to be placed on what [he] said' upon any given day. Tomorrow he may contradict himself. 'But even now', Keats writes, 'I am perhaps not speaking from myself; but from some character in whose soul I now live.'[56]

Byron recognized his own chameleon nature as early as 1814, in a letter of 22 October to Miss Milbanke, who did not either believe him or understand him when he informed her that he was a man of 'no character', 'no identity'. He wrote, 'I am sure that of my own character I know nothing – nor could I if my existence were at stake tell what my "ruling passion" is – it takes it's colours I believe from the circumstances in which I am placed'.[57] Two days earlier he had told her that he was 'not very illnatured *off the stage*'.[58] Here then, early in Byron's life, is the man of *mobilité*, self-consciously recognized as such, an actor capable of playing many roles, a chameleon player taking his colours from the circumstances of the moment, like Adeline with her country guests, charming in their presence, maliciously gossiping about them in their absence. But 'surely they're sincerest', Byron wrote in *Don Juan*, 'who are strongly acted on by what is nearest' (XVI, st. 97). Contradiction then is the price paid by the man of 'sincerity'. Even when he is *not* influenced by the presence of others he contradicts himself. In a passage already quoted from his journal of 6 December 1813, Byron wrote, 'God knows what contradictions it may contain. If I am sincere with myself (but I fear one lies more to one's self than to any one else), every page should confute, refute, and utterly abjure its predecessor.'[59] And so it was with the many-sided contradictions of his life and thought. His *mobilité*, his role-playing, the 'plurality of characters' he could assume – these were recognized by friends and acquaintances as different as Mary Shelley, Madame Albrizzi, Leicester Stanhope, Thomas Moore, Sir Walter Scott, and James Kennedy.[60] This *mobilité* represents an abnegation or annihilation of self, but the context is never apocalyptic, as with Blake.

Of all the Romantic poets Byron was the most secular-minded, that is, fewer things or relationships were sacred to him, it seems, and for those that were regarded as sacred, the feeling attached to them appears less intense or receives expression of less intensity. Although the Pilgrim's 'wanderings [are] done', his 'shrine . . . won' in Rome (*Childe Harold* IV, st. 164, 175), he expresses no sense of personal redemption, and Byron imagines in this poem no general redemption of mankind (or that portion worthy of it). Indeed, the word *redeem* in its several forms is usually secularized in meaning when used in his poetry. But Byron abhorred bonds as intensely as Blake, and his largest, most inclusive vision is political: the freedom of each nation and each individual to shape his own destiny. In this Byron expresses his eighteenth-century heritage of the human and national right to independence, even by revolutionary violence. He draws upon essentially the same tradition as Wordsworth in his tract on the *Convention of Cintra*, the title of which refers *to those Principles, by which alone the Independence and Freedom of Nations can be Preserved or Recovered.*

If for Byron poetry cannot redeem the world, a certain kind can preserve it – and that is Alexander Pope's kind. His ethical poetry is 'the Book of Life', the one best book to be rescued for posterity from the total disappearance of England from the face of the earth.[61] Pope's poetry is 'the Christianity of English poetry', and 'there will be found as comfortable metaphysics . . . in the *Essay on man* [as] in the *Excursion*'.[62] This is very high praise, but Byron's statements are not as startling as they might seem at first glance. Byron had read Wordsworth's 'Prospectus', appearing at the end of the Preface to *The Excursion* (1814), and recognized that both Pope's poem and Wordsworth's were addressed in important part to the same problem or theme as that of *Paradise Lost*, 'to justify the ways of God to man'. Pope uses a variation of this phrase at line 16 of his *Essay on Man* to announce his purpose, which is to 'vindicate the ways of God to man'. Wordsworth in his 'Prospectus' not only echoes *Paradise Lost* at least five times but also addresses the same audience: ' "fit audience let me find though few!" ' (l. 23).[63] All three poems in their different ways are intensely ethical, all three concerned with the philosophic problem of evil and with the way in which man should live in a world of obvious imperfection. All three, furthermore, propose for man some form of submission to the inevitable. At the end of *Paradise Lost* Adam has learned that 'to obey is best', and the spirit of Eve has been 'compos'd / To meek submission' (XII, ll. 561, 596–7). The final imperative of the first Epistle of Pope's *Essay on Man* is 'Submit', even as, by the clearest implication, the Solitary in *The Excursion* should submit to all the ills of life he has suffered and place his faith too in a Providence that can be trusted.[64] Byron, to be sure, achieved this trust himself only intermittently.

One feels certain, however, that it was not any enthusiastic dedication to Pope's 'comfortable' metaphysics that brought Byron rushing to his defence. The issue was again a personal one for him, involving his feelings about Wordsworth, Coleridge and Southey (not to mention Bowles, Hunt and Keats), but involving even more importantly his chosen image of the poet and of himself as one. In part it was a battle of town versus country, the urbane and amusing satirist versus the solemn-faced prophets of nature; and Byron's defence of works of art as superior to works of nature, in the Pope–Bowles controversy, as subjects or material of poetry may be regarded as his contribution to this battle, which was at once traditional and personal for him. But this is only part of the truth, for Byron had already decided when writing Canto IV of *Childe Harold* to emphasize art more than nature and to eliminate from this canto the kind of 'metaphysics' that was prominent in Canto III. Indeed, in 1817, he had intended to have dealt in Canto IV with 'the present state of Italian literature, and perhaps of manners', as he explained in his dedication. For Byron, finally, art had a decidedly and explicitly social role. Thus in *Don Juan* he 'will war . . . with all who war / With Thought' (IX, st. 24), even as Blake, in the Preface to *Milton*, 'will not cease from Mental Fight'. Byron's context here is again largely political, specifically, to war against tyranny.

If we accept Byron's position in the Pope–Bowles controversy as his final one in the great debate of his time upon man or art versus nature, he stood closer to Blake, surprisingly, than to Wordsworth, whose 'Prospectus' in its spousal verse had celebrated the marriage of man's mind and the natural world, the beauty of which surpasses 'the most fair ideal Forms / Which craft of delicate Spirits hath composed / From earth's materials' (ll. 43–5). (This, to be sure, is not wholly consistent with the doctrine of *The Prelude*.) 'English gardening', Byron asserted in the first letter to Bowles, 'is the purposed perfectioning of niggard *Nature*.'[65] For Byron (and Blake) the ideal images and art-products of the imagination regularly excel the merely natural, that which emerges from niggardly nature. Sculpture, for example, 'is more poetical than nature itself, inasmuch as it represents and bodies forth that ideal beauty and sublimity which is never to be found in actual Nature'.[66] This is not to deny that at other times and places he viewed or experienced nature as spiritualized, holy, or emblematic of the Divine.

What, then, do we make of Byron? Is he merely a bewildering conjunction of contradictions, a paradox of opposing qualities, or is there coherence to his being and art? Does the surface inconsistency mask, as Thomas Moore found, underlying harmony? Such questions have been, and probably always will be, debated. If Byron showed little interest in literary discussion, he had no equal as an ironic commentator on what went on around him. But how can we reconcile his acuteness as an observer of life with his relative failure as a literary theoretician? Even his need to express himself involved contradictions. He wrote, we have argued, not out of fullness but out of emptiness. A solitary and melancholy being, he expressed his thoughts in poetry and prose in order to achieve a meaningful and satisfying relationship with himself. What seems most artless in this work is often most artful, even in his apparently 'spontaneous' letters and journals. Contemplating his own contradictory self with candour, he hailed inconsistency as the key to fallen, flawed humanity. *Mobilité* – the word he coined to characterize Lady Adeline's behaviour – he also recognized captured his own. This life-long awareness of his nature, in poetry and in life, becomes the key to fathoming the Byronic paradox. He wrote out of and through himself and thus, in his person, exemplifies Keats's chameleon poet.

Byron stands apart from the other Romantics in his distrust of the imagination as a creative force. Yet, paradoxically, his poetry often praises imagination, even if he does not always call it by that name: in the passages on creation in *Childe Harold* III and IV, in the lines on Promethean creativity in *The Prophecy of Dante*, and, above all, in the ongoing imaginative–creative involvement with *Don Juan*. Byron also stands apart from the other Romantics in his liking for the dandies and, in later years, in his valuation of the ideal of 'gentlemanliness'. He stands with them in his veneration of the Old Testament and of *Paradise Lost*. Usually he places works of art above works of nature, but in one glorious summer, under the heady stimulus of Words-

7 Shelley: the Growth of a Moral Vision

It has been argued that the 'spirit of urbanity is so prevalent in Shelley that one learns to distrust the accuracy of any critic who finds Shelley's poetry shrill'.[1] In Shelley's prose, however, one finds repeatedly the shrillest of tones, and it does no one any good to point out the same shrill tone in some of his worst, propagandistic poems. The remarkable quality that distinguishes Shelley among the major Romantic poets is not any singleness of tone but the tremendous tonal range of his achievement. Among his successful poems we find the urbane conversational style of the two educated gentlemen in *Julian and Maddalo; A Conversation*, colloquial but at the same time precise, informed, or profound, revealing many of the qualities of good stage dialogue.[2] This is quite different from the linked sweetness of the modified Spenserian 'Stanzas written in Dejection – December 1818, near Naples', with its elaborate alliteration and assonance, marred only by the inurbane but Shelleyan lament of the last stanza: 'for I am one / Whom men love not' – direct, abstract, agonized, self-pitying. Different from this is the epistolary tone of *Letter to Maria Gisborne*, whimsical or otherwise humorous, retrospective but also optimistically anticipatory, self-depreciating and generous in its judgment of such figures as Leigh Hunt, Hogg, Peacock and Horace Smith, all named in the poem, along with Godwin and Coleridge. Here life, like a beautifully engraved cameo of a living person, becomes art without losing its direct link to life. This, in turn, is obviously different from the metaphorical complexities of *Epipsychidion*, as 'the noble and unfortunate lady', Emilia Viviani, is progressively and neoplatonically translated from an actual woman (who, according to Claire Clairmont, changed the saint she prayed to each time she changed her lover) into a cascade of increasingly idealized, abstract, and iridescent metaphors (ll. 115–23), then into the source of the poet's inspiration and song, finally into a sensual female dramatic figure uniting sexually with the first-person narrator, allegorical of the union of poet and inspiration that produces the poem called *Epipsychidion*. The stanzaic intricacies of 'Hymn to Intellectual Beauty' and the obscure syntax of 'Mont Blanc' differ from anything else Shelley ever wrote, as does the soaring triumphant song, rising out of the melancholy notes of stanza 18, of 'To a Skylark', a unique excursion into lyric definition worthy of comparison with Hopkins's 'The Caged Skylark'. It is hardly necessary here to remind the reader of Shelley's major achievements in the form of elegy, lyrical drama, tragedy, and the unfinished and unclassifiable *The Triumph of Life* – a vision poem, Shelley's *Purgatorio*, the tone of which is not urbane.

This remarkable tonal range is matched, perhaps, by the equally startling range of Shelley's philosophical positions, which are sufficiently varied or puzzling to have led scholars to call him 'an atheist and a believer in a personal God, a Platonist and a pseudo-Platonist, a Berkeleian Immaterialist and a Humean sceptic-empiricist, a "naturalistic pantheist" . . . and even something of a mystic'.[3] Between 9 May and 15 August 1811 he underwent a complete change of mind concerning the morality of the institution of marriage, becoming on the latter date, as he wrote Hogg, a 'perfect convert to matrimony'.[4] Ten days later he eloped with Harriet Westbrook. In the same year, 1811, his deism slipped with startling rapidity into self-proclaimed atheism. He would, of course, change his mind again on all these subjects. Clearly, the dates, many uncertain, of Shelley's major pronouncements are of the utmost importance, for even among the Romantic poets his capacity for radical intellectual growth was very great.

He began, with Hogg, at a point far removed from the basic assumptions of English Romanticism, as a kind of delayed eighteenth-century agnostic and rationalist, concerned in 'The Necessity of Atheism' with 'proofs' and 'the nature of Belief'.[5] The distance that separated the early Shelley from the early Blake (who is not mentioned by Shelley) is suggested by several statements on the senses and on the reason that the two poets made in their earliest expository prose. In the agnostic 'Necessity of Atheism', Shelley asserted in Lockean fashion, 'The senses are the sources of all knowledge to the mind; consequently their evidence claims the strongest assent' (SP, 38). Blake, on the contrary, in the second series of 'There is No Natural Religion', asserted with equal confidence, 'Mans perceptions are not bounded by organs of perception. He perceives more than sense (tho' ever so acute) can discover.'[6] For the young Shelley, 'no testimony can be admitted which is contrary to reason; reason is founded on the evidence of our senses' (SP, 38). Shelley would alter his opinion on this point, but early and late the unredeemed reason for Blake is no more at best than 'the ratio of all we have already known' and at worst such reason is represented by the title character of *The Book of Urizen*. Shelley concludes, 'Every reflecting mind must allow that there is no proof of the existence of a Deity' (SP, 39); Blake concludes, 'He who sees the Infinite in all things sees God.' Both agreed that deism or natural religion was unacceptable, but they reached their conclusions by very different routes, Blake objecting violently to its rationalistic and mechanistic aspects, Shelley in his early *Refutation of Deism* arguing that it is in fact no better than Christianity, for 'the evidences of the Being of a God are to be deduced from no other principles than those of divine revelation' (SP, 118) – which revelation the young Shelley did not accept.

Both poets objected, finally, to the mistaken epistemology of other men. Shelley protested, as fundamentally as did Blake, against the common or vulgar concept of God as 'a venerable old man, seated on a throne of clouds, his breast the theatre of various passions, analogous to those of humanity, his will changeable and uncertain as that of an earthly king' (SP, 77). The young Byron would have agreed. In his letter to Hodgson of 13 September 1811, one encounters, in addition, the Shelleyan (and Humean) assertion, 'As to miracles, I agree with Hume that it is more probable men should *lie* or be *deceived*, than that things out of the course of nature should so happen.'[7] Shelley had echoed Hume's famous sentence in the same year, 1811, in 'The Necessity of Atheism'. The mature Shelley would become more sympathetic to miracles: life itself would become 'the great miracle'. A 'mist of familiarity obscures from us the wonder of our being', he wrote in 'On Life' (SP, 172). This phrase is echoed again in his letter to Hunt of 27 September 1819, where, speaking of Boccaccio's descriptions of nature, he writes: 'It is the morning of life stript of that mist of familarity which makes it obscure to us.'[8] Similarly, but for a different purpose and in a different way, Byron in *Don Juan* 'strips off this illusion' of false sentiment and cant.[9] Shelley would also become much less certain and dogmatic, even in his scepticism or agnosticism: 'it is a mistake to suppose', he wrote in the preface to *Prometheus Unbound*, 'that I consider them [his 'poetical compositions'] in any degree as containing a reasoned system on the theory of human life' (SP, 328). One thinks here of Byron's distrust of systems – and of Blake's. Such humility had not always been evident in Shelley's thought.

Although Shelley, Byron and Blake were all (with reservations) poets of democracy and although the intensity of Shelley's passion for reforming the world was equalled by Blake's, Shelley differed in degree from the others in the extent of his interest in political reform. (This interest consumed less of the energy of Keats, it would seem, than of any of the other poets.) If Blake is an apocalyptic writer expressing his utopian ideals most typically in terms of a new Jerusalem, Shelley is the radical's radical, entertaining the most extreme views but concerned in the same essay with the most practical and possible reforms. Although in his prose he is eloquent in the cause of political liberty, master on the highest level of the rhetorical arts of political demagoguery, able to convey a tremendous sense (or illusion) of outrage, he is at the same time clearly aware of limits and knowledgeable concerning the art of the possible. The last two paragraphs of 'An Address to the People on the Death of Princess Charlotte' constitute a magnificent artifice designed for one purpose only: to arouse the emotions of the people, to excite their sense of injustice by contrasting the deaths by execution of three Derbyshire workmen for high treason with the death of the young princess, whose death is then transformed into the death of Liberty.

But in *A Philosophical View of Reform* he is concerned with the most down-to-earth realities or actualities: the right to vote, 'public credit' and the use of paper money, the resultant monetary inflation and its economic and social effects upon the lives of the poor.[10] The entire elaborate structure is erected upon an eminently sane psychology that recognizes man's egocentric nature ('a man loves himself with an overweaning love' [SP, 240]) but has full confidence in man's capacity to improve his lot. The true enemy emerges finally not as the king or the aristocracy as such but as the very rich, ruling by means of their control of money, specifically, debased and unredeemable paper money. Supporting the very rich is a second 'aristocracy of attorneys and excisemen and directors' (245), who must in turn be supported by the poor. These latter must now labour twice as many hours as in the past in order to stay alive, with the result that England's 'lowest and . . . largest class' now 'eat less bread, wear worse clothes, are more ignorant, immoral, miserable, and desperate' than every before (246). Among Shelley's solutions are the abolition of the national debt, to be paid off by the very rich, who alone incurred it in the first place. However, chapter II closes on a note of moderation: the sudden or abrupt introduction of universal suffrage, accompanied by the 'immediate abolition . . . of monarchy and aristocracy, and the levelling of inordinate wealth, and an agrarian distribution, including the parks and chases of the rich', might well be followed by a civil war and the brutalizing effects that war has upon the soldier (252–3).

Not even Shelley, who asserted that 'politics are only sound when conducted on principles of moraltiy' (SP, 71), believed that the equal distribution of all property was practically possible at present or under present conditions even desirable. It was an ideal, Christlike and Platonic. Similarly for universal suffrage: women (and children) were not yet ready for it. Indeed, as late as 1817, in 'A Proposal for Putting Reform to the Vote', he thought the franchise should be limited to male taxpayers, those 'paying a certain small sum in *direct taxes*' (161). To grant the right to vote 'to every male adult would be to place power in the hands of men who have been rendered brutal and torpid and ferocious by ages of slavery' (162). Although Shelley admitted that the arguments of the radical Major John Cartwright for immediate reform of Parliament were 'unanswerable', he tried nevertheless to answer them. But it was Byron who presented Cartwright's petition to the House of Lords and supported it in a speech.

The distinguishing quality of Shelley's mature political thought is its great respect for human limits: 'nothing is more idle than to reject a limited benefit because we cannot without great sacrifices obtain an unlimited one' (SP, 256). And after all the grand ideals have been achieved, 'there will remain the great task of accommodating all that can be preserved of antient forms . . . in legislation, jurisprudence, government, and religious and academical institutions' (260). Balancing their passionate interest (and confidence) in the future's changes, the Romantic poets had a deep reverence for the achievements of man in the past. Such a view leaves no possibility of reverence for primitive or savage, ignorant or uneducated man. Shelley firmly believed that society had progressed, but his passionate dedication to reform rested upon the conviction, expressed in the early 'Essay on Christianity', that 'the whole frame of human things is infected by the insidious poison' of 'regulations of precedent and prescription' in the present 'unequal system'. Hence 'man is blind in his understanding, corrupt in his moral sense, and diseased in his physical functions' (210–11). Government exists, he asserted in 'A Declaration of Rights', only 'to repress the vices of man. If man were today sinless, tomorrow he would have a right to demand that government and all its evils should cease' (72).

At different times and in different ways all the Romantic poets found abhorrent what organized religion had done to the teachings of Christ. In the 'Essay on Christianity', '*God* according to the acceptation of Jesus Christ is the interfused and overruling Spirit of all the energy and wisdom included within the circle of existing things. . . . mysteriously and illimitably pervading the frame of things' (SP, 201). Shelley does not disagree and gives to Christ the name of poet. The man who 'only aspires to that which the divinity of his own nature shall consider and approve – he has already seen God' (202). 'All deities', as Blake said, 'reside in the human breast'.[11] And those who have seen God, Shelley explains in Coleridgean terms, achieve within themselves the harmony of an Eolian harp and 'give forth divinest melody when the breath of universal being sweeps over their frame' (SP, 202).

Shelley's thought, then, is basically Christian at least in its primary assumption and in its chief or governing aspiration or anticipation. Man exists in a fallen state, but a new day will come: 'According to Jesus Christ, and according to the indisputable facts of the case, some evil Spirit has dominion in this imperfect world. But there will come a time when the human

mind shall be visited exclusively by the influences of the benignant power' (SP, 204). These are, then, the two focal points of
Shelley's thought: a realistic assessment of the present state of
affairs, and, for the future, a confident hope and faith.

Because of the basic sympathy Shelley felt for the thought of
Christ, he can find his own ideas in Christ's mind. Shelley's
Christ, for example, seems to believe in the future perfectibility
of man or of some men. If the latter, then this is of course quite
orthodox.

> Jesus Christ instructed his disciples to be perfect as their
> father in Heaven is perfect, declaring at the same time his
> belief that human perfection required the refraining from
> revenge or retribution in any of its various shapes. The per-
> fection of the human and the divine character is thus asserted
> to be the same.[12]

Christ, according to Shelley, also expressed belief in the equal-
ity of all men, and his hero, Rousseau, perhaps 'resembles most
nearly the mysterious sage of Judaea' (SP, 209). The thought of
neither Christ nor Rousseau is primitivistic: Christ did not teach
a 'return to the condition of savages', and Rousseau did not
advocate that men should destroy their cities and 'become the
inhabitants of the woods' (210). Nothing underlines more
clearly than this the basic sympathy Shelley felt for the teachings of Christ, since 'uncivilized man is the most pernicious and
miserable of beings' (211). In Shelley's opinion, Christ was the
great civilizer, and no office or function was higher. One may
compare Blake's address 'To the Christians': 'What are the
Treasures of Heaven? . . . are they any other than Mental
Studies & Performances? . . . What is the Life of Man but Art &
Science?'[13]

If Christ is the type of the great civilizer, giving to man, like
Prometheus, the arts and sciences, along with an expansive ethic
of love, the true Satan is not his contrary but his opposite, a
Blakean 'Accuser' and repressor. Furthermore, as Shelley writes
in his 'Essay on the Devil and Devils', Satan is 'at once the
informer, the attorney general [chief prosecutor], and the jailor
of the celestial tribunal' (SP, 269). The God of established religion and vulgar superstition is the great judge, using Satan for his
own purposes, and consequently is more satanic than Satan, his

creation and creature. Together they are responsible for the greatest injustice man knows: eternal damnation of millions of human spirits.

By contrast, Milton's Satan is a magnificent creature, as he is for Blake. In Shelley's opinion, 'Nothing can exceed the grandeur and the energy' of Satan's character, who as 'a moral being is . . . far superior to his God' (SP, 267). For to the extent that forgiveness is the central teaching of Christianity, Milton's God is himself monstrously satanic: his purpose is to inflict 'the most horrible revenge upon his enemy' (267). Shelley would have agreed with Blake that Milton was of Satan's party without knowing it, for he clothed Satan 'with the sublime grandeur of a graceful but tremendous spirit' (268), thus uniting in one figure the ideas of energy and grace.

When one attempts to isolate those other pieces of Shelley's prose that are of interest today, of absolute value that is, not merely of historical value, it is surely necessary to include the 'Speculations on Morals', the essays 'On Life' and 'On Love', perhaps the unfinished romance 'The Coliseum', the prefaces to *Alastor*, *Prometheus Unbound*, and *The Cenci*, and without question *A Defence of Poetry*. A remarkable number of these essays are concerned with the nature and necessity of love, a subject central to the *Defence*.

A single page from the first of these, the 'Speculations on Morals', refers to a number of Shelley's controlling ideas and anticipates the *Defence*. Here the links between the ethical and the aesthetic imagination are firmly established as Shelley associates the virtuous and civilized man, acquainted with poetry and philosophy, with the capacity for sympathetic identification with the pains and pleasures of others. Such a man is contrasted with 'an infant, a savage, and a solitary beast', all of whom are 'selfish', that is, without the power of imagination, which is the very foundation of civilization (SP, 188). 'Imagination or mind employed in prophetically [imaging forth] its object is that faculty of human nature on which every graduation of its progress, nay, every, the minutest, change depends' (189). Blake never elevated the imagination more highly, although he typically expressed himself less abstractly. For Shelley, 'the only distinction between the selfish man and the virtuous man is that the imagination of the former is confined within a narrow limit, whilst that of the latter embraces a comprehensive circumference' (189). The ethical imperative then demands an escape from the normal or natural limits of the self, and this escape is made possible by the 'exercise' that the arts provide for the imagination. Finally, 'disinterested benevolence is the product of a cultivated imagination and has an intimate connection with all the arts. . . . Virtue is thus entirely a refinement of civilized life' (189). The noble savage had little interest for Shelley, nor any other kind of primitivism.

All this is quite different from Shelley's concept of romantic love between man and woman, which has its origins in a quest for perfect sympathy and understanding and therefore is focused on the self rather than on others. To the extent that the self 'thirsts after its [own] likeness' it is narcissistic (SP, 170). The dangers of this condition Shelley explored in *Alastor*, in which the main character, as he wrote in the preface, rejects the human love of the Arab maiden and 'thirsts for intercourse with an intelligence similar to itself', embodying his own imagination in a vision that he seeks fruitlessly even unto death. In Shelley's short essay 'On Love' we encounter for the first time the concept of the epipsyche, 'a soul within our soul' (echoed in ll. 238 and 455 of *Epipsychidion*) 'that describes a circle around its proper paradise, which pain, and sorrow, and evil dare not overleap' (SP, 170). That 'paradise' Shelley depicted in the last long section of the poem addressed to Emilia Viviani, an anticipated imagined retreat into a bower of perfect love wholly free from pain. In plain prose, however, Shelley knew that such a perfect union is 'unattainable' and so described it in 'On Love'. Few major Romantic poems deal primarily with 'romantic' love. Those that do are usually poems of love found and lost, or rejected, destroyed or unfulfilled. One thinks of Blake's *Book of Thel* and his *Visions of the Daughters of Albion*, Wordsworth's *The Ruined Cottage*, Coleridge's *Christabel* perhaps, Byron's *Manfred* and the Haidée episode of *Don Juan*, Shelley's *Alastor*, and Keats's *Lamia*.

If for Shelley the circle of the epipsyche walls out the pain of other men, the 'comprehensive circumference' of the virtuous man's imagination embraces it (SP, 189). Shelley understood clearly the relationship between the two circles. In his moments of greatest insight he never doubted, he knew that the essential condition of man's life was a movement away from self in the direction of that which is not self. The old father in 'The

Coliseum', Shelley's incomplete romance begun in late 1818,
knows this and expresses it in terms of two very different circles
within the human psyche. One of these is 'not to be sur-
mounted' by other men, 'and it is this repulsion which constitutes the misfortune of the condition of life. But there is a circle
which comprehends, as well as one which mutually excludes,
all things which feel. . . . Happiness consists in diminishing the
circumference which includes those resembling [the individual]
himself, until they become one with him and he with them'
(227). This position approaches without duplicating Blake's
expanding vision of infinite multitudes of grains of sand, stone,
rocks, hills, fountains, mountains, and stars that are in reality
'Men Seen Afar' but to eyes that 'Continue Expanding . . .
Appear'd as One Man'.[14] So it is for Shelley that men can and
must '*enter into* the meditations, designs, and destinies of something beyond ourselves' (italics added); it is this power that
permits men to experience a 'tingling joy' in the presence of
natural beauty. 'And this is Love', the old father exclaims (SP,
227), meaning something very different from what Shelley
meant when in 'On Love', after defining the romantic love of
man and woman, he wrote, 'This is Love' (170). Instead, the old
father addresses this love as 'O Power! . . . which interpenetratest all things, and without which this glorious world were a
blind and formless chaos, Love, Author of Good, God, King,
Father' (227). Presumably all the vocatives in the sentence are
synonymous, and the speaker, who has our sympathy, thus
occupies a pantheistic universe in which love in its highest,
most exalted form pervades all things and unites all living creatures. Shelley, too, could believe that 'every thing that lives is
Holy'.[15]

Blake's words and those of the old father in Shelley's
romance are essentially expressions of wonder (not assertions of
knowledge) before the great miracle of life, which Shelley cele-
brates explicitly and with great intensity in his short essay 'On
Life', written in late 1819. Like Coleridge on Wordsworth, he is
aware of the 'mist of familiarity' that 'obscures from us [this]
wonder', the 'great miracle' of life.[16] And like both Coleridge
and Blake, he employs an optical metaphor to describe men's
ignorance, thus defining by implication an important function
of the poet: to open men's eyes. The nature of perception is as

important for Shelley as for Blake, and as interesting as it is for Byron.

Like Coleridge, the main thrust of Shelley's thought was in the direction of idealistic monism, at one time taking the form of a modified Berkelian position: 'nothing exists but as it is perceived', a statement Shelley regarded as important enough to repeat in 'On Life' (SP, 173, 174). Thus ideas and external objects are 'merely . . . two classes of thoughts'. Similarly, the 'I' of the essay who is now speculating and thinking is merely 'a portion' of the 'one mind' (174). Coleridge wrote, 'every Thing has a Life of it's own, & . . . we are all *one Life*'. Or, in other terms, he 'defined life *absolutely*, as the principle of unity in *multeity*'.[17] Byron in *Childe Harold* III lives not in himself but becomes 'portion of that around' him, and therefore he is 'absorbed, and this is life' (stanzas 72, 73), in a universe that is conceived for the time being in terms of pantheistic monism.

Therefore, for Shelley and for other poets like Wordsworth, the state of reverie, found more often in children than in adults, permits the individual to feel as if he were 'dissolved into the surrounding universe, or as if the surrounding universe were absorbed into their being. They are conscious of no distinction' (SP, 174). But for Shelley the benefits of both dissolution or annihilation of the sense of self and the absorption of the universe by and into the self (of which Byron has been accused) are the same. The experience is associated with 'an unusually intense and vivid apprehension of life' (ibid.). Thus those individuals who have carried this power of childhood over into their maturity live in a world of miracles in which they are completely at home. One thinks of 'Tintern Abbey', in which 'we are laid asleep / In body, and become a living soul' (ll. 45–6) or of Wordsworth's remarks to Miss Fenwick on his childhood sensations: 'I was often unable to think of external things as having external existence, and I communed with all that I saw as something not apart from, but inherent in, my own immaterial nature.' Wordsworth goes on to deplore the common loss of such powers or experiences in mature men, as Shelley does, and describes 'that dream-like vividness and splendour which invest objects of sight in childhood' as a universal experience once shared by all.[18]

Shelley's concept of love is thus broadly inclusive. It is any

movement or attraction 'beyond ourselves' in which we seek a
condition of 'community' – that condition in fact achieved by
the Ancient Mariner. Love is 'the bond and the sanction [i.e.,
that which sanctifies or makes sacred] which connects not only
man with man, but with everything which exists' (SP, 170).
Thus a love relationship is possible with human beings, nature,
and God. 'Communion' with the 'beautiful or . . . majestic' in
man, Shelley wrote in his 'Essay on Christianity', is the equivalent of 'intercourse with the Universal God' (202). The
apotheosis or deification of man's potentialities or aspirations is
no greater in Blake. By an implication perhaps not intended by
Shelley, the poet, concerned so vitally with the beautiful and
majestic, regularly communes 'with the Universal God'. Both
are essentially creative: 'Non merita nome di creatore, se non
Iddio ed il Poeta' (172), a quotation from Tasso that Shelley
liked so well that he used it again, underscoring it, in *A Defence
of Poetry*, where he develops more fully a number of these
ideas.[19] Perhaps the words of Tasso reminded Shelley of Coleridge on the primary imagination (of which the secondary or
poetic imagination is an echo), 'a repetition in the finite mind of
the eternal act of creation in the infinite I AM'.[20]

The *Defence* begins by distinguishing between reason and
imagination, the latter faculty identified with 'the principle
of synthesis', as in Coleridge, who was also interested in
'the similitudes of things' (SP, 277). Imagination is, in short, the
image-making power. Later in the essay Shelley asserts that the
perfection of Homer and Sophocles consists in a Coleridgean
'harmony of the union of all' the parts of their works (286).
Reason, by contrast, is quite similar to Blake's 'ratio': it is 'the
enumeration of quantities already known' (277), in other words
'a mode of Memory', close to Coleridge's Fancy as defined in
chapter XIII of the *Biographia*. This fundamental opposition
between the abstracting reason and imagination is also Wordsworthian. 'No officious slave / Art thou of that false secondary
power / By which we multiply distinctions', Wordsworth had
told Coleridge in Book II of *The Prelude* (ll. 215–17). In a later
passage of the same book he defines the function of imagination
as the 'observation of affinities / In objects where no brotherhood exists / To passive minds' (ll. 384–6).

The *Defence* next defines poetry as 'the expression of the
imagination'. The language of poets 'is vitally metaphorical;

that is, it marks the before unapprehended relations of things'
(SP, 278). Therefore, poets are teachers of ideal truth, creators
of new knowledge, discoverers of 'those laws according to
which present things ought to be ordered', thus 'legislators'.
But the poet also 'beholds the future in the present' and so has a
prophetic function (279). Again one is reminded of Blake, who
also was convinced that 'a poet participates in the eternal, the
infinite', as Shelley expressed it (279). Shelley's examples are
Aeschylus, the *Book of Job*, and the *Paradiso*. Milton he considers
a few pages later.

Shelley moves on to protest the popular distinction between
poets and prose writers, as both Wordsworth and Coleridge
had done in their different ways.[21] Poetry is concerned with 'the
unchangeable forms of human nature' (SP, 281), here echoing
Aristotle on the difference between history and poetry, as
Wordsworth had done in the 1800 Preface.[22] One thinks here of
Blake's 'Visions of these eternal principles or characters of
human life [that] appear to poets, in all ages.'[23]

Having thus defined poets and poetry, Shelley next considers
their 'effects upon society' (SP, 281). None of these poets had
ever heard of art for art's sake: poetry always exists for man's or
society's sake. For Shelley as for Wordsworth and Coleridge,
the primary end of poetry is 'pleasure', which opens the spirit of
the reader to receive the 'wisdom which is mingled with its
delight'.[24] Wisdom and delight exist in Coleridgean 'union'.
Before the paragraph has closed, Shelley, thinking of the *Iliad*,
has anticipated the central argument of the *Defence*: a sympathy
or admiration for the great heroes leads finally to an identification with them.

But the argument cannot be phrased in terms so historically
and ethically limited as the actions or ideals of the Homeric
heroes. As Coleridge had described the poetry of Wordsworth,
so poetry, for Shelley, 'lifts the veil from the hidden beauty of
the world and makes familiar objects be as if they were not
familiar' (SP, 282). With this beauty, made visible by a poetic
miracle of perception, we identify, and in one gigantic leap
Shelley has bridged the gap between aesthetics and ethics, even
as the Ancient Mariner had done. For 'the great secret of morals
is love, or a going out of our own nature', and this we achieve
when we identify 'ourselves with the beautiful which exists in
thought, action, or person, not our own' (282–3). Therefore, 'a

man, to be greatly good, must imagine intensely and com-
prehensively'. And for this reason:

> The great instrument of moral good is the imagination. . . .
> Poetry enlarges the circumference of the imagination. . . .
> Poetry strengthens that faculty which is the organ of the
> moral nature of man in the same manner as exercise strength-
> ens a limb (283).

Here then, beautifully argued, is one of the central assumptions
or doctrines of English Romanticism. The Shelleyan sympathetic or ethical imagination embraces by implication the Blakean
annihilation of self, the Wordsworthian blending or marriage of
man's mind with nature that will 'arouse the sensual from their
sleep / Of Death' and produce a new 'creation', the Coleridgean
expression of this same experience in the figure of the Mariner,
the chameleon quality of Byron (Shelley said all poets were
'camaeleonic'), and Keats's own 'camelion Poet' and his doctrine of empathy.[25]

This centre of *A Defence of Poetry* asserts or implies most of
Shelley's great attachments: his dedication to the beautiful, his
intense love for all living things, his ethical passion for doing
the world some good. All else in the *Defence* flows from this
centre. Therefore, as Shelley surveys the literary productions of
the centuries, he finds a correlation between artistic perfection
and moral greatness, as in the great age of Athenian drama.
Conversely, in periods of social decay, drama 'becomes a cold
imitation' (SP, 285). Blake understood the same truth: 'Nations
are Destroy'd, or Flourish, in proportion as Their Poetry Painting and Music, are Destroy'd or Flourish!'[26]

Poetry in fact redeems or recreates man, who needs to learn
the arts of love and civilization. In the familiar Romantic view,
the 'character of a poet participates in the divine nature' (SP,
286). If poetry is the redeemer, man clearly must stand in need
of redemption, and for Shelley he does. There is 'an inexplicable
defect of harmony in the constitution of human nature' (292);
'man, having enslaved the elements, remains himself a slave'
(293), bound as securely as in Blake. The 'principle of Self, of
which money is the visible incarnation', is the 'Mammon of the
world', adding 'a weight to the curse imposed on Adam' (293).
Once again, as with Blake, the calculators, the 'mere reasoners'

(like 'Locke, Hume, Gibbon, Voltaire' [292]), the inventors or physical scientists, 'for want of the poetical faculty', are among the villains. 'We want the creative faculty to imagine that which we know' (293).

The reality of evil established, poetry the redeemer is thus most greatly needed in periods when there is 'an excess of the selfish and calculating principle' (SP, 293). 'Poetry redeems from decay the visitations of the divinity in man' (295). (Even Count Maddalo, the Venetian nobleman meant to be Byron, is 'capable . . . of becoming the redeemer of his degraded country'.)[27] 'Poetry defeats the curse', which is defined in terms reminiscent of both Blake and Coleridge as that 'which *binds* us to be *subjected* to the *accident* of surrounding impressions', and so poetry 'creates anew the universe' (SP, 295; italics added), in effect producing a new Jerusalem within the individual.

Shelley first expressed the epistemological basis or cause of this effect in the essay 'On Life' and repeats it here: 'All things exist as they are perceived – at least in relation to the percipient' (SP, 295). Hence the great emphasis on perception, as in Blake, and on the importance of stripping 'the veil of familarity from the world', which recalls 'On Life'. Similarly, Coleridge asserted that Wordsworth sought in *Lyrical Ballads* to strip away the Shelleyan 'film of familiarity' that blinded the reader to the world's wonders.[28] Poetry, for Shelley, can achieve this miracle of altered perception because, in Coleridgean terms, 'it *marries* exultation and horror, grief and pleasure, eternity and change; it subdues to *union* . . . all irreconcilable things' (SP, 295; italics added).

Poetry conceived in such exalted terms clearly cannot be produced by 'the owl-winged faculty of calculation', the merely 'conscious portions' of the mind (SP, 294). It cannot be willed into existence, Shelley here seemingly disagreeing with Coleridge on the secondary imagination, which coexists 'with the conscious will'.[29] Poetic inspiration comes, instead, like 'some invisible influence, like an inconstant wind', which may remind us of Wordsworth's 'correspondent breeze' in *The Prelude* (I, l. 35). The art work, furthermore, grows organically in the mind of the artist 'as a child in the mother's womb' (SP, 294), with all that this implies concerning the absolute unity, the total fusion of the parts. One thinks of pages of poetry coming to Keats 'as naturally as the Leaves to a tree'.[30]

Even though turning away from the conscious, deliberate, and wholly rational origins of poetry in the mind of the poet, Shelley nonetheless suggests that the functons and purpose of poetry are intellectual. Poetry

> creates new materials of knowledge. . . . It is at once the center and circumference of knowledge: it is that which comprehends all science and that to which all science must be referred. It is at the same time the root and blossom of all other systems of thought (SP, 293).

It is no wonder then that 'poets are the unacknowledged legislators of the world', providing men with laws or standards to live by. They are however much more and much greater than this.[31] They are creators in the truest sense. *'Non merita nome di creatore, se non Iddio ed il Poeta'* (SP, 295). For they have not only reduced the 'chaos' of the familiar world to a state of 'order' (295, 293), even as in the Book of Genesis, when before Creation 'the earth was without form, and void': they have also 'create[d] anew the universe' (295), as in the Book of Revelation.

But the world must be created anew for each generation (for 'all things exist as they are perceived'), and Shelley believed, with Coleridge and Keats, that English poetry in his day had 'arisen as it were from a new birth' to produce 'a memorable age in *intellectual* achievements' (SP, 296; italics added), superior to anything since England's Civil War.

8 Keats the Humanist

Of the major Romantic poets, Keats was the latest born, the earliest to die, the shortest lived, the most likeable, the most easily lovable. His mature creative life was incredibly brief – his first perfect poem, 'On First Looking into Chapman's Homer', being written in October 1816, his last perfect poem, 'To Autumn', slightly less than three years later, on 19 September 1819. In his letters we observe a mind functioning at its best over a period of about three years, when Keats was aged twenty-one to twenty-four years. On 3 February 1820 he suffered a violent haemorrhage of the lungs; in September, dying, he sailed for Italy. Keats wrote some of the finest letters in the language, but until his illness they are the letters of a young man. There was much that he did not have time to read or to think about. These few dates suggest the tremendous intensity with which, for a startlingly brief period, Keats thought about his art and worked to create it.

Although Keats never systematized his literary theory and the thoughts about the nature of human existence that we find scattered and evolving in his letters, much of this theory and speculation possesses a remarkable harmony or unity that derives directly from certain basic qualities of his character. Perhaps chief among these personal qualities is one easier to name in negative than in positive terms: the usual and genuine absence in him of self-assertiveness. The dogmatic tone or spirit was not his, and he disliked dogmatic men and arguments, believing that it was more blessed to listen, learn, and explore than to preach in support of a pre-selected text. Thus we find an unusual gentleness about Keats's strength of mind. Because of the basically explorative thrust of his thinking, he was reluctant to reach closed-end conclusions.

These personal qualities derive finally, it would appear, from Keats's stalwart selflessness virtually without neurotic fears or the need to feel himself loved by everyone who came his way. In his letter to George and Tom Keats of 21, 27(?) December 1817, sandwiched between his remarks contrasting Benjamin West's painting *Death on the Pale Horse* with *King Lear* and his account of Negative Capability, is a description of a dinner with Horace Smith, 'his two brothers', and three other men of literary interests.[1] The letter suggests how easily Keats moved between the social world and the solitary world of literary theory. Of these six men, only Horace and James Smith, as co-authors of *Rejected Addresses* (1812) and *Horace in London* (1813), had any literary reputation. John Kingston, who was Deputy Controller of Stamps and to whom Wordsworth deferred, was also among those present. By and large, they were men of wit and fashion. But Keats felt little or no sympathetic identification with them, no admiration for them, no desire to become like them. At the age of twenty-two, he was already his own man, well acquainted with his own identity, feeling no need to impress these assembled wits of the fashionable world. It made no difference to him that his host Horace Smith, a friend of Shelley, was a highly successful satirist and stockbroker or that James Smith was reputed to be one of the wittiest of conversationalists in an age that elevated conversation to a fine art. 'These men', Keats observed,

> say things which make one start, without making one feel[;] they are all alike; their manners are alike; they all know fashionables; they have a mannerism in their very eating & drinking, in their mere handling a Decanter – They talked of Kean & his low company – Would I were with that company instead of yours said I to myself! I know such like acquaintance will never do for me (KL, I, 193).

Byron, who said he never drew well with literary men (except Scott and Moore), would have agreed.[2] Different as they were, both Keats and Byron (to say nothing here of the other major Romantics) were men of independent spirit.

Keats's equally Byronic reluctance to embrace some set of final conclusions and then live comfortably with it from that day forward, for better or for worse, may express itself as a kind of simple scepticism. Thus in the famous letter to Benjamin Bailey of 22 November 1817, he is 'certain of nothing but' two grandly epic concepts, 'the holiness of the Heart's affections and the truth of Imagination' (KL, I, 184). But four months later, on 13 March 1818, he is boldly sceptical of his own scepticism. After referring to his religious scepticism as a thing well known to Bailey, he in effect denies it – 'I do not think myself more in the right than other people' – and then he qualifies his denial: 'I must once for all tell you I have not one Idea of the truth of any of my speculations' (I, 242, 243). Keats was not of course a confirmed or philosophic sceptic, denying the possibility of arriving at certain kinds of knowledge; it is the questioning, questing nature of his mind that here expresses itself, his way of protecting himself against the dogmatic utterance of the assertive self. And so on 31 December 1818 as a kind of New Year's resolution, he 'made up [his] Mind never to take any thing for granted – but even to examine the truth of the commonest proverbs' (II, 18).

Distrusting, like Blake, the abstracting and deductive faculty of the reason as dogmatic and self-assertive, Keats sought other methods of grasping reality: 'I never can feel certain of any truth but from a clear perception of its Beauty' (31 December 1818: KL, II, 19). Almost inevitably, William Godwin becomes the enemy. Charles Wentworth Dilke, the true opposite not the contrary of the poet of negative capability, is 'a Godwin-methodist' (24 September 1819: II, 213) and elsewhere a 'Godwin perfectibil[it]y Man' (14 October 1818: I, 397). He 'was a Man who cannot feel he has a personal identity unless he has made up his Mind about every thing. The only means of strengthening one's intellect is to make up ones mind about nothing – to let the mind be a thoroughfare for all thoughts' (24 September 1819: II, 213). Even a preliminary consideration illustrates the fact that Keats's scepticism, his open-minded questing spirit, the natural enemy and antidote to dogmatic self-assertiveness, is linked with such important areas of his thought as religion, the nature and function of the imagination, the nature of the self, negative capability, and human reason.

Keats's concept of the chameleon poet, a concept he took over from Hazlitt, is also tied to all this.[3] Specifically, it appears in the absence in him of a strong streak of self-assertiveness, as in his distinction in *The Fall of Hyperion* between true poets and 'mock lyrists, large self-worshippers / And careless hectorers in proud bad verse' (KL, I, 207–8) – perhaps a reference to Byron. 'Man should not dispute or assert', Keats wrote to John Hamilton Reynolds, 'but whisper results to his neighbour, and thus. . . every human might become great, and Humanity . . . would become a grand democracy' (19 February 1818: I, 232). The world, in short, would be transformed. As for himself, he stated, with his usual insight into his own being, 'I shall never be a Reasoner because I care not be in the right, when retired from bickering and in a proper philosophical temper' (13 March 1818: I, 243).

Keats's distrust of the disputatious and assertive man, like Godwin or Dilke, surely explains much about his anti-clericalism. As early as December 1816 he composed a sonnet 'Written in Disgust of Vulgar Superstition'. He found the Bishop of Lincoln to be 'tyran[n]ical' and worse (3 November 1817: KL, I, 178); a parson 'must be either a Knave or an Ideot' (14 February 1819: II, 63); and the 'history' of Jesus, the only man Keats knew of with a completely disinterested heart, except for Socrates, was lamentably 'written and revised by Men interested in the pious frauds of Religion' (19 March 1819: II, 80). This is very like Shelley, who more than once paired Jesus and Socrates. No wonder that Keats wrote of himself on 22 December 1818, 'I am reckoned lax in my christian principles' (II, 14).

But in important ways he was knowledgeably Christian, as well as being a close student of the Bible like the other Romantic poets.[4] He was baptized in the Church of England, and on his deathbed his friend Joseph Severn read to him from Jeremy Taylor's *Holy Living and Holy Dying*. The headmaster of the school at Enfield, where Keats was a student from 1803 to 1811, was John Clarke, who influenced his development and from whom he probably received religious training.[5] Keats's letter to his sister on 31 March 1819, instructing her in preparation for her confirmation, demonstrates how very knowledgeable he was of Anglican doctrine and of the Bible. In answer to just one of her questions, he refers her to twelve Biblical passages.[6] His faith in an immortal afterlife seems firm; earthly happiness will then be repeated 'in a finer tone' (22 November 1817: KL I, 185). Among 'the grandeurs of immortality' will be the perfect understanding that the disembodied spirits will have of each other, existing outside space in the form of pure intelligence. On this day, 16 December 1818, he had 'scarce a doubt of immortality of some nature' (II, 5, 4). But even more significant and revealing is the fact that two of his most famous letters – the Mansion of Life letter and the Vale of Soul-Making letter – are conceived in important part in Christian terms and rest upon Christian assumptions.

The earlier letter, to Reynolds of 3 May 1818, is centrally concerned with comparing the virtues of Milton and Words-worth: the grounds are explicitly humanitarian or humanistic but implicitly they are Christian. Keats saw human life as pro-cess or growth of mind just as truly and habitually as Words-worth or Byron. It was a movement from innocence to experi-ence and beyond, as in Blake and as in Byron's *Don Juan*, how-ever great the disparities among each's interpretation – and symbolic representation – of that journey. In life's 'large Man-sion of Many Apartments', the first is 'the infant or thoughtless Chamber, in which we remain as long as we do not think'. When we begin to reflect upon life we move into 'the Chamber of Maiden-Thought', where 'we become intoxicated with the light and the atmosphere, we see nothing but pleasant wonders, and think of delaying there for ever in delight'. In that Chamber we also undergo a 'sharpening' of 'vision into the heart ⟨head⟩ and nature of Man'. The experience has the effect of 'convinc-ing' our 'nerves that the World is full of Misery and Heartbreak, Pain, Sickness and oppression' (KL, I, 280, 281). Eventually many doors open out of the Chamber of Maiden-Thought, 'all dark – all leading to dark passages – We see not the ballance of good and evil'.[7] To this point, Keats believed, Wordsworth had come when he wrote 'Tintern Abbey'. Because 'his Genius is explorative of those dark Passages', it is 'deeper' or more pro-found than Milton's (KL, I, 281). Keats judges Wordsworth superior because he has a greater 'anxiety for Humanity' and 'martyrs himself to the human heart' (I, 278–9), into which he has thought more deeply and more sympathetically than Mil-ton, even though Milton's philosophic powers were surely as great as Wordsworth's.[8] From this Keats concluded that 'a mighty providence subdues the mightiest Minds to the service of the time being' (KL, I, 282). Quite as significant in the present context is Keats's third and last Chamber of Life. Although he gave it but one isolated sentence (he says that at this time he could describe only two), it is obviously a chamber of redemption or salvation. It will be stored with the wine and bread of communion, 'the wine of love – and the Bread of Friendship' (I, 283).

The great Vale of Soul-Making passage of 21 April 1819 in Keats's long journal-letter to George and Georgiana Keats explicitly deals with central Christian questions and assumptions: the 'Protection of Providence' (uncertain), the nature of human nature (imperfect), the existence of evil (necessary). 'Man is originally "a poor [bare] forked creature" ', like Adam after the Fall, and 'subject to the same mischances as the beasts of the forest'. Even if mankind could achieve happiness, Keats argued, the approach of death would then become intolerable, and the individual 'would leave this world as Eve left Paradise'. 'But in truth', Keats adds, 'I do not at all believe in this sort of perfectibility – the nature of the world will not admit of it' (KL, II, 101). Keats, like Byron, also rejected the doctrine of Christ the Redeemer, whose rewards are to be had only in heaven.[9] At several points his tough-minded and realistic insight into the nature of human existence recalls Byron.[10] But the imperfect creature here described is obviously in need of redemption, and Keats provided his own 'system of salvation' in his concept of a 'World of Pains and troubles' as a 'vale of Soul-making' (not a vale of tears), which neatly justifies the ways of God to man and solves the philosophic problem of evil (KL, II, 102).

Imperfect though man is, however, he comes from God, like Adam, and on 21 April 1819 Keats's concept of man's divine origin was as exalted as William Blake's or that of any other Christian. Man, for both Keats and Blake, is a fallen creature, in need of salvation. Intelligences, as distinct from the souls that will be created, are 'sparks of the divinity'; they are 'atoms of perception . . . in short they are God', to whom they may return (KL, II, 102). As Blake said, 'All deities reside in the human breast.'[11] Because God is One, these sparks of the divinity 'must feel and suffer in a thousand diverse ways' in order to become unique 'individual beings', that is, to become souls possessed of '*the sense of Identity*' (KL, II, 102, 103). Thus Keats explains the infinite variety of man and, by implication, the unique value of each. Even though Christianity remains for Keats only one of many 'Schemes of Redemption', his 'system of salvation', which he argues is far grander 'than [that of] the chrystain religion', is essentially Christian in spirit and in its major assumptions.[12]

Keats, with his Christian background, must have found it easy to nourish the basically non-assertive, non-dogmatic nature of his personality. This background enabled him to gain new insights into poetry and the nature of 'the poetical Character' (KL, I, 386). Aesthetic and ethical insights become one. Although he phrases his discussion in terms of aesthetics (or the psychology of the creative process and person), its implications, as with Blake and Shelley, are ethical. The egotistical poet – Wordsworth, for example – is both bully and self-deceived (I, 223). Such a poet, as Keats understood the matter at this time, violates the sanctity of other human personalities. Similarly, Leigh Hunt's 'self delusions are very lamentable. . . . There is no greater Sin after the 7 deadly than to flatter oneself into an idea of being a great Poet' (11 May 1817: I, 143). Such literary criticism is clearly ethical in its assumptions, and self-deception or self-flattery became for Keats the worst possible sin for a poet. It became, in effect, the eighth deadly sin, the equivalent of Blake's sin of selfhood. 'Complete disinterestedness of Mind' or heart, he found, had been possessed only by Socrates and Jesus, great men both, though neither left to posterity writings of his own (19 March 1819: II, 79, 80). But the major critical insight that Keats's sensitivity to egotism allowed him to achieve was his distinction between the 'wordsworthian or egotistical sublime' and the 'camelion Poet' of 'no Identity' (27 October 1818: KL, I, 387) – or Keats himself. One feels it was inevitable that he should have perceived this, for Keats was in fact perceiving a fundamental aspect of his own being, his fearless selflessness, which would perhaps have permitted him, had he lived, to have excelled marvellously in the drama, creating a host of richly diverse characters.

Although Keats early gives evidence of his capacity for sympathetic identification with that or those outside the self, the Chameleon–Poet letter of 27 October 1818 is the first in which the phrase (verbally reminiscent of Shelley on Byron)[13] appears and thus deserves examination in detail. Significantly, the letter opens with a celebration of Richard Woodhouse's 'friendliness' and goes on almost at once to define Keats's kind of poetical character in terms of selflessness, the absence of the egotistical – 'it has no self' (KL, I, 386, 387). The implication is that the poet of 'the wordsworthian or egotistical sublime' is confined, bound by and to itself in subject, point of view, and tone. (Note Keats's use of the lower-case 'w' for Wordsworth's name, as the younger poet symbolically converts the older to his own doctrine, a 'conversion' comparable to Blake's of Milton in his *Milton*). This poet is, like Shakespeare's Ajax, 'a thing [i.e., a man] per se and stands alone'. By contrast, the chameleon Keatsian poet is a being of immense variety and breadth, delighting in every level of existence, unconfined by puritanical or rationalistic restraints. All his imaginative creations, whether dark or bright, treacherous or wronged, Iago or Imogen, 'end in speculation' for the reader and are accompanied by the ranging delight he feels in the poet of 'no Identity', 'no self'. This poet is the purified Blakean Milton, completely free of the sin of selfhood and escaped into or 'filling some other Body'. For such a poet, 'it is a wretched thing to confess; but is a very fact that not one word I ever utter can be taken for granted as an opinion growing out of my identical nature – how can it, when I have no nature?' Shakespeare is Keats's example *par excellence* of the poet who possesses Negative Capability. Such a poet quite literally lives not in the limited self but in other selves, where is his true home: when 'in a room with People . . . then not myself goes home to myself: but the identity of every one in the room begins to [*for* so?] to press upon me that, I am in a very little time an[ni]hilated – not only among Men; it would be the same in a Nursery of children' (I, 387). Thus did Keats carry out, in the great generous depths of his being, the Blakean, Christian command: 'Selfhood . . . must be put off & annihilated.'[14] None of this implies that Keats suffered gladly dull or uninteresting persons, 'unpleasant human identities . . . people who have no light and shade'. To be in such company is 'a capital punishment' (17 March 1819: KL, II, 77). He was of course selective.

The Byronic and the Shelleyan chameleon poet, each in his different way, could sometimes but not always attain this loss of the sense of identity. In his self-pitying 'Stanzas written in Dejection – December 1818, near Naples' Shelley failed. At the end of his journal kept for Augusta in September 1816 Byron recorded his own failure: nothing he had seen in his tour of the Alps had, he said, 'enabled me to lose my own wretched identity in the majesty & the power and the Glory – around – above – & beneath me'.[15] Keats's poet, by contrast, 'is continually in for – and filling some other Body – The Sun, the Moon, the Sea and Men and Women'. This is the expansionist urge to move outside the self, to unite with that which is the not-self, evident in all these poets, and of which one of Keats's great expressions is in *Endymion*, I, ll. 777–815. Such a selfless poet has a 'relish of the dark side of things' as well as a 'taste for the bright one'. He delights in all aspects of existence, unlike the 'virtuous philosop[h]er', who may be shocked within his rigidly moralistic system of thought (KL, I, 387).

The experience of self-annihilation may succeed or fail on any of several levels: the imaginative or artistically creative, the spiritual or religious, and the purely ethical. Keats could achieve it variously, sometimes as a temporary escape from a sense of unhappiness. He could not believe in any but present happiness. His sense of beauty awakened before the 'setting sun', and such an experience gave a rise to his spirits. 'If a Sparrow come before my Window I take part in its existince [sic] and pick about the Gravel.'[16] Imaginative identification with either sunset or sparrow could lift him out of depression. In these passages Keats describes an exercise in empathy. Experience of sorrow tests a man's resilience. 'The first thing that strikes me on hea[r]ing a Misfortune having befalled another is this. "Well it cannot be helped – he will have the pleasure of trying the resources of his spirit["]' (KL, I, 186). This same letter also generalizes on an intellectual and abstract level about the difference between men of power, 'who have a proper self', and men of genius, who are 'great as certain ethereal Chemicals operating on the Mass of neutral intellect – by [*for* but] they have not any individuality, any determined Character' (I, 184). They function as catalysts, in other words, and will alter the very nature of the relationship between man and society. This action is performed most effectively by means of poems of epic grandeur written by a poet with a dramatic or Shakespearean genius, able to efface himself and enter into a host of dramatic characters. Such poets are the Shelleyan 'unacknowledged legislators of the world'. The same kind of speculation, phrased in more personal or limited terms, appears near the end of the Chameleon–Poet letter: 'But even now I am perhaps not speaking from myself; but from some character in whose soul I now live' (I, 388).

The annihilation of self by means of empathy need not

involve identification with living persons: the imaginative experience may begin and end with the imagination. As Keats felt the power of his imagination strengthening, he felt increasingly that he did 'not live in this world alone but in a thousand worlds', *surrounded* by 'shapes of epic greatness'. 'Then "Tragedy, with scepter'd pall, comes sweeping by". According to my state of mind I am with Achilles shouting in the Trenches or with Theocritus in the Vales of Sicily' or with Shakespeare's Troilus, into whom he throws his 'whole being . . . and . . . melt[s] into the air' (24 October 1818: KL, I, 403–4). Here Keats speaks of himself as a kind of ideal reader interacting with the work of literature. Such interaction, he implies, should be a repetition of the poet's interaction with his own writing.

Whether as writer or reader, there is a dramatic outpouring of the self into some other being or thing, which may produce poetic results as different as the Blakean lines of 'Where's the Poet?' – ' 'Tis the man who with a bird, / Wren or eagle, finds his way to / All its instincts' (ll. 8–10) – and the 'Ode to a Nightingale'. The lesser poem is an exercise in definition: to the Keatsian poet even 'the tiger's yell / Comes articulate, and presseth / On his ear like mother-tongue' (ll. 13–15). The Nightingale Ode, by contrast, is structured like the record of an exploration, ending on a question. It was written by a Shakespearean poet of Negative Capability, who 'is capable of being in uncertainties, Mysteries, doubts, without any irritable reaching after fact & reason. . . . With a great poet the sense of Beauty overcomes every other consideration, or rather obliterates all consideration' – or calculation, or deliberation (21, 27[?] December 1817: KL, I, 193, 194). Dilke, with whom Keats had had a 'disquisition', was again the catalyst for a new insight. The opposing terms or concepts are of interest, suggesting as they do a quite Byronic distrust of elaborate intellectual systems of thought: a fine isolated truth versus systematic fact and reason (or, put another way, the single unique insight versus a consideration'.[17] So far had Keats come by the end of 1817; as late as 24 September 1819 he could still find in Dilke the very opposite of the man of Negative Capability (KL, II, 213). Nevertheless, Keats came increasingly to reconcile such opposite or seemingly discordant pairs of elements as beauty and truth, 'consequitive reasoning' and the real need for knowledge. And, paradoxically, it was Keats's talent for avoiding the 'irritable reaching' after self-justification in argument that encouraged him to seek reconciliation of his contraries.

An example of such reconciliation occurs even in the letter on Negative Capability, where Shakespeare's *Lear* provides the example of 'the excellence of every Art', which is 'its intensity, capable of making all disagreeables evaporate, from their being in close relationship with Beauty & Truth' (KL, I, 192). To evaporate, one may recall, is to change a liquid (or a solid) into gaseous form by means of heat, to transform, in other words, the apparent nature of reality, even as Wordsworth and Coleridge had planned to do in *Lyrical Ballads*, as they divided up their labours, 'by awakening the mind's attention from the lethargy or custom, and directing it to the loveliness and the wonders of the world before us'.[18] The world, in short, was to be transformed in the mind by the poem and its beauty truly revealed. So it was also, Keats perceived, in *Lear*, a play not only of transformation (Lear himself) but also of revelation (Cordelia reveals her true self to Lear, Edgar to his father Gloucester) and reconciliation.[19] Unlike West's painting of *Death on the Pale Horse*, in *King Lear* the 'unpleasantness', the 'repulsiveness' is buried – it is dead, not alive – by the 'momentous depth of speculation excited' by the play. The 'disagreeables' have been transformed because of the 'speculation' to produce finally an imaginative thing of 'Beauty' (KL, I, 192).

Keats wrote a great deal about beauty, associated with truth not only by the Grecian Urn. When he said that he could never 'feel certain of any truth but from a clear perception of its Beauty' (31 December 1818: KL, II, 19), he meant that the effect of beauty was therapeutic and ethical. 'The mighty abstract Idea I have of Beauty in all things stifles the more divided and minute domestic happiness' (24 October 1818: I, 403), which is to say, as Blake expressed it, 'You must leave Fathers & Mothers & Houses & Lands if they stand in the way of Art.'[20] As late as February 1820, he expressed regret that he had created 'no immortal work', but, he added as a kind of counterweight, 'I have lov'd the principle of beauty in all things' (KL, II, 263). Such love also strengthens the spirit by making it independent or inner-oriented: 'Praise or blame has but a momentary effect on the man whose love of beauty in the abstract makes him a severe critic on his own Works' (8 October 1818: I, 373). But Keats's most extended and profound exploration of beauty and associated subjects occurs in his letter of 22 November 1817 to Bailey, which expresses a good part of his aesthetics. Here we learn that it is love, like all the other 'Passions' in their sublime form or aspect, that is 'creative of essential Beauty' (I, 184), thus transforming our vision of life and revealing its true nature. Keats refers to a passage in *Endymion* (I, ll. 777–815) where love is sung and celebrated as the great creative force that activates the imagination and permits rich and 'self-destroying' 'enthralments'.[21] These lead Endymion to his final realization that Cynthia and the Maid of Sorrow are one. The feminine characters have been reconciled – heaven and earth have been reconciled – and Endymion finally sees the truth, led to it by his imagination. As Keats explained to his publisher John Taylor, the writing of this passage toward the end of the first book of *Endymion* 'was a regular stepping of the Imagination towards a Truth' (30 January 1818: KL, I, 218). Thus the creative imagination, as Keats had written Bailey on 22 November 1817, 'may be compared to Adam's dream' of the creation of the beautiful Eve: 'he awoke and found it truth' (I, 185). There she was, the first female universal particular, palpable and meaningful, symbol of all others to follow.

As for the Maid of Sorrow, subject of Keats's 'little song' of Book IV, Endymion's relations with her extend his knowledge of all that Cynthia represents: the essential beauty, the ultimate truth or reality, includes the 'human' maiden. This is the truth that the imagination first seized or recognized as Beauty. Sorrow has been transformed, as in *Lear*, and opposite or discordant qualities reconciled in union at the end.

Keats's highly speculative discussion in the letter to Bailey, which includes the exclamation 'O for a Life of Sensations rather than of Thoughts' (KL, I, 185), begins with a statement on beauty, truth and imagination.

> I am certain of nothing but of the holiness of the Heart's affections and the truth of Imagination – What the imagination seizes as Beauty must be truth – whether it existed before or not – for I have the same Idea of all our Passions as of Love[.] they are all in their sublime, creative of essential Beauty. (I, 184)

The latter part of this statement illuminates the earlier and says essentially the same thing. Love, Keats writes, is 'creative of' – it does not create – the essence of Beauty. But it is the imagination that is the precedent term, and *it* is the primarily creative power. For 'what the imagination seizes as Beauty', or makes its own or apprehends as beauty, *must* exist – 'whether it existed before or not'. That which is newly or freshly apprehended is in fact newly created. As Blake said, 'Mental Things are alone Real' or truly existent.[22] Shelley expressed the idea somewhat differently: 'nothing exists except but as it is perceived'.[23] The imaginative and sensual apprehension of that which is ideal – ' "a Vision in the form of Youth", a Shadow of reality to come' – is clearly different from truth arrived at by 'consequitive reasoning' (KL, I, 185). Although Keats had 'never yet been able to perceive how any thing can be known for truth' by such means, he recognized that 'it must be'. This same letter moves on to describe 'a complex Mind – one that is imaginative and at the same time careful of its fruits – who would exist partly on sensation [experience acquired through the senses] partly on thought – to whom it is necessary that years should bring the philosophic Mind' (I, 186), as in Wordsworth's Intimations Ode. The extreme, discordant elements have again been reconciled.

This is not to deny that Keats's thought has in it a strain of antirationalism, which may express itself in terms quite Wordsworthian in their wise passiveness: 'let us not therefore go hurrying about . . . buzzing here and there impatiently from a knowledge of what is to be arrived at: but let us open our leaves like a flower and be passive and receptive – budding patiently under the eye of Apollo' (19 February 1818: KL, I, 232). 'Diligent Indolence' may become a richly productive state of mind reconciling opposite, normally discordant qualities (I, 231). All poets wait passively for the Spirit of the muse to descend upon them, including Byron when the *'estro'* is upon him.[24] However, we may read Keats's 'What the Thrush Said' in the same way that we read Wordsworth's 'The Tables Turned'. Neither poem asserts that every man on every day will learn more from a single impulse of a vernal wood than all the sages can teach. Keats was capable of writing on 27 February 1818 that 'if Poetry comes not as naturally as the Leaves to a tree it had better not come at all' (KL, I, 238–9). Similarly, the effect of the poem upon the reader should seem to be a natural thing: 'the rise, the progress, the setting of imagery should like the Sun come natural [to the reader] – shine over him and set soberly' (I, 238). One is reminded here of Shelley's great painting growing as naturally 'under the power of the artist as a child in the mother's womb'.[25]

Nevertheless, Keats did indeed fret after knowledge. The need to possess it became urgent for him. However, he drew a distinction between systematic, abstract reasoning, distrusting it as deeply as Blake and Byron distrusted it, and genuine knowledge. Temperamentally, all three poets were unfitted to put on the show of logic that Godwin, for example, was capable of. Keats wrote, as we have seen, that he did not wish to be a 'Reasoner' because he did not care 'to be in the right' (KL, I, 243). Apollonius is his fallen Urizen-figure. Keats's 'Read me a lesson, Muse', written upon the top of Ben Nevis, measures the distance between his mind and Wordsworth's on Mount Snowdon, the elder poet finding there with magnificent certainty 'the emblem of a mind / That feeds upon infinity, that broods / Over the dark abyss' (*Prelude*, XIV, ll. 70–2). Keats upon the summit of Ben Nevis wrote a symbolist poem also, but the sullen mist he found provided him with a symbol of ignorance (to be overcome), not knowledge. Dilke, whose mind ran on nothing but *Political Justice* and his son, was one of 'the stubborn arguers' of the world who 'never begin upon a subject they have not preresolved on' (24 September 1819: KL, II, 213). This way of proceeding allows for no progress at all, of course, and illustrates the kind of sterile, uncreative thinking that is the opposite of the insight characteristic of the poet of Negative Capability.

Such a poet or poetic thinker thirsts after knowledge, the highest form of which is knowledge of the suffering human heart. The felt need of such knowledge or understanding can be almost overwhelming in its intensity: 'I find that I can have no enjoyment in the World but continual drinking of Knowledge' (24 April 1818: KL, I, 271). In the Mansion of Life letter 'an extensive knowledge . . . helps . . . to ease the [Wordsworthian] Burden of the Mystery' (3 May 1818: I, 277). Wordsworth 'is a Genius and superior [to] us, in so far as he can, more than we, make discoveries, and shed a light in them', that is, illuminate

the 'dark Passages' of human life that the older poet explored in
'Tintern Abbey'. In Keats's view as in Sidney's before him,
England has produced 'the finest writers in the world' because
the English have caused them to suffer and to observe the suffering of 'the festerings of Society' (9 June 1819: II, 115). Thus
when 'Knowledge enormous makes a God of' Apollo, it is
chiefly knowledge of human suffering, of 'gray legends, dire
events, rebellions, / . . . agonies, / Creations and destroyings'.[26]
Apollo's 'aching ignorance' (l. 107) before his transformation
precisely parallels Keats's own state of mind when composing
his sonnet 'Why Did I Laugh Tonight': 'it was written with no
Agony but that of ignorance; with no thirst of any thing but
knowledge' (19 March 1819: KL, II, 81).

Although Keats thought that poetry 'should strike the Reader
as a wording of his own highest thoughts, and appear almost a
Remembrance' (27 February 1818: KL, I, 238), he also knew that
'Memory should not be called knowledge' (I, 231). Blake called
reason 'the ratio of all we have already known', but insisted that
it 'is not the same that it shall be when we know more'.[27] Knowledge, Keats wrote, is created by 'original Minds' and expresses
itself in the form of 'a tapestry empyrean – full of Symbols for
[the] spiritual eye' (19 February 1818: KL, I, 231, 232). Keats
had confidence that such originality, although obscured 'by
Custom', is possessed by many men.

Except allegorically, and not very clearly, as Apollo dies into
new life, Keats does not explain the nature of the new percep-
tion that transforms the Endymion-like youth into a god.
However, despite Apollo's passivity, Keats's own theories of
perception assumed a most *active* mind and imagination, very
different from the pale personification of Memory, which is
Mnemosyne and with whom Keats was obviously dissatisfied.
With one great revisionary leap from Mnemosyne to Juno
Moneta (the admonisher), Keats achieved that point where
Blake began: 'Imagination has nothing to do with Memory.'[28]
Moneta also recalls one of Blake's giant forms, and her allocu-
tion implies clearly that the poetic imagination cannot truly
exist unless it is an ethical imagination, feelingly alive to the
'giant agony of the world' (*The Fall of Hyperion*, I, l. 157). This
ethical imagination presupposes that the poet feels empathetically with all that lives. Then 'sure a poet is a sage; / A human-
ist, physician to all men' (I, 189–90).

9 English Romanticism: the Grounds of Belief

In the realm of belief, the second generation of Romantic poets moved beyond their distinguished predecessors toward scepticism. Although Wordsworth and Coleridge returned to the Anglican Church of their birth, neither Byron, Shelley, nor Keats was of any church in his maturity. All three had rejected organized Christianity. Shelley stated he had once been an enthusiastic deist but never a Christian.[1] For Keats the Christian was merely one of many 'Schemes of Redemption',[2] and Byron, characteristically, in the last years of his life was still conducting within himself an interior dialogue between the deistic and the Christian points of view. He requested Murray to send him a copy of Charles Leslie's *Short and Easie Method with the Deists*, but he also told James Kennedy, the Methodist minister who was attempting to bring him to accept orthodox Christianity, that he was 'not perfectly satisfied' with the author's 'mode of reasoning'.[3]

Unlike the earlier poets, no one of this later generation accepted Christ the Redeemer, though each spoke with the highest respect of Him. Keats, we remember, linked Christ and Socrates, even as Shelley had done in line 134 of *The Triumph of Life*. For Shelley, Christ is an 'extraordinary person' whose doctrines were 'quickly distorted' by the Church.[4] Byron as early as 13 September 1811 objected to the '*injustice*' of a diverse 'tyrant'[5] even as Keats objected to 'a certain arbitrary interposition of God . . . What a little circumscribe[d] straightened notion!' (KL, II, 101–2).

As had the first generation of English Romantic poets, the second generation also expressed the greatest reverence for the

Bible and for _Paradise Lost_. Byron indicated in his preface to _Cain_ that he had read Milton 'so frequently' before he was twenty that that poet had had a lasting influence upon him. He could not have written his _Vision of Judgment_, despite Southey, if _Paradise Lost_ had not been written earlier, and even _Don Juan_, in which, according to Paul Elmer More,[6] Byron adopted the only epic manner left for a poet of the nineteenth century, owes at least a negative debt (and probably much more) to Milton's poem. For Shelley, Milton is in the preface to _Prometheus Unbound_ 'the sacred Milton', and Shelley's great 'Lyrical Drama' is in fact more epic than dramatic. Finally, Keats did indeed achieve a Milton-like 'tenour and deep organ tone' in _Hyperion_ (I, l. 48).

Like their predecessors, each of the younger poets accepted as a fact the fallen or basically imperfect state of man. Byron wrote his _Cain_ in the impassioned terms and tones of a very nearly internal debate between Reason (Lucifer–Cain) and Faith (Adam–Abel). Shelley in _Prometheus Unbound_ has man himself responsible for the evil Jupiter, whom he empowers and thus in effect creates. _The Triumph of Life_ depicts a defeated and fallen race, without an effective Saviour, and the 'curse imposed on Adam' lives on in _A Defence of Poetry_, where we also learn that there is 'an inexplicable defect of harmony in the constitution of human nature' (SP, 293, 292). Keats's Vale of Soul-Making letter describes a 'System of Salvation' for 'a World of Pains and troubles' obviously in need of it. 'Man is originally "a poor forked creature" subject to the same mischances as the beasts of the forest' (KL, II, 103, 102, 101). Nature likewise is fallen for Keats on 21 April 1819, although not merely in the eye of the beholder: the fish can no more 'philosophise the ice away from the Rivers in winter time' than man can 'exterminate' the 'Poles . . . the sands of Africa, Whirlpools and volcanoes' (I, 101). Similarly cognizant of the destructive forces of nature external to man was Byron. We may recall his 'Darkness', the role of Ocean in _Childe Harold_ IV, and the shipwreck canto of _Don Juan_. Shelley was likewise aware, in a note to _Queen Mab_, of the 'wide-wasting earthquake, the storm'.[7] At one time he believed that 'the depravity of the physical and moral nature of man' could be traced back to 'unnatural diet' (such as that of Adam and Eve), which in turn originated in 'some great change in the climates of the earth' (SP, 81, 82).

All the Romantic poets agree then upon the flawed nature of man: it is essentially the sin of pride, Blake's selfhood, the absence of love for others. Evil in man is viewed in terms of separation or separateness, or of solitaries. Thus Wordsworth in *The Excursion* creates the Solitary, disillusioned, disappointed, and somewhat cynical, to be 'educated' by the other main characters, and in *The Recluse* the Wordsworthian persona finds 'a true Community' (I, l. 615), even as the Mariner at the end of Coleridge's poem comes to acknowledge his community with others. The proud and solitary Byronic hero normally achieves no lasting spiritual salvation. Manfred is guilt-laden and tormented, seeking above all else an escape from his remorse. Of the three younger poets, Byron is the most concerned with the suffering inherent in the human condition. For Shelley, 'the principle of self . . . is . . . the Mammon of the world', worshipped by all but the few in a time when there is 'an excess of the selfish and calculating principle' (SP, 293); as long as Prometheus is ruled by hatred, he is separated from Asia, the love-principle. Keats expresses his views on the question of self in an aesthetic context. Unlike the Wordsworthian poet of the egotistical sublime, the Keatsian poet has 'no self'. This chameleon dramatic poet of greatest empathy is 'an[ni]hilated' by the identity of others and enters fully into their existence (KL, I, 387), even as the spirit of Milton entered into Blake and eventually is redeemed. (As a result, the fictive Blake is also transformed.) But Keats believed, with Shelley, that 'complete disinterestedness of Mind' had been achieved perhaps only by Socrates and Christ (II, 79–80).

For all six poets, then, the solution to the problem of selfhood is the empathetic involvement that Keats suggested. No less than the older generation, the younger sought to escape from the self. This escape may be achieved by a union, communion, or marriage with that which is outside self, essentially an expansionistic urge away from the single centre of consciousness. The Keatsian poet 'is continually in for —and filling some other Body' (KL, I, 387). If a sparrow comes and picks away at the gravel before Keats's window, he picks away too. The spirit of the bird that cuts its airy way through the heavens is *not* closed to Keats's senses five. A key passage here, unlocking much of Keats's art, is that already examined toward the end of Book I of

Endymion (l. 777ff.). If the final goal is 'fellowship with essence', a union of the human and the divine spirits, the means to such salvation is 'self-destroying' love, with which 'we blend, / Mingle, and so become a part of it'; our souls 'interknit' and 'combine' with it. As Douglas Bush has pointed out, the 'clear religion of heaven' is 'Keats's version of Wordsworth's view of nature'[8]–the great difference being of course a difference in emphasis upon nature. The similarity resides in the metaphor of sexual union, with the resulting sensation of 'a sort of oneness' with man and, loosely, with the universe. Keats's 'Platonic' ascent begins with a sensuous apprehension of natural beauty, moves on to art (music and poetry), friendship, and love both mortal and divine, with the greatest number of lines in the passage being given to the love between man and woman. Upon all this one might speculate endlessly and compare with it such pronouncements of Blake's in *The Marriage* as his 'where man is not nature is barren' and 'if the doors of perception were cleansed every [natural] thing would appear to man as it is, infinite';[9] or his complex concept of contraries and their 'marriage', specifically his notions about the sexual union of man and woman, surprisingly like Coleridge's and, less surprisingly, like Shelley's.[10] One thinks also of Coleridge's pious hope of man's 'Reconciliation from this Enmity with Nature' and his persuasion that 'a *Poet's Heart & Intellect* should be . . . *intimately combined & unified*, with the great appearances in Nature'.[11]

Similarly, Shelley understood that 'the great secret of morals is love, or a going out of our own nature' (SP, 282) so as to achieve an imaginative identification with the non-self. Comparable to Keats's 'enthralments' in *Endymion*, love is, for Shelley, 'the bond and the sanction which connects not only man with man but with every thing which exists' (170). After Prometheus is unbound, the poem ends, as does *Endymion*, with union and marriage. Byron's 'Prometheus', written in July 1816, does not take the story that far and leaves the hero still bound: 'Thy Godlike crime was to be kind' (l. 35).

For a while during the summer of 1816, Byron viewed love as the great principle of the universe, and the narrator of *Childe Harold* III learns temporarily to live not in himself but to become 'portion' of that around him. With that he can 'mingle' and therefore he is 'absorbed' (stanzas 72, 73), even as Shelley's child

or poet in reverie feels as if he 'were dissolved into the surrounding universe, or as if the surrounding universe were
absorbed into [his] being' (SP, 174). He is 'conscious of no
distinction' between the two experiences. Such visionary union
assumes a monistic universe, the essence of which is love,
Endymion's quest; or as Shelley has the old man in 'The Coliseum' say, love is the 'Power . . . which interpenetratest all
things, and without which this glorious world were a blind and
formless chaos' (227).

We enter into such a world and become one with it in an
experience that is clearly imaginative, transcending the limited
world of outward sense but beginning in it. The impact of the
great basilica of St. Peter at Rome Byron experiences in stanzas
153–9 of *Childe Harold* IV. There his mind 'dilate[s]' and grows
'colossal', even as, earlier, it had expanded in the Alps, which
throne 'Eternity in icy halls / Of cold Sublimity' (III, st. 62).
Similarly, Coleridge, standing imaginatively in the Vale of
Chamouni (where he had never actually been) and gazing up at
Mont Blanc, *hears* the 'dread and silent Mount' 'blending with
[his] Thought',

> Till the dilating Soul, enrapt, transfused,
> Into the mighty vision passing – there
> As in her natural form, swelled vast to Heaven.[12]

The persona then calls upon the 'thousand voices' of Earth to
praise God, which in the poem's last line they do.

Although the aesthetic, the ethical, and the spiritual (or wor-
shipful or devout) are distinct, they may be closely associated
and often are. The imagination of Keats's poet of empathy,
'continuously in for – and filling' such symbolic bodies as sun,
moon, or sea but also the divine or holy bodies of men and
women, may function on the aesthetic, ethical, or spiritual
levels. Perhaps Shelley stated the concept most clearly: we go
out of ourselves and identify ourselves 'with the beautiful
which exists in thought, action, or person, not our own. A man,
to be greatly good, must imagine intensely and comprehen-
sively' (SP, 283). For Blake, the only life was the life lived
imaginatively, the existence that annihilated and transcended
self. In Book XIV of *The Prelude* Wordsworth finds that
'spiritual Love acts not nor can exist / Without Imagination' (ll.

188–9), a text well illustrated and adorned by Coleridge's Mariner.

The charity of Byron's imagination began at home, it would seem, with himself or with his own mind, or so, maybe, he would have it seem. It permitted that mind to escape from itself in the imaginative contemplation of nature or art in the act of poetic composition. Both Lady Blessington and Shelley saw a 'chameleon' in Byron of some similarities with Keats's chameleon poet of no self or identity. Indeed, Shelley, we may recall, not only discovered a chameleonic quality in all true poets but also concluded that Canto V of *Don Juan* set Byron 'far above all the poets of the day'.[13] Byron's volume including *Cain*, he believed, 'contains finer poetry than has appeared in England since the publication of Paradise Regained. – Cain is apocalyptic – it is a revelation not before communicated to man.'[14] Of himself, Byron wrote, 'like all imaginative men, I, of course, embody myself with the character while I *draw* it'.[15] At the very least, for himself, the Byronic imagination transformed the world; and the tremendous influence of his poetry makes it clear that it could do the same thing for his readers. Nor did Byron will such imaginative poetry into existence. It is not the product of the calculating reason but 'the feeling of a Former world and Future',[16] thus dependent in important part on experience or memory. It is also, significantly, prophetic, as Shelley said of *Cain*.

The poet who celebrated and exalted the poetry of Pope emphasized even more than Wordsworth the emotional origins of poetry. 'It is the lava of the imagination whose eruption prevents an earth-quake', he told his future wife.[17] 'Are not the *passions* the food and fuel of poesy?' he asked,[18] and obviously expected the answer to be affirmative. Here Byron approaches Keats, who claimed that 'all our Passions . . . are . . . creative of essential Beauty' (KL, I, 184). Elsewhere, Byron wrote that 'poetry is the expression of *excited passion*' and that 'poetry is itself passion, and does not systematize . . . does not argue'.[19] On another occasion he seems to express an impersonal theory of poetry: 'a man's poetry is a distinct faculty, or soul, and has no more to do with the every-day individual than the Inspiration with the Pythoness when removed from her tripod'.[20] At times Byron will even speak of poetry as if he were describing a

Wordsworthian recollection in tranquillity: 'As for poesy – mine is the *dream* of my sleeping Passions – when they are awake – I cannot speak their language – only in their Somnambulism.'[21] More colourfully, he expresses to Trelawny his more usual position, 'I can only write when the *estro* is upon me.'[22] The term derives from the Greek meaning *gadfly*, hence *stinging frenzy*, and today refers to the period of sexual heat in female animals. In Byron's opinion, then, the imaginative or poetry-producing faculty conceives in a very female and earthy or natural fashion. All these comments suggest that he believed in an organic conception of poetic origin. It is not surprising, then, to find that Byron wished 'to let [his] Genius take its natural direction'.[23]

The other Romantics also endorsed the idea that poetry must come spontaneously. For Keats, 'the Genius of Poetry must work out its own salvation in a man: It cannot be matured by law & precept' (KL, I, 374). In short, it is essentially self-creative, although as Keats well knew it must be nurtured by knowledge and discipline. Blake expressed the autonomous quality of poetic composition in somewhat less organic terms. Referring, it seems, to his *Milton*, he said: 'I may praise it, since I dare not pretend to be any other than the Secretary; the Authors are in Eternity.'[24]

If we view poetry in its origins and end as a process of natural growth or change, so we may also view life. The villain, the tempter, the accuser thus becomes any force that attempts to bind, limit, confine, or inhibit. The second generation of poets shared with the first a strong dislike for bonds or limits upon the individual's natural growth and so also produced a poetry celebrating process, growth and change: for example, Byron's *Don Juan*, Shelley's *Prometheus Unbound*, and Keats's two *Hyperion* poems. The tension between creativity and restriction expresses itself in the conflict between Coleridgean organic and mechanical form, the latter resulting when the poet imposes a system of predetermined rules upon his material. One thinks of Urizen's ten restrictive rules, the thou-shalt-nots.[25] Byron's *Don Juan* may be and has been read as a poem whose central rhythm and controlling concept are determined by his 'sense of life as endless movement and change'. The poem repeatedly satirizes attempts 'to restrain life, to bind and force it into some narrow, permanent form'.[26] Precisely at this point, by sharing their most important assumption, does Byron most easily and inevitably take his place again in the company of the Romantic poets: with Blake breaking the bonds imposed by Urizen, with Wordsworth escaping from the depressing limitations of Godwinian rationalistic theory, with Coleridge celebrating repeatedly the life principle itself.

We recall that Inez ridiculously limited Juan's education, Lambro sold him into slavery, Gulbeyaz forced him to disguise himself as a slave girl in a Turkish harem, and that every one of the heroines, in fact, attempted to capture and bind him. Not in all its cantos does the poem offer a single successful marriage. Indeed, during his entire life Byron resisted artificial restraints upon man's full development as compulsively as did Blake. One thinks of his recurrent interest in the figure of Promethean defiance[27] and of his near obsession with the notion of a vengeful deity who unjustly predetermines the fate of men and thus inhibits their freedom to grow. His own Romantic heroes are usually fated and sometimes very frustrated characters. Byron is, then, the poet and advocate of growth largely because of his insight into the elements that inhibit it. The education of Juan is clear nonetheless: he moves from innocence to experience, even if we are not allowed to look often or deeply into his mind.

Keats's Mansion of Life letter also moves, in its different way, from innocence to experience and beyond. Central to *Hyperion* is the theme of evolution or growth: ''tis the eternal law / That first in beauty should be first in might' (II, ll. 228–9). In that poem the deification of Apollo (which is also the birth of a poet) takes place *because* 'Knowledge enormous' becomes his (III, l. 113). Here and in other Romantic poems the growth is a growth in knowledge of human agony and strife. 'Sorrow is Knowledge', said Manfred (Act I, scene i, l. 10), and over the course of the poem he learns the full extent of that sad truth. As much might be said of *The Prelude*, which Coleridge in a letter to Wordsworth called 'the Poem on the growth of your own mind'[28] and which came about as a result of the agonies of Wordsworth's experiences in France and their aftermath. Like Coleridge's 'old Navigator', Wordsworth underwent growth through and as a result of suffering.

At best, following such a growth experience or enlargement of vision, the poet or his poetic character may finally perceive what Keats called 'the ballance of good and evil' (KL, I, 281).

Byron observed in 1821 that 'good and evil are pretty equally balanced in this existence',[29] a conclusion he may well have reached shortly after completing *Cain*. Shelley's *Prometheus Unbound* restores the balance of good and evil or imperfection, rejecting any Godwinian theory of man's perfectibility. At the end of the climactic passage closing Act III, after Jupiter has fallen, 'man remains', his lot immeasurably improved, but still man, subject as always to his human passions, to 'chance and death and mutability'. Keats also rejected the doctrine of the perfectibility of man: 'the nature of the world will not admit of it' (KL, II, 101). And Byron never considered such a doctrine: the facts were all against it.

To achieve an insight into the balance of good and evil is to achieve a variety of Coleridgean reconciliation of opposite or discordant qualities, coexisting together and even interpenetrating each other. Such an insight is not wholly distinct from Blake's contraries, 'necessary to Human existence', like his Reason and Energy, the former being in one guise the fallen, satanic Urizen but in another guise the essential 'bound or outward circumference of Energy'.[30] 'In the very temple of Delight', Keats discovered, 'Veiled Melancholy has her sovran shrine.' The inhuman Lamia, possessed of a 'sciential brain' able 'to unperplex bliss from its neighbour pain' (Part I, ll. 191–2), is kin to Urizen, who, unaware of the law of contraries, 'sought for a joy without pain'.[31] Byron also understood the mixed character of human nature: 'at the very height of . . . human pleasure . . . there mingle[s] a certain sense of doubt and sorrow'.[32] He concludes that Hope cannot exist without Fear. Keats, in an early sonnet 'To Lord Byron', found Byron's melody 'sweetly sad', his tale one of 'pleasing woe'. Shelley observed, 'tragedy delights by affording a shadow of the pleasure which exists in pain. This is the source also of the melancholy which is inseparable from the sweetest melody' (SP, 292). The idea finds its way into 'To a Skylark': 'Our sweetest songs are those that tell of saddest thought.' Blake had said it all more vividly and violently, Coleridge more philosophically when he found that 'one great principle is common to all' life and all the arts, the 'ever-varying balance, or balancing, of images, notions, or feelings . . . conceived as in opposition to each other; in short, the perception of identity and contrariety'.[33]

At times the Romantic poets adopted a formal, ornate, or Miltonic style. But no one of them permitted himself to be bound or limited by a single style. The rich variety of their insights demanded an equally rich variety of styles or modes. A poetry of process, recognizing the mixed nature of human experience and expressing the theme of growth or natural change, will most often express itself in a 'natural' diction, one nourished, however indirectly, by the living spoken language, and in generally informal styles, which, avoiding the elaborate, ornate, and rigidly structured, will nevertheless allow for simplicity and naturalness. Blake professed to be proud that his 'Visions. . . have been Elucidated by Children'[34] and some poems in *Songs of Innocence* do appear to be addressed to an audience of children. But aside from these, Blake's diction, once we subtract the proper names of places and persons, seems to be even simpler in numerous passages of the prophecies, which may be without all but the most obvious symbolism or irony. 'No man', Blake asserted, 'can think write or speak from his heart, but he must intend truth.'[35] The ballad style of the *Ancient Mariner* is recognizably akin to that of most of Wordsworth's contributions to *Lyrical Ballads* but easily distinguishable from it. Similarly, the style of Coleridge's conversation poems can never be confused with the conversational style of *Don Juan* or that of Shelley's *Julian and Maddalo*, subtitled *A Conversation*.

Obviously the notion of a conversational style implies tremendous variety, the variety of life itself. Every individual is capable of a number of styles: the Shelleyan voice of Julian is different from that of the *Letter to Maria Gisborne*, and the difference is determined in important part by the differences between Maddalo and Maria. Shelley wrote in the preface to *The Cenci*: 'I entirely agree with those modern critics who assert that in order to move men to true sympathy we must use the familiar language of men. . . . But it must be the real language of men in general,' he continues in a more Coleridgean strain, 'and not that of any particular class'. Shelley further stresses the element of the artificial when he recommends that his own contemporaries study 'our great ancestors the ancient English poets' (SP, 324). This advice Shelley himself followed, for as much as anything else the style of *The Cenci* is pseudo-Shakespearean. Saying this by no means damns the play, one of the best of the century, for its blank verse can be effectively spoken and the play has had successful productions. The style is 'natural', using 'the familiar language of men' to the extent that it permits a willing suspension of disbelief on the part of an actual theatrical audience. To conclude with the last and first of these poets, Keats called for a return to 'the old Poets' (KL, I, 225). He came to regard the style of *Paradise Lost* as 'a curruption [sic] of our Language' and left *Hyperion* incomplete, for he now believed that Miltonic verse could only be written in an 'artful or rather artist's humour'.[36]

The Romantic period was an expansive age, and all its major poets sought to express their free spirits in large, long poems of heroic proportions or implications. Coleridge, the seeming exception, teemed with thoughts in the 1790s for an epic poem, 'The Fall of Jerusalem', but never got it written.[37] In attempting an ambitious poem, the poet might himself become a hero and live heroically. We may note at this point the veneration in which all the Romantic poets held the great seminal writers of Western civilization. Blake, we have seen, valued Moses, Solomon, Homer and Plato. Among the poets of the second generation, one thinks of Byron's love of the Old Testament, Shelley's magnificent translations from Plato, the sense of high adventure that Keats found in Homer. In short, the Romantic poets were not eccentrics (as most of their contemporaries thought) but at the centre of Western literary tradition.

The second generation of Romantic poets had read their Wordsworth and Coleridge, comprehended their questions and answers, and felt a clear need to move on into pastures new. They more or less deliberately built new structures upon a number of typically Wordsworthian and Coleridgean bases. Or at times they refused to build. Quantitatively, they theorized less than their elders. They had little or nothing new to say, for example, about the nature of the symbol, about the relationships among the reason, imagination and fancy, about the reconciliation of man and nature. Byron wrote only two significant critical essays (one of which was not published during his lifetime); Shelley's major critical contributions are his Prefaces and his *Defence of Poetry*, the latter first published in 1840; and Keats left us his letters. This relative paucity of theoretical writing suggests that the second generation distrusted intellectual systems to a greater extent than did the first or had less need of them. Even Blake felt the need to construct an admittedly highly elastic system of his own or be enslaved, he thought, by another man's. Wordsworth was no philosopher but he created a 'philosophy' that is recognizably Wordsworthian, however inconsistent or vague it seems at times. Coleridge's mature philosophy and literary criticism we find magnificently consistent. But Byron clearly distrusted intellectual systems, as did Keats, and Shelley denied in his preface to *Prometheus Unbound*, completed near the end of 1819, that his 'poetical compositions' contained 'a reasoned system on the theory of human life. Didactic poetry is my abhorrence'.[38] Since the second generation of poets shared an unwillingness to submit to intellectual systems, a reductive force inevitably exerts itself in this brief recapitulation of the grounds of belief shared by all six major poets.

We have seen that Byron, Shelley and Keats, hardly less than their three predecessors, pored over the Bible and reverenced *Paradise Lost*. But even though the broad foundations of their Romanticism are both Christian and humanistic, they could not attain the security of belief that their predecessors had attained. They were basically less inclined to arrive at final conclusions. And yet the younger poets agreed with Blake, Wordsworth and Coleridge that man's nature was significantly imperfect and thus in need of redemption. Despite Byron's persisting interest in deistic thought, he is the most orthodox of his contemporaries on the subject of man's inherent imperfections and the need for redemption. Shelley's greatest document of redemption is *Prometheus Unbound*, whereas Keats's is his Vale of Soul-Making letter.

The three younger poets were nearly as interested in the nature of perception as their predecessors, although they were less clearly persuaded that an improved perception would produce a redeemed nature. However, as we have seen, Byron analyzed with great acuity the perceptual experience of Childe Harold in St. Peter's Basilica, where his mind, 'expanded by the Genius of the spot, / Has grown colossal'. For Shelley, nothing exists except as it is perceived, and Keats's old sophist Apollonius in *Lamia* is clearly a counterpart of Blake's Angel in *The Marriage*, whose metaphysics produced the monstrous Leviathan, indeed all that 'we saw'.[39] 'Do not all charms fly', Apollonius asks, 'At the mere touch of cold philosophy?' (Part

II, ll. 229–30). We may take his relentless gaze to be a metaphor
for his metaphysics, which causes Lamia to disappear and
Lycius to die. All this suggests that the younger poets, as well as
the older, understood that the mind does not merely mirror a
reality external to itself but engages in genuine creative acts of
perception. These acts alter the nature of human existence and
also transform nature by humanizing it, by rendering the external internal, bringing it indoors, as it were, and thus again
reconciling the great polar opposites.

As much as had the earlier, the later generation of Romantic
poets viewed the poetic imagination as an ethical or religious
imagination. The expansive empathetic power persists as the
only power capable of subduing the old enemy, Blakean selfhood, and annihilating the self in man's continuing quest for
community. The Romantic poets were repeatedly going away
from themselves and from each other, walking away or running
away, sometimes in silence and sometimes in despair; but they
hungered after community and recognized that the important
thing was to know where home was and to try to come back
again.[40] The larger structure in several of Blake's poems – *The
Book of Urizen, Ahania,* and *America,* among others – is circular,
ending in a coming together, a coming home, a return to unity
and harmony. The conversation poems of Coleridge – who
thought the best poems were circular in structure – illustrate his
awareness of the need for a return to community. Byron expresses his sense of community most clearly in terms of his
guilt-laden, suffering, solitary heroes, who never find a home.
(He succeeded in going home again – to Norman Abbey –
only through his persona in Canto XIII of *Don Juan*.) Poetically,
the sense of community, the felt desire or ability to identify
sympathetically and deeply with others, takes the metaphoric
form of a chameleon, which is virtually identical with the
Byronic concept of *mobilité*.

It would be unwise to close with an image of Romanticism as
some massive, transparent triangle constructed of such blood-
less concepts as organicism, dynamicism and diversitarianism, or
a similarly massive and transparent four-sided figure built of
dynamic organicism, imagination, symbolism and the unconscious mind.[41] Rather, it is salutory to remember the ages at
death of Byron, Shelley and Keats: thirty-six, twenty-nine and
twenty-five respectively. They were, chronologically, young

men, unlike Blake in 1824 (the year of Byron's death), aged sixty-seven; Wordsworth, aged fifty-four; and Coleridge, aged fifty-two. We are concerned, in short, not merely with two generations but with an older generation that outlived by many years the younger and lived through experiences that the younger could not duplicate. For whatever reasons, the writers of the first generation achieved a poetically expressed sense of security that we do not find in the later poetry of the second generation. Blake saw the New Jerusalem and described it more than once in his poetry – in 'Night the Ninth' of *The Four Zoas*, for example, and at the end of *Jerusalem*; Wordsworth solved his deepest problems and succeeded in finding 'Home at Grasmere'; the old Mariner had preceded him by several years in going home, where he found a new purpose in life, as Coleridge himself was to do in the Christian church. But Byron, as first-person narrator viewing events at Norman Abbey, returned to his boyish antics as 'the Abbot' of Newstead Abbey, and at the end Juan discovers, concealed beneath the robes of the ghostly Black Friar, only the too solid flesh of 'her frolic Grace – Fitz-Fulke'; Shelley's Prometheus withdraws to his cave with Asia, not to reappear, and we are left with the magnificently inhuman ballet of earth and moon; and Keats's poet-persona can communicate only with the goddess Moneta (the admonisher) and overhear the sadly weakened voices of the fallen Titans.

Notes and References

PREFACE

1. Morse Peckham, 'Romanticism: The Present State of Theory' (1965), in *The Triumph of Romanticism: Collected Essays* (Columbia: University of South Carolina Press, 1970) p. 58.
2. Earl R. Wasserman, 'The English Romantics: The Grounds of Knowledge', *Studies in Romanticism,* 4 (Autumn 1964) p. 17.
3. Walter Jackson Bate, *From Classic to Romantic: Premises of Taste in Eighteenth-Century England* (1946; New York: Harper, 1961) p. 164.

CHAPTER 1: INTRODUCTION

1. Shelley, *The Revolt of Islam,* VIII, st. xix.
2. Charles Tomlinson, 'A Meditation on John Constable', in *Selected Poems 1951–1974* (London: Oxford University Press, 1978) p. 21.
3. A large bibliography has attached itself to the beliefs of the Romantic poets. Modern discussions often begin with T. E. Hulme's definition of Romanticism as 'spilt religion'. A standard study for this period, somewhat vitiated by its firmly Anglican viewpoint, remains Hoxie Neale Fairchild's *Religious Trends in English Poetry,* vol. III, *1780–1830 Romantic Faith* (1949). An important related study is James Benziger's *Images of Eternity: Studies in the Poetry of Religious Vision from Wordsworth to T. S. Eliot* (1962). Of the Romantics, he has chapters on Wordsworth, Shelley and Keats, prefaced by one on the 'Transcendentalizing Imagination'. The chapter, 'The Romantics: 1780–1840', in A. S. P. Woodhouse's *The Poet and His Faith: Religion and Poetry in England from Spenser to Eliot and Auden* (1965) I found too generalized to be of much use. Stephen Prickett's chapter on 'The Religious Context' in *The Romantics* (New York: Holmes & Meier, 1981), ed. Prickett, provides the best recent overall discussion that I have seen. 'For evidence that Romanticism . . . was primarily a religious phenomenon,'Prickett writes, 'we need to look not merely at contemporary changes in the emotional climate but also at the transformation of the whole way of understanding religious belief that underlay those changes' (p. 143). The latter part of this statement sums up one of the purposes behind this book.

161

In notes to subsequent chapters I mention a number of studies that focus on the beliefs of the individual poets.

4. Any discussion of selfhood needs of course to be supplemented by an antithetical view: that the self is genius as well as demon. This central Romantic contradiction appears in its completed form as early as Goethe's *Werther*.

5. Jerome J. McGann, 'On Byron', *Studies in Romanticism*, 16 (Fall 1977) pp. 576, 577. This position by no means excludes others that argue for continuities between the Enlightenment and the early nineteenth century, e.g., most recently, James Engell's *The Creative Imagination: Enlightenment to Romanticism* (1981) and, earlier, Walter Jackson Bate's *From Classic to Romantic* (1946).

6. SP, p. 318. Cf. Shelley's comment in a letter of 15 October 1819 to his publisher, Charles Ollier: 'A certain similarity all the best writers of any particular age inevitably are marked with, from the spirit of that age acting on all' (SL, II, p. 127).

7. 'Southey's Colloquies on Society', in Macaulay, *Selected Writings*, ed. John Clive and Thomas Pinney (Chicago and London: University of Chicago Press, 1972) p. 36.

8. 'Recollections of Charles Lamb', in *Collected Writings of Thomas De Quincey*, ed. David Masson, 14 vols (London: A. & C. Black, 1896–7) III, p. 42.

9. Walter Jackson Bate, *The Burden of the Past and the English Poet* (London: Chatto & Windus, 1971) p. 52.

10. Donald Davie, *Articulate Energy: An Inquiry into the Syntax of English Poetry* (London: Routledge & Kegan Paul, 1955) p. 165.

11. 'On Shakspeare and Milton', in *Lectures on the English Poets, Complete Works of William Hazlitt*, ed. P. P. Howe, 21 vols (London and Toronto: Dent, 1930–4) V, p. 53.

12. *Collected Writings*, ed. Masson, XI, p. 56.

13. BPP, p. 5.

14. Cited from *The Prelude to Poetry*, ed. Ernest Rhys, Everyman's Library (1927; London/New York: Dent/Dutton, 1951) p. 15.

15. *The Faerie Queene*, I, X, st. 55, in *Edmund Spenser's Poetry*, ed. Hugh Maclean (New York: Norton, 1968) pp. 122–3.

16. *Devotions Upon Emergent Occasions*, ed. Anthony Raspa (Montreal and London: McGill–Queen's University Press, 1975) p. 86.

17. 'On the Living Poets', in *Lectures on the English Poets, Complete Works*, ed. Howe, V, p. 146.

18. SP, p. 314; K. N. Cameron, *Shelley: The Golden Years* (Cambridge, Mass.: Harvard University Press, 1974) p. 115.

19. John Hollander, 'Blake and the Metrical Contract', in *From Sensibility to Romanticism: Essays Presented to Frederick A. Pottle*, ed. Frederick W. Hilles and Harold Bloom (New York: Oxford University Press, 1965) p. 301.

20. E. D. Hirsh, *The Wordsworth Circle*, 3 (Winter 1972) p. 19. Morse Peckham, reviewing *Natural Supernaturalism* in *Studies in Romanticism*, 13 (Fall 1974), levels the same charge (pp. 364–5).

21. M. H. Abrams, *Critical Inquiry*, 2 (Spring 1976) p. 455.

22. E.g., Thomas McFarland, 'The Symbiosis of Coleridge and Wordsworth', *Studies in Romanticism*, 11 (Fall 1972) pp. 262–303; William

Heath, *Wordsworth and Coleridge: A Study of Their Literary Relations in 1801–1802* (1970); Charles E. Robinson, *Shelley and Byron: The Snake and Eagle Wreathed in Flight* (1976). As Donald H. Reiman has recently observed: 'If a poet "is a man speaking to men", then such humane examination of the mortal entanglements and struggles of the writers of the Romantic era should add to the resonance of their highly individual voices' ('Introduction' to *The Evidence of the Imagination: Studies of Interactions between Life and Art in English Romantic Literature,* ed. Michael C. Jaye, Reiman, and Betty T. Bennett [New York University Press, 1978] p. svi).

23. CL, III, p. 216. Coleridge–Thomas W. Smith, 22 June 1809.
24. BLJ, VIII, p. 132; IX, pp. 119, 189–90; X, p. 69.
25. 'Recollections of Charles Lamb', in *Collected Writings,* ed. Masson, II, pp. 41–2, 43.
26. In a review of Albert Gérard, *L'Idée romantique de la poésie en Angleterre* (1955), in the *Times Literary Supplement,* 21 September 1956, p. 552.
27. Jack Stillinger, 'Refurbish or Perish', *The Wordsworth Circle,* 2 (Spring 1971) p. 47. Walter Jackson Bate makes a case against another kind of artificial division: 'The persisting myopia of compartmentalized literary studies, especially English studies, is constantly seducing us into forgetting that Kant, Beethoven, Goethe, Schiller, Blake, Wordsworth, Coleridge – not to mention many others that we routinely associate with the "nineteenth century" – were all born and educated, and in some cases produced their major works, in the eighteenth century' (*The Burden of the Past and the English Poet,* p. 33).
28. BLJ, VIII, p. 201. Byron–Octavius Gilchrist, 5 September 1821.
29. *Don Juan*, III, st. 88; cf. *Marino Faliero: 'true* words are *things'* (Act V, scene i, l. 289).
30. The past two decades have witnessed an increasing divergence in Romantic studies between theorists, often associated with the Yale school or their epigones, and practitioners of historial scholarship. Much of the theoretical criticism practised by the Structuralists and the Deconstructionists resembles, as D. J. Enright recently put it, a 'sphere where secondary ingenuity tends to drive out primary texts' (*Times Literary Supplement,* 14 April 1978, p. 412). I consider various twentieth-century approaches to Romanticism in 'The "Folklore" of English Romanticism', *Mosaic,* 14 (Summer 1981), pp. 95–112. For a more extended analysis of recent trends in criticism, see Gerald Graff, *Literature Against Itself: Literary Ideas in Modern Society* (1979), and Frank Lentriccia, *After the New Criticism* (Chicago and London: University of Chicago Press, 1981). Lentriccia rightly criticizes the Yale school for its 'refusal to credit the historical . . . dimension of discourse'. He observes: 'On the matter of history, the deconstructionist position . . . appears equivalent to the position of the literary know-nothing, newly reinforced with a theory of discourse that reassures him that history-writing is bunk' (p. 182).

   Jonathan Swift seems to have foreseen the problem, *mutatis mutandis,* in Book I of *Gulliver's Travels.* The King 'asked the opinions of his learned men . . . , which were various and remote, as the reader may well imagine without my repeating; although indeed I could not very well understand them' (ch. 2).

31. M. H. Abrams, *Natural Supernaturalism* (New York: Norton, 1971) p. 13; *Critical Inquiry*, 2 (Spring 1976) p. 459.
32. Elsewhere, I have written: 'Romanticism is as much a European phenomenon as it is a congeries of national movements, and . . . it is folly to try to understand so complex and varied a phenomenon without seeing how it evolved within social, political, and cultural manifestations, within currents of ideas, that transcend national borders' (Clubbe, 'Romanticism Today', *Mosaic*, 7 [Spring 1974] p. 138). This I believe more than ever, but *that* book will be work for another day. It seemed wiser for the purposes of this one to adopt the above limitations.

CHAPTER 2: BLAKE AND THE NATURE OF PERCEPTION

1. David Erdman, in *Poetry and Prose*, p. 713. Blake permitted himself a comparable freedom of arrangement in his *Songs of Innocence and of Experience*. Citations to his poetry are usually given parenthetically to plate and line number, the abbreviated title of Erdman (BPP), followed by the page in Erdman's edition: thus JERUSALEM 6, 5–9: BPP, 147 means *Jerusalem*, plate 6, lines 5–9: page 147. When it proved impossible to give useful line numbers, I give only the page reference to the Erdman edition.
2. Among those who did use the figure is Wordsworth, who in a letter to Mrs Clarkson of January 1815 protested against the conception of a Supreme Being 'bearing the same relation to the universe as a watch-maker bears to a watch' (*Letters . . . The Middle Years [1812–1820]*, part II, ed. de Selincourt, rev. Mary Moorman and Alan G. Hill [1970], III, p. 189). And Coleridge inveighed against 'the mechanical system of philosophy which has needlessly infected our theological opinions, and teaching us to consider the world in its relation to God, as of a building to its mason, leaves the idea of omnipresence a mere abstract notion in the state-room of our reason' (*Biographia*, II, p. 59). But Byron wrote his publisher John Murray in 1819, 'It is an odd World – but the Watch has its mainspring after all' (BLJ, VI, p. 209).
3. BPW, I, pp. 29–30. Byron's poem often echoes Pope's 'The Universal Prayer'.
4. CPW, I, p. 429.
5. Thomas McFarland, *Coleridge and the Pantheist Tradition* (Oxford: Clarendon, 1969) pp. 27, 28. On this point, see discussion by René Wellek in *The English Romantic Poets: A Review of Research,* ed. Frank Jordan, 3rd rev. edn (New York: Modern Language Association, 1972) p. 236.
6. On Blake's views regarding the fall of man, see J. G. Davies, *The Theology of William Blake* (1948), ch. VI.
7. Shelley, Preface to *The Cenci;* Byron in a letter to Francis Hodgson, 13 September 1811, in BLJ, II, p. 97.
8. *Shakespearean Criticism,* II, p. 103.
9. BL, p. 28. Subsequent references to pages in this edition given parenthetically.
10. *Shakespearean Criticism,* II, pp. 103, 104.
11. WPW, II, p. 428.
12. SP, pp. 173, 174.

13. BPP, p. 555. In *The Valley of Vision: Blake as Prophet and Revolutionary* (University of Toronto Press, 1961), Peter F. Fisher elaborates on the relationship between the senses and the imagination (pp. 116–18, 241, 245). See also Robert F. Gleckner, 'Blake and the Senses', *Studies in Romanticism*, 5 (Autumn 1965) pp. 1–15.

14. 'A Skeptical Patrician [review of *The Education of Henry Adams*]', *The Athenaeum*, 23 May 1919, p. 362.

15. The classic account remains Northrop Frye's in *Fearful Symmetry: A Study of William Blake* (Princeton University Press, 1947) pp. 14–29. An intriguing recent study, on Byron but indirectly illuminating the problem of perception in Blake and the other Romantics, is Frederick W. Shilstone's 'Byron's *The Giaour*: Narrative Tradition and Romantic Cognitive Theory', *Research Studies*, 48 (June 1980) pp. 94–104. Shilstone's bibliographical notes cover recent developments in cognitive theory.

16. P. Medawar, *The Hope of Progress* (London: Methuen, 1972) p. 53.

17. R. Gregory, *Times Literary Supplement*, 23 June 1972, p. 707.

18. J. G. Taylor, *Times Literary Supplement*, 23 June 1972, p. 721.

19. CCL, II, p. 709. To Thomas Poole, 23 March 1801.

20. R. Gregory, *Times Literary Supplement*, 23 June 1972, p. 707.

21. BL, p. 69. On this distinction in Coleridge, see 'On Poesy and Art', reprinted in the Shawcross edition of the *Biographia*, II, pp. 256–8; *Shakespearean Criticism*, II, pp. 53–4; and the discussion in Chapter 4.

22. BL, p. 57. Compare Wordsworth's similar position: 'TASTE, . . . like IMAGINATION, is a word which has been forced to extend its services far beyond the point to which philosophy would have confined them. . . . Proportion and congruity, the requisite knowledge being supposed, are subjects upon which taste may be trusted; it is competent to this office. . . . But the profound and exquisite in feeling, the lofty and universal in thought and imagination; or, in ordinary language, the pathetic and the sublime; – are neither of them, accurately speaking, objects of a faculty which could ever without a sinking in the spirit of Nations have been designated by the metaphor – *Taste*' (WPW, II, p. 427).

23. Gilpin, *Three Essays* (London: R. Blamire, 1792) pp. 64–5.

24. WL, I, p. 500. To Sir George Beaumont, 31 August 1804.

25. Or, as he wrote to Trusler: 'I feel that a Man may be happy in This World' (BL, p. 30). Wordsworth reached a similar conclusion. Man finds happiness

> Not in Utopia, – subterranean fields. . . .
> But in the very world, which is the world
> Of all of us, – the place where, in the end,
> We find our happiness, or not at all!
> (*Prelude*, XI, ll. 140–4)

26. First published in *Romanticism Reconsidered* (1963), ed. Northrop Frye; reprinted in *Romanticism and Consciousness* (1970), ed. Harold Bloom.

27. Revelation, ch. 21: 1. For a brief but illuminating discussion of the Book of Revelation's influence on Blake's longer epics, see Joseph Anthony Wittreich, Jr, 'Opening the Seals: Blake's Epics and the Milton Tradition',

in *Blake's Sublime Allegory: Essays on 'The Four Zoas', 'Milton', 'Jerusalem'*, ed. Stuart Curran and Joseph Wittreich, Jr, (Madison: University of Wisconsin Press, 1973) pp. 37–8.

28. Compare Wordsworth on Pope: 'Having wandered from humanity in his Eclogues with boyish inexperience, the praise, which these compositions obtained, tempted him into a belief that Nature was not to be trusted, at least in pastoral Poetry' (WPW, II, p. 418).

29. 'Public Adress', BPP, p. 565. Coleridge returned again and again to the distinction between copy and imitation. 'An imitation is not a copy, precisely as likeness is not sameness, in that sense of the word "likeness" which implies difference conjoined with sameness' (*Shakespearean Criticism*, II, p. 123). Elsewhere: 'The pleasure [derived from poetry] may be traced to three exciting causes. . . . The second is the apparent naturalness of the *representation,* as raised and qualified by an imperceptible infusion of the author's own knowledge and talent, which infusion does, indeed, constitute it an *imitation* as distinguished from a mere *copy'* (*Biographia*, II, p. 30).

30. J. A. Froude, as late as the 1880s, ascribed Carlyle's inability to write inspired poetry to his want of 'invention' (*Froude's Life of Carlyle*, ed. Clubbe [Columbus: Ohio State University Press, 1979] pp. 206, 307).

31. KL, I, pp. 169–70.

32. BPP, p. 532. Wordsworth observes that the false taste of the age has led to poets focusing on 'those points wherein men differ from each other, to the exclusion of those in which all men are alike, or the same'. The true poet will establish 'that dominion over the spirits of readers by which they are to be humbled and humanised, in order that they may be purified and exalted' (WPW, II, p. 426).

33. BPP, p. 544. We should point out, as does Frye, that Blake uses the term 'allegory' somewhat ambiguously. See Frye's 'The Road of Excess' in *Myth and Symbol,* ed. Bernice Slote (Lincoln: University of Nebraska Press, 1963) p. 13.

34. CCL, II, p. 709.

35. Ibid., II, p. 864. To William Sotheby, 10 September 1802.

36. BPP, p. 555. This of course is only one of a number of ways in which Blake defines the Last Judgment. 'To different People it [the Last Judgment] appears differently as everything else does' (ibid., p. 544).

37. BPP, p. 267. 'But why Homers is peculiarly so, I cannot tell', Blake continued in 'On Homers Poetry': 'he has told the story of Bellerophon & omitted the Judgment of Paris which is not only a part, but a principal part of Homers subject[.] But when a Work has Unity it is as much in a Part as in the Whole. the Torso is as much a Unity as the Laocoon' (ibid.).

38. For Coleridge's distinction between the *natura naturata* (God reflected) and the *natura naturans* (God creating), see discussion in Chapter 4.

CHAPTER 3: WORDSWORTH: THE BLAKEAN RESPONSE

1. WL, I, p. 76. To William Mathews, 19 May [1792]. In 1798 Christopher, Wordsworth's youngest brother, became a fellow of Trinity College,

Cambridge, and in 1820 was elected Master of Trinity. In *Wordsworth's 'Natural Methodism'* (New Haven and London: Yale University Press, 1975), Richard E. Brantley takes up Wordsworth's indebtedness to Evangelical Anglicanism and argues with some cogency that he was at least as much Methodist as Anglican in his sensibility. For Brantley Wordsworth is fundamentally a Christian poet. So he becomes also for John A. Hodgson, who in *Wordsworth's Philosophical Poetry, 1797–1814* (Lincoln and London: University of Nebraska Press, 1980) finds that 'more and more after' 1805 Wordsworth 'modifies his metaphysical assumptions', arriving finally at 'something very like the God of Christianity' (p. xvi). No one can deny Wordsworth's powerful expression of pantheist or near-pantheist belief during the great decade, 1798–1807. But we wish to stress, against much current thinking, both the pervasiveness and the durability of his Christian background. Still an excellent commentary on Wordsworth's religious beliefs is Stopford A. Brooke's *Theology in the English Poets: Cowper – Coleridge – Wordsworth and Burns* (1874).

The religious orthodoxy of Coleridge, a friend like no other Wordsworth ever had, we discuss in the next chapter.

2. WPW, II, p. 240. Subsequent citations are given parenthetically by line numbers. Citations from the prose (unless otherwise indicated) are given parenthetically by volume and page number of this edition. Many of Wordsworth's key critical essays may be found in the second volume.

3. *The Prose Works of William Wordsworth*, ed. W. J. B. Owen and Jane Worthington Smyser, 3 vols (Oxford: Clarendon, 1974) I, pp. 41, 37, 45. This is not to deny that Wordsworth's prefaces and poems are filled with his faith in the natural goodness of the human heart and that he often sings of such goodness and virtue (e.g., *Prelude*, XIII, ll. 182–5). On this point, see Carl Woodring, *Wordsworth* (Boston: Houghton Mifflin, 1965) p. 113.

4. BPP, p. 655.

5. Henry Crabb Robinson, *Blake, Coleridge, Wordsworth, Lamb, Etc.*, ed. Edith J. Morley (Manchester University press, 1922) p. 15. In the passages reprinted in this book, Crabb Robinson enables us to gain a vivid sense of how Blake and Wordsworth responded to each other in conversation. See also *Henry Crabb Robinson on Books and Their Writers*, ed. Morley, 3 vols (London: Dent, 1938) I, p. 327.

6. The reader should keep in mind, in light of the discussion that follows, that Blake's not annotating a passage in Wordsworth does not necessarily prove anything.

7. See WPW, II, p. 429. Blake wondered over the neglect of genius in a letter to William Hayley of 7 October 1803: 'How is it possible that a Man almost 50 Years of Age, who has not lost any of his life since he was five years old without incessant labour & study, how is it possible that such a one with ordinary common sense can be inferior to a boy of twenty, who scarcely has taken or deigns to take a pencil in hand . . . . Such is somewhat like my fate & such it is likely to remain' (BL, p. 78). But he knew where his compensations lay. 'Yet I laugh & sing, for if on Earth neglected I am in heaven a Prince among Princes, & even on Earth beloved by the Good as a Good Man.'

8. As Blake had written in *The Marriage:* 'But first the notion that man has a body distinct from his soul, is to be expunged; this I shall do, by printing in the infernal method, by corrosives, which in Hell are salutary and medicinal, melting apparent surfaces away, and displaying the infinite which was hid' (BPP, p. 38).

9. WPW, II, p. 426. Wordsworth had made the point in a letter of 14 June 1801 to C. J. Fox: 'Michael' and 'The Brothers', he said, show 'that our best qualities are possessed by men whom we are too apt to consider, not with reference to the points in which they resemble us, but to those in which they manifestly differ from us' (WL, I, p. 315).

10. 'Tradition and the Individual Talent', in *The Sacred Wood* (1920; London: Methuen, 1948) p. 50.

11. How exquisitely the individual Mind
    (And the progressive powers perhaps no less
    Of the whole species) to the external World
    Is fitted: – and how exquisitely, too –
    Theme this but little heard of among men –
    The external World is fitted to the Mind.
                        (WPW, V, p. 5)

12. – Such grateful haunts foregoing, if I oft
    Must turn elsewhere – to travel near the tribes
    And fellowships of men, and see ill sights
    Of madding passions mutually inflamed;
    Must hear Humanity in fields and groves
    Pipe solitary anguish; or must hang
    Brooding above the fierce confederate storm
    Of sorrow, barricadoed evermore
    Within the walls of cities – may these sounds
    Have their authentic comment; that even these
    Hearing, I be not downcast or forlorn! –
                        (ibid.)

13. *Paradise Lost,* II, l. 622. Coleridge came to a somewhat similar conclusion. 'The philosophy of mechanism . . . in every thing that is most worthy of the human Intellect strikes *Death*', he wrote Wordsworth on 30 May 1815 (CCL, IV, p. 575). In *The Prelude* Wordsworth described mechanical materialism substituting a 'universe of death / For that which moves with light and life informed, / Actual, divine, and true' (XIV, ll. 160–2).

14. Presumably Blake has in mind the Newtonian mechanical universe of single vision.

15. *Times Literary Supplement,* 23 June 1972, p. 707. See also discussion of this point in the previous chapter.

16. Both italicized quotations are taken from 'On the Principles of Genial Criticism Concerning the Fine Arts', reprinted in the Shawcross edition of the *Biographia* (II, pp. 230, 239).

17. SP, pp. 282–3.

18. *Henry Crabb Robinson on Books and Their Writers,* ed. Morley, I, p. 327.

19. *Letters . . . The Middle Years (1806–1811)*, part I, ed. Ernest de Selincourt, rev. Mary Moorman (Oxford: Clarendon, 1969) II, 146, 150.

20. *Letters . . . The Later Years (1821–1828)*, part I, ed. Ernest de Selincourt, rev. Alan G. Hill (Oxford: Clarendon, 1978) III, p. 546. To William Rowan Hamilton.

21. *Letters . . . The Later Years (1829–1834)*, part II, ed. Ernest de Selincourt, rev. Alan G. Hill (Oxford: Clarendon, 1979) II, p. 704. To William Maynard Gomm.

CHAPTER 4: THE UNITY OF COLERIDGE'S CRITICAL THEORY

1. CCL, I, p. 354.
2. CCW, VI, pp. 468–9.
3. *Biographia*, I, p. 27. Elsewhere, we observe that Coleridge distinguishes between his purpose in the *Biographia* – 'an application of the rules, deduced from philosophical principles, to poetry and criticism' (I, p. 1) – and that of contemporary reviewers concerned to apply 'fixed canons of criticism, previously established and deduced from the nature of man' (I, p. 44). Yet, upon examination, these are not contradictory or mutually exclusive purposes: Coleridge did *both*.
4. WPW, V, p. 2. Preface to *The Excursion*.
5. See also Wordsworth's mention of 'Imagination' and 'fancy' in *The Prelude*, VIII, ll. 366, 373, and Jack Stillinger's note in *William Wordsworth: Selected Poems and Prefaces*, Riverside Edition (Boston: Houghton Mifflin, 1965) p. 558. The lines are alike in the 1805 and 1850 versions of the poem.
6. WPW, II, p. 441. Preface to the edition of 1815.
7. SP, pp. 173, 174; 'On Life'.
8. *Biographia*, I, pp. 15–16. Coleridge's mature view of Bowles would be far less favourable. Cowper remained a favourite.
9. Cited from the Shawcross edition of the *Biographia*, II, p. 253.
10. 'On the Principles of Genial Criticism', Essay Third (1814), cited from the Shawcross edn of the *Biographia*, II, p. 230.
11. CCW, I, p. 392. For discussion of the scientific controversies out of which Coleridge's 'essay' emerged, see Alice D. Snyder, *Coleridge on Logic and Learning* (New Haven: Yale University Press, 1929) pp. 16–23.

    Valuable studies on Coleridge's thought that take up several of the questions raised in this chapter include John H. Muirhead, *Coleridge as Philosopher* (1930); Thomas McFarland, *Coleridge and the Pantheist Tradition* (1969); and Owen Barfield, *What Coleridge Thought* (1971).
12. I do not wish to minimize the very great differences between Coleridge's and Blake's methods of argument. Richard Harter Fogle has pointed out to me that Coleridge, as an orthodox thinker, reasons in *threes* (thesis–antithesis–synthesis), whereas Blake's numbers are *two* and *four*. His sense of opposition is more violent than Coleridge's and he is likely to use the term *contrary*. Coleridge's opposites can be reconciled, but for him contraries are incompatible and therefore irreconcilable. He is not totally consistent in this policy.

13. CCW, I, p. 411.
14. *Shakespearean Criticism,* I, p. 181.
15. CCL, V, p. 35. To Thomas Allsop. The bracketed word is an editorial addition.
16. Wordsworth had a far more complex sense of language than he gives evidence of in the 1800 Preface – as many passages on language in *The Prelude* and his elaborate note to *The Thorn* testify. The problem lies more in his awkward and critically unsophisticated presentation of his ideas than in the ideas themselves.
17. WPW, II, p. 392.
18. CCW, VI, p. 312, *Table Talk,* 12 May 1830.
19. CCL, IV, p. 834. To the Rev. H. F. Cary, 6 February 1818.
20. CCW, V, p. 16. Although Coleridge accepted the fall, he avowed that he could not fully understand it from within.
21. CCL, I, p. 396. To George Coleridge, *c.* 10 March 1798. On Coleridge's religious beliefs, see Charles Richard Sanders, *Coleridge and the Broad Church Movement* (1942); James D. Boulger, *Coleridge as Religious Thinker* (1961); J. Robert Barth, S. J., *Coleridge and Christian Doctrine* (1969); David Pym, *The Religious Thought of Samuel Taylor Coleridge* (1978); and Stephen Prickett, *Romanticism and Religion: The Tradition of Coleridge and Words-worth in the Victorian Church* (1976), chs 1 and 2. E. S. Shaffer, *'Kubla Khan' and The Fall of Jerusalem: The Mythological School in Biblical Criticism and Secular Literature, 1770–1880* (1975) valuably supplements all of the above.
22. CPW, I, p. 116. Charles Lamb, who valued 'Religious Musings' as a significant theological statement, thought 'it the noblest poem in the language, next after the Paradise lost' (letter to Coleridge, [5 February 1797], in *The Letters of Charles and Mary Anne Lamb,* ed. Edwin W. Marrs, Jr, 3 vols to date [Ithaca and London: Cornell University press, 1975–] I, p. 95).
23. 'Religious Musings', ll. 147–55. 'Fancy's wing', we observe, has not yet become the wings of the Imagination.
24. BPP, p. 555. 'A Vision of the Last Judgment'.
25. CCL, II, p. 864. To William Sotheby, 10 September 1802.
26. 'The Eolian Harp', ll. 44–8. Humphry House in *Coleridge* (London: Rupert Hart-Davis, 1953) p. 76, points out that these lines did not form part of the poem as published in 1796. They are, however, close to the 1797 version published in CPW, II, p. 1022.
27. 'On Poesy and Art', *Biographia,* II, p. 258. For discussion of this idea in the Romantics and afterwards, see M. H. Abrams, *The Mirror and the Lamp: Romantic Theory and the Critical Tradition* (1953; New York: W. W. Norton, 1958) pp. 21–6.
28. The discussion here, as well as elsewhere in this chapter, is indebted to the brilliant *tour de force* that is Richard Harter Fogle's *The Idea of Coleridge's Criticism* (1962).
29. CCW, I, p. 402.
30. BL, p. 163. To George Cumberland, 12 April 1827. Compare also Blake's account of the origin of the Priesthood, an account strikingly similar to Coleridge's idea, in plate 11 of *The Marriage* (BPP, p. 37). Robert F.

Gleckner discusses the ramifications of this passage in the article cited in note 13 to chapter 2.

31. *The Notebooks of Samuel Taylor Coleridge: 1794–1804*, ed. Kathleen Coburn, 2 vols (New York: Pantheon, 1957) part I (text), no. 1618. Entry of 26 October 1803.

32. 'Hints Towards the Formation of a More Comprehensive Theory of Life', CCW, I, p. 396.

33. In the *Biographia* Coleridge spoke of the 'despotism of the eye' as well as of 'the despotism of outward impressions, and that of senseless and passive memory' (I, pp. 74, 77).

34. 'Hints . . . Life', CCW, I, p. 396.

35. 'Hints . . . Life', CCW, I, p. 373.

36. 'On Poesy and Art', *Biographia*, II, p. 253.

37. CCL, II, p. 864. To William Sotheby, 10 September 1802. As earlier the youthful Coleridge had praised Bowles's poems, so now, ten years later, he realizes that though Bowles 'has indeed the *sensibility* of a poet, . . . he has not the *Passion* of a great Poet' (ibid.).

38. 'On Poesy and Art', *Biographia*, II, p. 257.

39. CCL, II, p. 709. To Thomas Poole [23 March 1801].

40. Ibid., p. 707. To Thomas Poole [16 March 1801].

41. Ibid., p. 709. To Thomas Poole [23 March 1801].

42. CCL, VI, pp. 574, 575. To William Wordsworth, 30 May 1815.

43. *Statesman's Manual*, CCW, I, p. 433.

44. *Stateman's Manual*, CCW, I, pp. 437–8.

CHAPTER 5: BLAKE, WORDSWORTH AND COLERIDGE:
A PRELIMINARY SYNTHESIS

1. CCL, IV, pp. 833–4. To H. F. Cary, 6 February 1818. In an 1809 letter Dorothy Wordsworth mentioned a book in which several of Blake's songs of innocence and experience were first printed (*Letters . . . 1806–1811*, part I, ed. de Selincourt, rev. Moorman [1969], II, p. 368). Crabb Robinson in 1812 remembered reading Blake's poems to Wordsworth, who 'was pleased with some of them' (*Blake, Wordsworth, Coleridge, Lamb, Etc.*, ed. Morley [Manchester University Press, 1922] p. 1).

2. *The Romantics on Milton: Formal Essays and Critical Asides*, ed. Joseph Anthony Wittreich, Jr (1970), documents this enthusiasm by reprinting the key primary materials. Three essays in *Milton and the Line of Vision*, edited by Wittreich (1975), supplement this book: on the prophetic tradition in poetry after Milton (by Wittreich himself), on Wordsworth (James Rieger), on Shelley, Mary Shelley and Byron (by Stuart Curran). Specifically on Blake is Wittreich's *Angel of Apocalypse: Blake's Idea of Milton* (1975).

3. BL, p. 30, To Dr John Trusler, 16 August 1799.

4. WPW, II, pp. 439, 440. Preface to the edition of 1815.

5. CCL, II, pp. 866, 865. To William Sotheby, 10 September 1802.
6. *Table Talk,* 12 May 1830, in CCW, VI, p. 312. Suggesting the reverence with which Blake, Wordsworth and Coleridge regarded Milton by no means delimits his importance for them. In their view, Milton invariably 'needed correction'. One can argue with equal force that Blake had to redo Milton to free himself, that Wordsworth had to throw off Milton to find his epic subject in himself, and that Coleridge's failure to do either leaves his poetic achievement seriously incomplete.

   M. H. Abrams in *Natural Supernaturalism* (1970) p. 33 briefly details other instances of the first generation's intense interest in the Bible and in Milton. I discuss the response of the second generation in the chapters on each that follow and in Chapter 9.
7. T. S. Eliot, 'Dante', in *Selected Essays* (New York: Harcourt, Brace and Company, 1951) p. 231.
8. *Biographia,* II, pp. 215, 218. Cf. a letter of 1 October 1803 to Sir George and Lady Beaumont, where Coleridge states that his 'Principles' 'were Christian, for they demanded the direct reformation & voluntary act of each Individual prior to any change in his outward circumstances . . . : they were philosophical, because I contemplated a possible consequent amelioration of the Human Race in it's present state & in this world; yet christian still, because I regarded this earthly amelioration as important chiefly for it's effects on the future State of the Race of man so ameliorated' (CCL, II, pp. 999–1000). And in an essay on Milton Coleridge wrote: 'In all modern poetry in Christendom there is an under consciousness of a sinful nature, a fleeting away of external things, the mind or subject greater than the object, the reflective character predominant.' In *Paradise Lost* 'the love of Adam and Eve in Paradise is . . . a union of opposites, a giving and receiving mutually of the permanent in either, a completion of each in the other' (CMP, pp. 164, 164–5).
9. Of the many excellent discussions of this vexatious issue, see particularly Earl R. Wasserman's 'The English Romantics: The Grounds of Knowledge', *Studies in Romanticism,* 4 (Autumn 1964) pp. 17–34, and the last chapter of Bate's *From Classic to Romantic* (1946).
10. CCL, IV, pp. 574, 575. To Wordsworth, 30 May 1815.
11. In the 'Essay, Supplementary', WPW, II, p. 412.
12. *The Friend,* I, pp. 520–1, 520; BL, p. 163 (to George Cumberland, 12 April 1827); *Jerusalem* 10, ll. 13–15, 10: BPP, 151.
13. Douglas Bush, *Mythology and the Romantic Tradition in English Poetry* (1937); Hoxie Neale Fairchild, *Religious Trends in English Poetry,* vol. III (1949); T. E. Hulme, *Speculations* (1924).
14. Ronald Schuchard, 'T. S. Eliot as an Extension Lecturer, 1916–1919', *Review of English Studies,* n.s., 25 (May 1974) p. 165. Eliot's views on Romanticism were strongly influenced by the lectures of his Harvard professor Irving Babbitt, whose *Rousseau and Romanticism* (1919) is arguably the book most hostile to Romanticism, if not to Rousseau, ever written. For later manifestations of Eliot's dislike of the Romantics, see Clubbe, 'The "Folklore" of English Romanticism', *Mosaic,* 14 (Summer 1981) pp. 99–101.
15. CCL, I, p. 396. To George Coleridge [*c.* 10 March 1798].

16. *Letters . . . 1806–1811,* part I, ed. de Selincourt, rev. Moorman (1969) II, pp. 150, 146.
17. 'Hints Towards the Formation of a More Comprehensive Theory of Life', CCW, I, p. 396.
18. Only the passage in Corinthians speaks of 'the heart of man'. The closest of the other passages is John 12:40 – which would have Coleridge announcing the Messiah himself!
19. *Biographia,* II, p. 123; *Paradise Lost,* III, l. 44.
20. Not explored here is the relation between the 'Eden' of the first genera-tion of Romantic poets and the great burst of millennial enthusiasm set in motion by the French Revolution. E. P. Thompson places the numerous millennial movements in England within a larger historical context in his impressive study, *The Making of the English Working Class* (1963). See also J. F. C. Harrison's excellent *The Second Coming: Popular Millenarianism 1780–1850* (1979). For a brief discussion of Byron's ambivalent attitude toward 'Eden', see Clubbe, *Byron's Natural Man: Daniel Boone & Kentucky* (Lexington: King Library Press, 1980 [1982]) pp. 16–24.
21. 'Preface to the Edition of 1815', WPW, II, pp. 439–40.
22. 'A Vision of the Last Judgment', BPP, p. 545.
23. *Shakespearean Criticism,* II, p. 54; *Biographia,* II, p. 33.
24. CCL, II, p. 990. To Thomas Wedgwood, 16 September [1803].
25. BL, p. 69. To Thomas Butts, 6 July 1803.
26. SP, p. 186.
27. WPW, II, p. 390. 1800 Preface.
28. *Shakespearean Criticism,* I, p. 198.
29. BLJ, VI, p. 207. To John Murray, 12 August 1819.
30. *The Statesman's Manual,* in CCW, I, p. 436.
31. *The Notebooks of Samuel Taylor Coleridge: 1804–1808,* ed. Coburn (1962), part I (text), no. 2546. Entry of 14 April 1805.
32. *Biographia,* I, p. 11; *Table Talk,* 3 July 1833, in CCW, VI, p. 468.
33. BL, p. 57. To Thomas Butts, 22 November 1802. Elsewhere, Blake re-ferred to 'Popes Metaphysical Jargon of Rhyming' ('Public Address', in BPP, p. 565).
34. 'On the Principles of Genial Criticism concerning the Fine Arts', in *Bio-graphia,* II, p. 230; 'Preface to the Edition of 1815', in WPW, II, p. 439.
35. 1800 Preface, WPW, II, p. 400.
36. *The Statesman's Manual,* in CCW, I, p. 437.
37. Ibid., p. 438, and *Biographia,* I, p. 202.
38. WPW, II, p. 390.
39. WPW, II, pp. 387–8.
40. CCL, II, p. 864. 10 September 1802.
41. The problem can be in part one of degree: Wordsworth in 'Tintern Abbey' refers to what we 'half create, / And what perceive' (ll. 106–7).
42. CCL, II, p. 864. 10 September 1802.
43. 'Preface to the Edition of 1815', WPW, II, p. 436.
44. *Shakespearean Criticism,* II, p. 54.
45. BL, p. 69. To Thomas Butts, 6 July 1803.
46. BL, p. 163. To George Cumberland, 12 April 1827.
47. 'On Poesy and Art', *Biographia,* II, p. 253.

48. For a related perspective on the poem's Christian themes, see Jerome J. McGann, 'The Meaning of The Ancient Mariner', *Critical Inquiry,* 8 (Autumn 1981) pp. 35–67. McGann argues convincingly that the 'context' of Coleridge's 'religious and critical thought shows quite clearly . . . that the poem is, as it were, an English national Scripture' (p. 57). He finds in it 'a religious, a Christian, and ultimately a redemptive meaning' (p. 60).

49. *The Marriage,* in BPP, p. 34.

CHAPTER 6: BYRON AS A ROMANTIC POET

1. BLJ, III, p. 240.

2. LJ, I, pp. 341–3.

3. Ibid., II, p. 430.

4. As Byron wrote to Murray on 23 March 1820: 'I am now foaming an answer (in prose) to the Blackwood Article of last August.' He concludes the letter, 'I must now put myself in a passion to continue my prose' (BLJ, VII, pp. 59, 60).

5. BLJ, VI, p. 46. Byron–Thomas Moore, 1 June 1818. Byron frequently expressed his dislike of rigid codifying and of metaphysics, e.g., his parody of the Decalogue in *Don Juan,* I, st. 204–6. It was a constant in his thinking.

6. On Wordsworth's Preface, see *English Bards and Scotch Reviewers,* ll. 241–4, 250, and note; on the *Biographia,* see *Don Juan,* 'Dedication', st. 2; Canto I, st. 91, 205.

7. BLJ, IX, pp. 22, 30. 'Detached Thoughts', nos 29 and 53.

8. For a fuller account of the Byron–Scott relationship, see Clubbe, 'Byron and Scott', *Texas Studies in Literature and language,* 16 (Spring 1973) pp. 67–91.

9. Two unfinished sonnets written by Shelley in the summer of 1816 have recently turned up in a notebook found in a chest belonging to Byron's friend, Scrope Berdmore Davies. Judith Chernaik and Timothy Burnett published the sonnets in 'The Byron and Shelley Notebooks in the Scrope Davies Find', *Review of English Studies,* n.s., 29 (February 1978) pp. 36–49. See also Roland A. Duerksen, 'Thematic Unity in the New Shelley Notebook', *Bulletin of Research in the Humanities,* 83 (Summer 1980) pp. 203–15. On Byron and Shelley, see John Buxton, *Byron and Shelley: The History of a Friendship* (1968), and Charles E. Robinson, *Shelley and Byron: The Snake and Eagle Wreathed in Flight* (1976). The latter study probes Shelley's despair at 'rivalling Lord Byron'.

10. BLJ, VIII, p. 85.

11. BPP, p. 675.

12. See, for example, BLJ, I, pp. 179–80; II, p. 9; III, pp. 243, 257; IV, p. 219.

13. Ibid., III, p. 257.

14. Hazlitt thought that Byron's 'only object seems to be to stimulate himself and his readers for the moment – to keep both alive, to drive away *ennui*' ('Lord Byron' in *The Spirit of the Age, Complete Works,* ed. Howe, XI, p. 72). Goethe thought that 'Byron was indebted for the profound views he took of the Bible to the ennui he suffered from it at school.' See *Henry*

Crabb Robinson on Books and Their Writers, ed. Morley, I, p. 372. In an ironical epigram, Goethe calls ennui (*Langeweile*) the mother of the muses.

15. The prophetic poet, for one thing, does not contradict himself. Nor is he – as is Byron – pervasively ironic. Yet, as both Blake and Shelley recognized, Byron *can be* a prophetic poet. After reading *Cain,* Blake saw Byron as a true poet-prophet, a distinction he accorded no other contemporary poet, and in *The Ghost of Abel* he hailed Byron as Elijah. On Byron and Blake, or rather on Blake's response to Byron, see Leslie Tannenbaum, 'Lord Byron in the Wilderness: Biblical Tradition in Byron's *Cain* and Blake's *The Ghost of Abel*', *Modern Philology,* 72 (1975) pp. 350–64; Irene Taylor, 'Blake meets Byron on April Fool's', *English Language Notes,* 16 (December 1978) pp. 85–93; and Martin Bidney, '*Cain* and *The Ghost of Abel*: Contexts for Understanding Blake's Response to Byron', *Blake Studies,* 8 (1979) pp. 145–65. For Shelley, who found *Cain* 'apocalyptic', see SL, II, p. 388.
16. *LJ,* V, p. 591. Cf. IV, pp. 486–7.
17. Ibid., IV, p. 491.
18. Ibid., V, p. 560.
19. Ibid., p. 550.
20. M. H. Abrams, *Natural Supernaturalism* (New York: Norton, 1971) p. 13.
21. In Keats and Shelley – who died in their twenties, Shelley a month short of thirty – the pattern does not emerge with clarity, though the last poems of both give evidence of a change of mind on fundamental questions of belief. Still useful on Byron's speculations is Edward Wayne Marjarum, *Byron as Skeptic and Believer* (1938). Jerome J. McGann in *Fiery Dust: Byron's Poetic Development* (University of Chicago Press, 1968) pp. 247–55, considers Byron's religious beliefs from a perspective different from the one found in this chapter.
22. BLJ, III, p. 233. Cf. *Don Juan,* II, st. 209–15.
23. BLJ, II, p. 88.
24. BLJ, IX, p. 45, no. 96.
25. BLJ, VIII, p. 51.
26. BLJ, II, p. 89.
27. LJ, V, p. 554.
28. BPP, p. 792.
29. BLJ, II, p. 98. Byron–Hodgson, 13 September 1811.
30. BPP, p. 579. Annotation to Lavater's *Aphorisms on Man.*
31. BLJ, II, p. 97.
32. For discussion of Byron's fascination with the notion of a God of vengeance, see Lovell, *Byron: The Record of a Quest* (Austin: University of Texas Press, 1949) p. 198ff.
33. BLJ, VIII, p. 115. Byron quotes from Johnson's life of Dryden.
34. LJ, V, p. 470. Byron–John Murray, 3 November 1821.
35. BP, V, p. 210. Preface to *Cain.*
36. BLJ, IX, pp. 46–7.
37. See, for example, BLJ, I, pp. 114–15; II, p. 136; III, p. 64; VIII, p. 98; IX, pp. 46, 118–19, 123; X, pp. 137–8; and James T. Hodgson, *Memoir of the Rev. Francis Hodgson, B.D.,* 2 vols (London: Macmillan, 1878) I, p. 220.
38. Abrams, *Natural Supernaturalism,* p. 257.

39. LJ, V, p. 575. Italics added.
40. Ibid., p. 588. 'Entusymusy' is Byron's play – after John Braham – on 'enthusiasm' (see BLJ, III, p. 209).
41. See Abrams, *Natural Supernaturalism*, pp. 257–8.
42. *Memoirs, Journal, and Correspondence of Thomas Moore*, ed. Lord John Russell, 8 vols (London: Longman, 1853–6) III, p. 161. Michael G. Cooke in 'Byron and Wordsworth: The Complementarity of a Rock and the Sea' (in *Lord Byron and His Contemporaries*, ed. Charles E. Robinson [Newark: University of Delaware Press, 1982]) provides the best recent analysis of the two poets.
43. BLJ, V, p. 105.
44. *Oeuvres Complètes*, ed. Bernard Gabnebin and Marcel Raymond, 4 vols, Bibliothèque de la Pléiade (Paris: Gallimard, 1959) I, p. 1141.
45. See *Manfred*, Act I, scene ii, ll. 66–7, 85–7; Act II, scene ii, ll. 1–8.
46. BPW, II, p. 312.
47. Walter Jackson Bate, *From Classic to Romantic*, p. 154.
48. Abrams, *Natural Supernaturalism*, p. 258.
49. *Table Talk*, in CCW, VI, p. 312. 12 May 1830.
50. KL, I, p. 387. Keats–Richard Woodhouse, [27 October 1818].
51. *Don Juan*, XVI, note to stanza 97. E. P. Thompson has pointed out that the word has a political sense: ' "Mobility" was a term proudly adopted by 19th-century Radicals and Chartists for their peaceable and well-intentioned demonstrations' (*The Making of the English Working Class*, p. 73).
52. *Lady Blessington's 'Conversations of Lord Byron'*, ed. Ernest J. Lovell, Jr (Princeton University Press, 1969) pp. 71, 72.
53. SL, II, p. 358. Shelley–Byron, 21 October 1821.
54. KL, I, p. 387.
55. Ibid.
56. Ibid., p. 388.
57. BLJ, IV, p. 221.
58. Ibid., p. 219.
59. BLJ, III, p. 233.
60. See Lovell, *Byron: The Record of a Quest*, pp. 26–7. Moore's observation is penetrating: 'That he was fully aware not only of the abundance of this quality in his own nature, but of the danger in which it placed consistency and singleness of character, did not require the note on this passage [*Don Juan*, XVI, st. 97], where he calls it "an unhappy attribute", to assure us. The consciousness, indeed, of his own natural tendency to yield thus to every chance impression, was not only forever present in his mind, but . . . had the effect of keeping him in that general line of consistency, on certain great subjects, which, notwithstanding occasional fluctuations and contradictions as to details of these very subjects, he continued to preserve throughout life' (*Letters and Journals of Lord Byron*, 2 vols [London: John Murray, 1830] II, pp. 787–8).
61. LJ, V, pp. 590, 560.
62. Ibid., IV, pp. 486, 489.
63. Cf. *Paradise Lost*, VII, l. 31, and LJ, IV, p. 488.
64. So Francis Jeffrey read the poem in his largely unfavourable review: 'a

firm belief in the providence of a wise and beneficent Being must be our great stay and support under all afflictions and perplexities upon earth – and that there are indications of his power and goodness in all the aspects of the visible universe, whether living or inanimate – every part of which should therefore be regarded with love and reverence, as exponents of those great attributes' (*Edinburgh Review*, 24 [November 1814] p. 5).
65. LJ, V, p. 587.
66. Ibid., p. 547.

CHAPTER 7: SHELLEY: THE GROWTH OF A MORAL VISION

1. Harold Bloom, *The Visionary Company: A Reading of English Romantic Poetry*, revised and enlarged edition (Ithaca: Cornell University Press, 1971) p. 284, following Donald Davie's discussion in *Purity of Diction in English Verse* (1952).
2. See Shelley's discussion of the poem's 'familiar style of language' in his letter to Leigh Hunt, 15 August 1819, in SL, II, p. 108.
3. Joseph DeRocco, in his review of *Shelley's Theory of Poetry: A Reappraisal* by Earl A. Schulze: *Keats–Shelley Journal*, 17 (1968) p. 128.
4. SL, I, p. 135.
5. SP, p. 37, Shelley left many of his prose pieces incomplete and untitled, and we have not always adopted Clark's often unreliable dates, titles, or spellings of titles. James A. Notopoulos, 'The Dating of Shelley's Prose', *PMLA*, 58 (1943) pp. 477–98, dates several of Shelley's prose pieces more accurately than does Clark. We have drawn upon the notes to the three prose pieces ('On Love', 'On Life', and *A Defence of Poetry*) that are included in new texts in the Reiman–Powers edition of *Shelley's Poetry and Prose* and upon John E. Jordan's edition of *A Defence of Poetry* (1965). Jordan points out many of Shelley's debts to Sidney, to the other Romantic poets, and to eighteenth- and early nineteenth-century critical theory.

   The most thorough study of Shelley's beliefs, including his attitude towards Christianity and Christ, remains Ellsworth Barnard's *Shelley's Religion* (1937).
6. BPP, p. 2. References to Blake in this paragraph are to this page.
7. BLJ, II, p. 97.
8. SL, II, p. 122.
9. BLJ, VIII, p. 148. Byron–John Murray, 6 July 1821.
10. Donald H. Reiman has published a new text of this essay and of 'On Love' in volume VI of *Shelley and His Circle 1773–1822*, ed. Reiman (Cambridge, Mass.: Harvard University Press, 1973). Reiman dates 'On Love' to the summer of 1818, probably after 20 July (p. 639); 'A Philosophical View of Reform' he dates to the period from November 1819 to January 1820 (p. 954).
11. *The Marriage,* in BPP, p. 37.
12. SP, p. 207. For Blake 'the Covenant of Jehovah' was this: 'If you forgive one another your Trespessas [sic] so shall Jehovah forgive you . . . but if you Avenge you Murder the Divine Image.' 'The Everlasting Gospel', in BPP, p. 792.

13. BPP, p. 229. In other words, the corporeal does not exist for Blake: 'Mental Things are alone Real' ('A Vision of the Last Judgment', in ibid., p. 555).
14. BL, p. 47. Blake–Thomas Butts, 2 October 1800.
15. The last line of 'A Song of Liberty', in BPP, p. 44. Blake used the phrase in other poems.
16. SP, p. 172. Cf. *Biographia,* II, p. 6. Elsewhere, Coleridge in a 'Definition of Miracle' analyzed the various kinds of miracles, observing in a footnote that his definition has been compared to Dr Johnson's in the life of Sir Thomas Browne. Johnson wrote: 'There is undoubtedly a sense in which all life is miraculous, as it is an union of powers of which we can image no connection, a succession of motions of which the first cause must be supernatural' (cited from CCW, V, p. 543). In his 'Theory of Life' Coleridge posed the same question that intrigued Shelley: 'What is Life?' (ibid., I, p. 385). Shelley considered the question at least twice, once in 'On Life' and once at l. 544 of *The Triumph of Life.*
17. Coleridge–William Sotheby, 10 September 1802, in CCL, II, p. 864; 'Theory of Life'', in CCW, I, p. 387.
18. WPW, IV, pp. 463–4. Wordsworth's observations were made as a gloss to the Intimations Ode. Although Shelley's essay first saw publication in 1832 and Wordsworth dictated his note to Miss Fenwick in 1843, it is inconceivable that the older poet was recalling the words of the younger.
19. He also used it twice in his *Letters* (SL, II, pp. 30, 152).
20. *Biographia,* I, p. 202.
21. Wordsworth, in WPW, II, pp. 391–2; Coleridge, in chapters XVIII and XIX of the *Biographia.*
22. 'Poetry, therefore, is a more philosophical and a higher thing than history, for poetry tends to express the universal, history the particular', in *Aristotle on the Art of Poetry,* trans. S. H. Butcher, ed. Milton C. Nahm (New York: Liberal Arts Press, 1948) p. 13. Compare Wordsworth's 1800 Preface in WPW, II, p. 395
23. BPP, p. 527.
24. SP, p. 281. WPW, II, pp. 395–6; *Biographia,* II, pp. 9–10.
25. *Milton,* plate 38, ll. 34–49, and plate 40, l. 36 in BPP, pp. 138, 141; Wordsworth's 'Prospectus', ll. 60–1, 69, in WPW, V, p. 5. Shelley said all poets were 'camaeleonic' in a letter to [John and Maria Gisborne] [13 July 1821] in SL, II, p. 308. For Keats, see KL, I, p. 387.
26. BPP, p. 144.
27. SP, p. 325. Manfred, however, is unable to 'make my own the mind of other men, / The enlightener of nations' (Act III, scene i, ll. 106–7).
28. *Biographia,* II, p. 6. Both poets use the same phrase.
29. *Biographia,* I, p. 202.
30. KL, I, p. 238.
31. That Shelley took over almost verbatim from *A Philosophical View of Reform* (pp. 239–40) the final paragraph of his *Defence* suggests that he conceived poetry as emanating from, and crucial to, a nation's spiritual vitality. In regard to present-day England, a poetical 'new birth' heralded a political one.

CHAPTER 8: KEATS THE HUMANIST

1. KL, I, pp. 191–4.
2. BLJ, IX, p. 30. 'Detached Thought', no. 53.
3. See Hazlitt's 'On Shakspeare and Milton', the third of his *Lectures on the English Poets* (1818): *Complete Works*, ed. Howe, V, p. 47.
4. In 1963 Walter Jackson Bate spoke of Keats's poetry as being 'largely untouched by any direct interest in religion' (*John Keats* [Cambridge, Mass.: Harvard University Press, 1963] p. 133). Recent scholarship has argued convincingly for a life-long interest. For a comprehensive study of this subject, see Robert M. Ryan, *Keats: The Religious Sense* (Princeton University Press, 1976). Ronald A. Sharp in *Keats, Skepticism, and the Religion of Beauty* (Athens: University of Georgia Press, 1979) focuses more on the poetry than (as had Ryan) on the life and the letters. Specifically on one poem is Gail McMurray Gibson, 'Ave Madeline: Ironic Annunciation in Keats's "The Eve of St. Agnes" ', *Keats–Shelley Journal*, 26 (1977) pp. 39–50.
5. Of Clarke's father, Ryan notes that he was 'deeply interested and involved in the scriptural scholarship of the time' (p. 36). Enfield Academy provided Keats, 'on the one hand, . . . with much of his formal grounding in Christian doctrine and his familiarity with the contents of the Bible. On the other, the liberal atmosphere of Clarke's school provided a matrix for his initial questioning of his religious heritage' (ibid., pp. 44–5).
6. KL, II, pp. 49–51. In 'Keats and the Bible' Lloyd N. Jeffrey lists numerous allusions by Keats to the Bible in his poetry and letters (*Keats–Shelley Journal*, 10 [1961] pp. 59–70). Even Ryan, who finds Keats almost totally rejecting Christianity, is forced to admit, in regard to this letter, that 'there is not a single indication that the writer had any personal difficulty with the doctrines of which he was speaking' (p. 188).
7. Compare Byron: 'All history and experience, and the rest, teaches us that the good and evil are pretty equally balanced in this existence, and that what is most to be desired is an easy passage out of it.' 'Detached Thought', no. 95, in BLJ, IX, p. 45.
8. On Keats and Wordsworth, see Clarence D. Thorpe, 'Wordsworth and Keats – A Study in Personal and Critical Impressions', *PMLA*, 42 (1927) pp. 1010–26. John Middleton Murry's *Keats* (1955) has a suggestive chapter on Keats and Wordsworth – and one on Keats and Blake. The best recent brief discussion is at the end of the last chapter of Jack Stillinger's *The Hoodwinking of Madeline and Other Essays on Keats's Poems* (1971).
9. See KL, I, p. 137, and Ryan's discussion in *Keats* (pp. 112–13). On Byron's Christless Christianity, see Chapter 6, note 37.
10. For example, in a letter to his publisher John Murray of 24 August 1819, Byron compares himself to the Aztec chief Guatimozin, who, along with a favourite companion, was being tortured by Cortes to make them reveal the location of the royal treasure. When he saw his companion weakening, Guatimozin checked him by asking, 'Am I now reposing on a bed of flowers?' See BLJ, VI, p. 216, and William Robertson, *A History of America*, 3rd edn, 3 vols (London: W. Strahan, etc., 1780) II, p. 427.

Matthew Arnold observed 'flint and iron' in Keats's character. See *The Complete Prose Works,* ed. R. H. Super, 11 vols (Ann Arbor: University of Michigan Press, 1960–77) IX, p. 211.

11. BPP, p. 37.
12. KL, II, pp. 103, 102. Ryan in *Keats* provides an excellent discussion of this letter (pp. 196–209), seeing it as Keats's deliberate attempt to move beyond the Christian thinking of his day. Our reading stresses the Christian foundations upon which Keats based that attempt.
13. See discussion in Chapter 6.
14. *Milton,* plate 40, l. 36, in BPP, p. 141. Much of plate 38 also insists upon the need to put off selfhood.
15. BLJ, V, p. 105.
16. KL, I, p. 186. 22 November 1817. Keats's empathetic power was of such intensity that he could see himself frying in a 'Gridiron' (KL, I, p. 162) and as 'a sort of ethereal Pig' (ibid., I, p. 223). He once imagined himself a 'Billiard-Ball' (I, p. 147), which he conceived might 'have a sense of delight from its own roundness, smoothness volubility. & the rapidity of its motion' (*The Keats Circle,* ed. Hyder Edward Rollins, 2nd edn. 2 vols [Cambridge, Mass.: Harvard University Press, 1965] I, p. 59). On another occasion Charles Cowden Clarke, who introduced Keats to Spenser's *Faerie Queene,* noted in his *Recollections of Writers* (1878) that Keats 'hoisted himself up, and looked burly and dominant, as he said, "What an image that is – *'sea-shouldering whales!'* " ' (Fontwell, Sussex: Centaur Press, 1969, p. 126).
17. We may compare Keats's unease before reason unaided to Blake's marginalia, 'To Generalize is to be an Idiot [,] To Particularize is the Alone Distinction of Merit' (BPP, p. 630) and to Wordsworth's fears of the rational intellect in 'Expostulation and Reply', 'The Tables Turned', and 'A Poet's Epitaph'.
18. *Biographia,* II, p. 6.
19. The transformation of the world as it seems to exist within the individual consciousness also occurs within the context of the appearance versus reality theme in *Don Juan.*
20. In 'The Laocoön', BPP, p. 272.
21. *Endymion,* ll. 799, 798. Stanley C. Russell, ' "Self-Destroying" Love in Keats' (*Keats–Shelley Journal,* 16 [Winter 1967] pp. 79–91), surveys Keats's alternating attraction and repulsion to love.
22. BPP, p. 555.
23. SP, pp. 173, 174.
24. Byron's word. See BLJ, X, p. 157, and elsewhere. We may set Byron's 'For what is poesy but to create / From overfeeling good or ill' (*The Prophecy of Dante,* IV, ll. 11–12) against Wordsworth's 'spontaneous overflow of powerful feelings'. Each poet implied a state of previous passivity.
25. SP, p. 294.
26. *Hyperion,* III, ll. 113–16. Keats's awareness of human suffering was of course firmly grounded in his medical training. It is worth pointing out that Apollo is not only the god of music (including poetry) but also has traditional associations with medicine.
27. BPP, p. 2. Cf. *Milton,* plate 26, l. 46, and plate 29, l. 18 (ibid. pp. 123, 126).
28. BPP, p. 655.

CHAPTER 9: ENGLISH ROMANTICISM: THE GROUNDS OF
BELIEF

1. SL, I, p. 89. Shelley–Janetta Phillips [? May 1811].
2. KL, II, p. 103.
3. BLJ, VIII, p. 238 (Byron–Murray, 9 October 1821); James Kennedy, *Conversations on Religion with Lord Byron* (London: John Murray, 1830) p. 231.
4. SP, p. 288.
5. BLJ, II, p. 97. See also pp. 88–9.
6. In *The Complete Poetical Works of Byron,* ed. Paul Elmer More (1905; Boston: Houghton Mifflin, 1933) p. 744.
7. SP, p. 112.
8. *John Keats: Selected Poems and Letters* (Boston: Houghton Mifflin, 1959) p. 319.
9. BPP, pp. 37, 39.
10. On Coleridge, see Jonas Spatz, 'The Mystery of Eros: Sexual Initiation in Coleridge's "Christabel" ', *PMLA,* 90 (January 1975) pp. 107–16.
11. CCL, IV, p. 575; II, p. 864.
12. 'Hymn before Sun-rise, in the Vale of Chamouni,' ll. 13, 19, 21–3. The poem is all the more impressive since it took its origin not in personal experience but, as is well-known, in Frederike Brun's quite dreadful 'Chamouny beym Sonnenaufgange', itself inspired by Klopstock.
13. SL, II, p. 323. Shelley–Mary Shelley [8–10 August 1821].
14. Ibid., II, p. 388. Shelley–John Gisborne, 26 January 1822.
15. BLJ, IX, pp. 118–19. Byron–Thomas Moore, 4 March 1822.
16. Ibid., VIII, p. 37.
17. Ibid., III, p. 179. Byron–Annabella Milbanke, 29 November 1813.
18. Ibid., VII, p. 132. Byron–John Murray, 17 July 1820.
19. Ibid., VIII, p. 146, and LJ, V, p. 582.
20. BLJ, IX, p. 64. Byron–Moore, 16 November 1821.
21. Ibid., V, p. 157. Byron–Murray, 2 January 1817. Equally suggestive of recollection in tranquillity is this passage: 'my first impressions are always strong and confused – & my Memory *selects* & reduces them to order – like distance in the landscape – & blends them better – although they may be less distinct' (ibid., V, p. 221; Byron–Murray, 9 May 1817). Compare an earlier statement: 'While you are under the influence of passions, you only feel, but cannot describe them' (ibid., III, p. 245; journal entry, 20 February 1814).
22. *Records of Shelley, Byron, and the Author,* 2 vols (London: Basil Montagu Pickering, 1878) I, p. 33. The word, a favourite, appears in BLJ, V, pp. 131, 157, 165; VI, p. 49; VIII, p. 166.
23. BLJ, VIII, p. 221. Byron–Murray, 24 September 1821. Although in his satirical poetry he makes a great show of reason and assumes towards its satiric object the superior position of the analyzer and evaluator, Byron, like Shelley and Keats, sensed a fundamental opposition between the faculties of reason and imagination: for example, 'it is only by the excess of imagination they [poets] can arrive at being poets, and this excess debars reason' (*Lady Blessington's 'Conversations of Lord Byron',* ed. Lovell, p. 115).
24. BL, p. 69. Blake–Butts, 6 July 1803.

25. In *America*, plate 8, BPP, p. 53. See also pp. 26 ('The Garden of Love') and 43 ('A Song of Liberty').

26. Alvin B. Kernan, *The Plot of Satire* (New Haven and London: Yale University Press, 1965) pp. 176, 205.

27. Explored in Clubbe, ' "The New Prometheus of New Men": Byron's 1816 Poems and *Manfred*', in *Nineteenth-Century Literary Perspectives* (1974), ed. Clyde de L. Ryals, John Clubbe and B. F. Fisher IV.

28. 30 May 1815, in CCL, IV, p. 573.

29. BLJ, IX, p. 45. 'Detached Thought', no. 95.

30. BPP, p. 34.

31. BPP, p. 70.

32. BLJ, VIII, p. 37. Journal entry, 28 January 1821.

33. *Shakespearean Criticism*, I, p. 181.

34. BL, p. 30. Blake–Trusler, 23 August 1799.

35. BPP, p. 2. On the eighteenth-century roots of Blake's language, see Josephine Miles, *Eras and Modes in English Poetry* (1957), chapter 5, 'The Sublimity of William Blake'.

36. KL, II, pp. 212, 167. Brian Wilkie nicely observes that Keats's self-correction is helpful (*Romantic Poets and Epic Tradition* [Madison: University of Wisconsin Press, 1965] p. 154).

37. E. S. Shaffer, *'Kubla Khan' and The Fall of Jerusalem: The Mythological School in Biblical Criticism and Secular Literature, 1770–1880* (1975), ch. 1.

38. SP, p. 328. Cf. his statement to Keats: 'In poetry *I* have sought to avoid system & mannerism' (SL, II, p. 221: 27 July 1820).

39. BPP, p. 40.

40. Hermione de Almeida explores this point in relation to Byron and Joyce. Following C. R. Beye, she writes of the early Greeks: 'The immense emphasis they placed upon the *polis* was derived from their fast-held notions of man's inseparable connections with place, of his need for a source or center to which he could always return' (*Byron and Joyce through Homer: 'Don Juan' and 'Ulysses'* [New York: Columbia University Press, 1981] p. 184). Maynard Solomon in *Beethoven* (1977) sensitively discusses the significance of Beethoven's desire to return, late in life, to his birthplace, Bonn.

41. For the former, see Arthur O. Lovejoy, 'The Meaning of Romanticism for the Historian of Ideas', *Journal of the History of Ideas*, 2 (June 1941), especially pp. 272–8; for the latter, René Wellek, 'The Concept of Romanticism in Literary History', *Comparative Literature*, 1 (1949), and Peckham, 'Toward a Theory of Romanticism', *PMLA*, 66 (1951), reprinted in his *Triumph of Romanticism* (1970). See, particularly, section II of Peckham's essay.

Index